You Can Truly Be Saved Too

My Spiritual Journey

George S. Chiou

Peace from Jesus Publishing ™

YOU CAN TRULY BE SAVED TOO: *MY SPIRITUAL JOURNEY*

Copyright © 2022 by George S. Chiou

Published by Peace from Jesus Publishing, Oldsmar, FL 34677
peacefromjesus7@gmail.com

All rights reserved.
No part of this book may be reproduced, stored in a retrieval system, or transmitted in any form or by any means, electronic, mechanical, photocopying, recording, or otherwise, without the express prior written permission of the publisher. The only exception is very brief quotations embodied in critical articles and reviews, as permitted by law.
ISBN-13: 979-8-9870298-1-7 (softcover)
ISBN-13: 979-8-9870298-0-0 (e-book)

All Scripture quotations, unless otherwise indicated, are taken from the Holy Bible, New International Version®, NIV®. Copyright ©1973, 1978, 1984, 2011 by Biblica, Inc. ™ Used by permission of Zondervan. All rights reserved worldwide. www.zondervan.comThe "NIV" and "New International Version" are trademarks registered in the United States Patent and Trademark Office by Biblica, Inc. ™

(Remarks added in parentheses or brackets are mine. Emphases indicated by italics or underlining, for certain words of the quoted Scripture from the Bible or other sources, such as Bible commentaries and news articles, are mine.)

Excerpts from The World's Religions: Worldviews and Contemporary Issues, third edition, by Young, William A., ©2011, reprinted by permission of Pearson Education Inc.

Printed in the United States of America

For those who seek the truth . . .

"The truth will set you free."

(John 8:32)

Contents

PART ONE

How I Was Truly Saved

1. Grandfather Thrown into Jail   *1*
2. Sparkling Stars in the Night Sky   *3*
3. Saw Father Sweating Profusely   *6*
4. The Joy of Being Born Again   *9*

PART TWO

What Is It Like to Be Saved?

5. To Have Life, and Have It to the Full   *17*
6. Loud Pounding on My Door   *18*
7. A Note on Prayers   *22*
8. "Don't Tell Her!"   *33*

9. "Why Does She Look So Particularly Beautiful Today?" *37*
10. A Note about Marriage *40*
11. Peace from Jesus *49*
12. What Is the Purpose of Our life? What Brings Real Happiness? *63*
13. What Is the Christians' Objective of Life? *78*
14. Concluding Thoughts for Part Two *105*

PART THREE

Questions You Might Be Asking

15. Introduction *111*
16. Questions about Science and Other Related Issues *113*
17. Are Science and Religion Compatible? *124*
18. Are All Religions Not the Same? *144*
19. What Are the Differences Between Major Religions in the World? *147*
20. Judaism *149*
21. Christianity *164*
22. Islam *166*
23. Hinduism *183*
24. Theravada Buddhism *195*
25. Mahayana Buddhism and Vajrayana Buddhism *215*
26. Traditional Chinese Worldview *222*

27. Philosophical Daoism (Dao jia) *227*
28. Religious Daoism (Dao jiao) *235*
29. Confucianism *237*
30. Questions about Christianity *246*

PART FOUR

You Can Truly Be Saved Too

31. Everyone Is Cherished in God's Eyes *333*
32. How You Can Truly Be Saved *338*
33. Seek and You Will Find *354*

PART ONE - How I Was Truly Saved

1 - GRANDFATHER THROWN INTO JAIL

I am originally from Taiwan. Most people on the island, except for the indigenous population, migrated from the mainland, including my ancestors. It was part of China for many years before 1895.

Unfortunately, in 1895, China lost the First Sino-Japanese War, and Taiwan was ceded to the Imperial Japan.

During the Japanese occupation, my mother said that every morning, all citizens of Taiwan were required to bow down facing Tokyo, where the Emperor resided, to honor him.

At the time, Shinto, the state religion of Japan, said that the Emperor was the manifestation of the Sun Goddess, and all must worship him as a deity.

My maternal grandfather was the pastor of a Christian church. He refused, saying he would only bow down to God, not man. Japanese police arrested him and threw him into jail.

Although the Japanese authority did allow Christians to attend church, it had rules on the State Shintoism, which people were required to obey.

Thankfully, in 1945, the Allies, led by the United States, defeated Japan, ending the Second World War. Taiwan became part of China again, and the citizens regained their full freedom of religion.

I was born after the War.

(Note: In 1949, after the Chinese Communist Party took over China, the Chinese Nationalist Party (Kuomintang) and the government (the Republic of China) withdrew to Taiwan.

Martial law was then declared, and the sole Nationalist Party ruled the island. Fortunately, religious freedom was still permitted.

In 1996, Taiwan became democratic after citizens elected their president directly for the first time, from a pool of candidates chosen by multiple political parties. Since then, the government of Taiwan has been a clear contrast to the still authoritarian communist regime on the mainland.)

Traditional Christian

Growing up, my mother took us to church every Sunday. I still have very fond memories of it. We got to play with other kids at the church, and the Christmas holidays brought about joyous celebrations. We would receive beautiful Christmas cards and eat special cakes (made in pink color!).

However, it was more like a family tradition than something I really understood and felt in my heart.

If she had taken me to a Buddhist temple, I would have gone there too.

2 - SPARKLING STARS IN THE NIGHT SKY

Then, one summer night, while I was a college student, I happened to stand in our home's backyard, looking up to the sky. I was amazed and awestruck by the numerous glittering stars up there. I wondered: What is beyond those stars? And what is further above that?

I suddenly felt very strongly and firmly that there must be God. I told my mother that I would like to be baptized. Our church pastor asked me why I wanted to do so. I cited my encounter and the conviction that night.

Shortly afterward, I was baptized and was called a "Christian".

In retrospect, I was perhaps only halfway in the right direction in terms of Christianity. Yes, those brilliant stars in the night sky did convince me that there must be a creator of the universe.

Just like the passage in the Bible that says:

"[19] since what may be known about God is plain to them, because God has made it plain to them. [20] For since the creation of the world God's invisible qualities—his eternal power and divine nature—have been clearly seen, being understood *from what has been made*, so that people are without excuse" (Romans 1:19-20).

(In this book, if a Bible verse is mentioned, the text of the Scripture will typically be included. However, a passage may be referred to without quoting the detailed content. To know what it says, visit Bible Gateway (www.biblegateway.com). It is an outstanding website, with over 200 versions of translations in 70 languages. This book uses the New International Version (NIV))

Those countless shining stars in the night sky revealed the existence of God to me. Still, other religions teach about a creator, too.

I did not really know Jesus. Yes, there is a creator, but who is Jesus?

I heard of his name in the church and read about his story in the Bible. Nonetheless, it did not register in my mind, let alone in my heart.

My life did not change because of the baptism I had. In fact, I was once caught cheating in an exam at the college, but I did not feel any guilt about it at all.

Prayed to God Earnestly for the First Time

In 1977, after earning a bachelor's degree in electronic engineering, I came to the United States to attend Texas Christian University's Graduate School of Business in Fort Worth, Texas.

I soon found myself amid American food and had a hard time getting used to it. In Taiwan, for example, we had rice every day; yet over here, at the school's cafeteria, there were only mashed potatoes most of the time.

I lost 20 pounds in less than two months. I was not sure if it was the food or my own health issues, but I became really worried, since I was all alone here and had no friends or relatives to call for help.

I decided to turn to God and prayed fervently to Him, "God, if you would grant me good health and the ability to study well, I would serve you."

That was the first time I ever prayed deeply from my heart. When I was in Taiwan, saying a prayer was often just a ritual to me.

Amazingly, in a few months, I regained all the 20 pounds and then some! Not only that, but I also received straight A's for all the courses I took at TCU.

Looking back on that prayer, it was like making a deal with God. It was naïve and immature. However, God is merciful. He granted my wish, not that He "needs" my service!

3 - SAW FATHER SWEATING PROFUSELY

After attending Texas Christian University for the spring and summer semesters, I decided to transfer to the University of Texas at Austin in the fall of that year. I received my graduate degree three years later, in 1980.

I then accepted an offer from an electronic manufacturing company in Dallas, Texas, and started working there.

One night, in my apartment, I asked God, "What would you want me to do for you, now that you have blessed me with good health and the academic ability to complete my studies?"

Shortly after, I learned of a Chinese Christian fellowship that was aiding refugees from Indochina. I joined them and began teaching English to the new immigrants there.

Then, one evening, when I happened to read a diary I wrote while at college in Taiwan, suddenly, a vision appeared in my mind:

I saw my dad, who had just come in through the door of our apartment in Taipei (the island's capital). He was sweating profusely and looked exhausted while I was sitting comfortably on the sofa in the living room and reading a newspaper with my feet propped up on the coffee table.

All of a sudden, I burst into tears.

I asked myself, "Why didn't I think of helping my dad?" He was close to 60 years old and overweight, while I was 19, young and strong. Although he had not asked me, I could have offered to lend a hand.

That summer, both of my older sisters were getting married. Perhaps Dad had been quite busy preparing for the weddings all summer long.

After the weddings, one of my sisters was to join her husband in the United States. When we stood on a platform outside a building at the airport in Taipei, watching her plane take off, my father, standing beside me, suddenly collapsed on the floor.

He died that very day of a massive heart attack.

I remember not crying that day, but now I could not stop weeping. I had never cried like that before, and I have not cried like that since.

At that moment, I realized that I am not better than anybody else in the world, just as the Bible points out in Romans 3:23,

"*All have sinned* and fall short of the glory of God."

Growing up, I had never caused any trouble. I studied diligently, received good grades, and helped with house chores. Nonetheless, now I wish I had done something to help my dad that summer.

Although I had done nothing illegal, I could now clearly see and feel my sinful human nature, like being self-centered, not being thoughtful, and not caring enough about others.

Thinking back, I was like that person in the famous hymn, "Amazing Grace," crying out: "was blind, but *now I see*."

Romans 1:28-32 describes a depraved mind:

"²⁸ Furthermore, just as they did not think it worthwhile to retain the knowledge of God, so God gave them over to *a depraved mind*, so that they do what ought not to be done. ²⁹ They have become filled with every kind of wickedness, evil, greed and depravity. They are full of envy, murder, strife, deceit and malice. They are gossips,

"³⁰ slanderers, God-haters, insolent, arrogant and boastful; they invent ways of doing evil; they disobey their parents; ³¹ they have no understanding, no fidelity, no love, no mercy. ³² Although they know God's righteous decree that those who do such things deserve death, they not only continue to do these very things but also approve of those who practice them."

Although I did not commit some of the serious acts mentioned in the passage, I could feel my fallen condition deeply just the same.

Besides seeing my sinful nature, most importantly, I now understood why Christ came into this world. He came to die for my sins. In retrospect, was it not about what Romans 5:8 says, "But God demonstrates his own love for us in this: While we were still sinners, Christ died for us"?

At the age of 32, I cried so hard that I could not stop. I felt I was like the string on a bow that was being stretched and stretched, and was about to be broken.

Then the phone rang. I glanced at the clock; it was around midnight, a strange phone call from out of state at an odd time indeed.

To this day, I do not know who that person was, nor do I recall what the conversation was about. But it stopped my sobbing. I understand it sounds mysterious; I felt the same way, too, but that was what actually happened.

4 - THE JOY OF BEING BORN AGAIN

Immediately after I stopped crying, I felt as if I had just taken a shower. My sins were like dirt washed away from my body, and I felt a tremendous sense of relief, peace, and joy.

I was a changed person: at peace with my Creator, no longer condemned; at peace with myself, sins forgiven. I was what Jesus says in John 3:3, "born again".

I was truly saved.

As soon as I woke up the next morning, I called my mother in Taiwan and told her I was coming home for a week or two.

She thought I was coming back to find someone to marry. I said, "No, Mom, I am coming home to go to Dad's grave to say I am sorry."

Soon after returning to Taiwan, I bought flowers and laid them at my father's graveside. Then, I went straight to a Christian bookstore and started picking out dozens of books to buy. Some were biographies of great Christians; some were commentaries for studying the Bible.

I bought so many books, that the store clerk grew curious and asked me if I was a pastor. Thinking back, I now know that even though I was not a pastor, I was like a newborn baby, so hungry and eager to take in all the spiritual milk I could get!

Remarkably, I later found that Scripture, in fact, talks about this phenomenon:

"¹ Therefore, rid yourselves of all malice and all deceit, hypocrisy, envy, and slander of every kind. ² *Like newborn babies, crave pure spiritual milk*, so that by it you may grow up in your salvation, ³ now that you have tasted that the Lord is good" (1 Peter 2:1-3).

By the way, now I know the Bible indeed also has a specific answer to the question I pondered that night in Taiwan, when I was looking up at that fascinating starry sky, asking, "What is beyond those stars?"

Apostle Paul says,

"² I know a man [Paul himself speaking in the third person] in Christ who fourteen years ago was caught up to *the third heaven*. Whether it was in the body or out of the body I do not know—God knows.

"³ And I know that this man—whether in the body or apart from the body I do not know, but God knows— ⁴ was caught up to *paradise* and heard inexpressible things, things that no one is permitted to tell" (2 Corinthians 12:2-4).

When Christ was hung on the cross with the other two condemned criminals beside him, Jesus said to the one who repented,

"'Truly I tell you, today you will be with me in paradise'" (Luke 23:39-43).

Revelation 2:7 writes,

"Whoever has ears, let them hear what the Spirit says to the churches. To the one who is victorious, I will give the right to eat from the tree of life, which is in the paradise of God."

It is evident that paradise is the dwelling place of God and the saints, and that paradise is in the third heaven - the heaven, I believe, beyond those stars.

My conviction that night was correct, that God exists, and that He resides beyond those stars, although I did not know about these passages then.

When I was at the airport departing Taiwan, the customs official at the gate, peering at my bulky luggage, full of nothing but books, became suspicious and thought I might be a political activist.

Taiwan, at the time, was still under martial law. Citizens were prohibited from engaging in anti-government activities. The news media and all forms of publication were subject to censorship. He directed me to another officer for further inspection.

Fortunately, perhaps because none of the books were about politics, I was allowed to exit Taiwan and return to the States.

Follow Christ Fervently

Back in America, I felt a burning desire to share Christ with others. I bought many copies of the Bible and gave it to whoever would like to have it, even to a taxi driver.

At the church I attended, I started to serve the people there. I taught first the children, and then the adult Sunday school; led a home evangelistic group, and later organized an annual church evangelistic event.

Hundreds of people attended that gathering in three days. Many responded to the call to repent and be saved. It was exciting to witness people's lives changed by the power of Jesus' love! Many of them were students from Communist China.

I also started systematically reading the Bible from the first book to the last. Almost every Saturday morning, I would get up early, bring a chair, go outside my house, and read it for hours.

The morning air was especially fresh, and the view from our house, which was on the top of a small hill, was gorgeous. I could see all the way to the distant DFW (Dallas and Fort Worth) airport, where planes flew in and out.

It was such an enjoyable time every Saturday morning! I remember my neighbor across the street got so curious that one day, he couldn't help but walk directly over to me and ask to see what I was reading.

In 1982, I got married. I am thankful that it happened after my conversion. Because when I was thinking about starting a family, I had this strong conviction that I must make sure that my wife was a genuine Christian, and that she was as committed to marriage as I was.

In hindsight, given so many divorces nowadays, without that firm pledge, our marriage might not have withstood the challenges of life. (In Part Two, I will share my experiences on how I met my wife and how we raised our children in more detail.)

On another note, now I could see that it was wrong and embarrassing that I cheated on a test at the college in Taiwan. It is like after taking a bath, you can now easily spot dirt on your body. You want to be clean. You are now sensitive to sin.

However, I am now also aware that being born again does not mean I am now perfect and could not sin again. Christians still have the sinful nature, just like everybody else.

Nonetheless, it does mean that I can learn to choose to overcome this inclination in my daily life, if I would depend on the power of the Holy Spirit to overcome it.

In fact, no Christian will be perfect until Jesus comes again, when we will be resurrected and transformed into a glorious body without sinful nature anymore. (I will explain this in Part Two and Part Three.)

In 1996, responding to God's calling, I quit my well-paying job in the computer field to attend Dallas Theological Seminary, a non-denominational Protestant Christian seminary. I received my second master's degree, Master of Theology, in January 2001.

Since then, I have served as a pastor, taught at a Bible college, and, for several years before retirement in 2015, taught world religions at a community college in Florida.

I miss the over one thousand students I taught. I can recall many of their faces. I also cannot forget those moments, when their eyes lit up and they smiled or nodded, seemingly understanding what I had just shared.

I remember vividly an incident that occurred one evening in the classroom. It was a two-hour class with a 10-minute break. After the break, a student sitting in the front said, "Can we go home?"

I understood it was tough for students to sit in the class for hours in the evening, especially for some who also worked a day job.

But I paused a second and said, "If there is only one person willing to learn tonight, this class is worth having." Then, I saw a student sitting in the middle of the room raise his hand. I still can clearly recall his face. It was quite meaningful and encouraging to me. I felt my effort was not in vain.

I wish them the best. They are our next generation. They are our future.

We have been married for over 39 years. God blessed us with two daughters, one son-in-law, and two grandchildren. Both daughters, while in their teens, wholeheartedly asked to be baptized. We are very happy for them.

I Am Very Thankful

Looking back, I am very thankful to those Western missionaries, who began to travel thousands of miles across the oceans, far away from their own homes, to come to Taiwan to share the good news of Christ's love more than three hundred years ago, and continue to do so today. It was through their Christian love that my grandparents had the opportunity to be saved.

I am also grateful to my grandparents, who stood firm against religious persecution, even at the risk of possibly losing their lives, and my parents, who were faithful and took us to church every Sunday and lived exemplary lives.

It was because of my mother, who took me to church as a child, that I knew whom I could pray to, when I was in need at Texas Christian University later on in my life.

But above all, I am most thankful to the merciful God, who not only answered my earnest prayer for a physical need at TCU, but also gave me the spiritual gift of the Holy Spirit, by *revealing* and *convicting me of my sins* later, while I was working in Dallas.

It thus enabled me to be truly saved, and not let me continue to be only a nominal Christian.

Just as what Jesus says in Luke 11:5-13:

"[5] Suppose you have a friend, and you go to him at midnight and say, 'Friend, lend me three loaves of bread; [6] a friend of mine on a journey has come to me, and I have no food to offer him.' ⁷ And suppose the one inside answers, 'Don't bother me. The door is already locked, and my children and I are in bed. I can't get up and give you anything.'

"⁸ I tell you, even though he will not get up and give you the bread because of friendship, yet because of your shameless audacity, he will surely get up and give you as much as you need.

"⁹ So I say to you: Ask and it will be given to you; seek and you will find; knock and the door will be opened to you. ¹⁰ For everyone who asks receives; the one who seeks finds; and to the one who knocks, the door will be opened.

"¹¹ Which of you fathers, if your son asks for a fish, will give him a snake instead? ¹² Or if he asks for an egg, will give him a scorpion? ¹³ If you then, though you are evil, know how to give good gifts to your children, *how much more will your Father in heaven give the Holy Spirit to those who ask him!*"

I was like that person, who desperately knocked on his friend's door in the middle of the night, asking for bread.

It is astounding that, even today, we can still *personally* receive and experience what Jesus promised almost two thousand years ago!

PART TWO - What Is It Like to Be Saved?

5 - TO HAVE LIFE, AND HAVE IT TO THE FULL

In Part One, I shared the joy of being born again and the earnest desire to follow Christ afterward. However, some might wonder, "What is it like in the believer's daily life?" and "What is the difference?"

Jesus declares, in John 10:10,

"The thief comes only to steal and kill and destroy; I have come that they may have life, and have it to the full."

It means that believers are no longer condemned to permanent death and will have eternal life when the end of time comes. (I will elaborate on end times in Part Four.)

In addition, it also means that, before that time comes, while we are still on this Earth, believers will be able to experience and learn to live their lives to the full, beginning right at the moment of being born again.

So, what does it look like to live it to the full?

The following chapters will share some of my pivotal and unforgettable spiritual experiences.

6 - LOUD POUNDING ON MY DOOR

While attending the University of Texas, I first worked as a research assistant and later on as an assistant instructor of computer technology.

One day, when I was in my apartment, suddenly, someone pounded on my door fiercely. The door was made of light metal, so it was quite loud. Bang! Bang! Bang! Bang! Bang! Bang! I was shocked. "Is it the police, or is some bad guy trying to break into my apartment?"

I opened the door; there stood a big, tall Chinese guy. He pointed his finger at me and angrily shouted, "YOU ROBBED MY RICE BOWL!" (In Mandarin, "rice bowl" means someone's job or way of making a living.) He then yelled again, "YOU ROBBED MY ASSISTANTSHIP!"

I was stunned by his angry accusation, yet also puzzled. Because there was no way you could "rob" someone's assistantship. It was a position you applied for at the school, and the department would decide who would get it. There was nothing I could have done about it. I did not even know who had submitted the applications.

I let him in and asked him to sit down beside me. As I remained silent, he continued screaming, "I am much more qualified than you! I came to this country earlier, I speak better English, I am in the Doctorate program, and YOU are JUST a master's student! YOU robbed MY assistantship!"

Although I did not know this person personally, I did hear about him. I heard that he had beaten up people on the campus. Since he was sitting right in front of me, I knew if I did not say or do something quickly, he might get violent at any moment. My silence would not work much longer.

I asked myself aloud in my mind, "How am I going to handle this situation?" At that moment, I said a simple, silent prayer, "God, please give me the wisdom to respond to his accusation, in Jesus' name, Amen."

Guess what happened next? I thought, since he had been ranting and raving for some time, he must be really thirsty by now. So, I turned and opened the little refrigerator beside me, took out an apple, and handed it to him.

He looked surprised, hesitated for a few seconds, then took the apple and started eating it. As he was munching on it, I saw tears running down his cheeks. I could not believe this mad, macho man, who was shouting minutes ago, was now weeping silently before me.

Ever since then, he has been very friendly to me, though I still had the teaching assistantship. He would spot me on the campus at a distance, wave at me, and shout, "Hi, George!" I do not know where he is now, but I wish him the best.

To this day, I am still amazed at how much an apple could do for me, and how marvelous it was that God let me witness His wisdom in times of need.

At that time, I had not been born again yet. Nonetheless, I had begun praying to God and attending church on Sundays regularly.

Just like my first prayer at TCU, God had let me experience, once again, his grace and care.

As Philippians 4:6-7 assures us:

"⁶ Do not be anxious about anything, but in every situation, by prayer and petition, with thanksgiving, present your requests to God. ⁷ And the peace of God, which transcends all understanding, will guard your hearts and your minds in Christ Jesus."

God promises believers that He will answer our prayers if we pray to him for help. There is no need to panic. We are His children, and He cares about us.

There is even a specific assurance regarding asking for wisdom in James 1:5, "If any of you lacks wisdom, you should ask God, who gives generously to all without finding fault, and it will be given to you."

Can we only pray for big issues?

While on this subject, some may ask, "Can we only pray for big issues?" The answer is "No," because the passage states that "in every situation," we can petition God.

I can clearly recall those seemingly small incidents when our first daughter was just a baby. For example, sometimes she would cry and would not stop.

I checked if she was hungry. Nope, she had been fed. I would then check if her diaper was soiled. Not at all; it looked clean. I then tried to make sure if she was just tired and wanted to nap, so I put her head on my shoulder for her to rest. That did not work either. At that point, I asked God to comfort her.

Remarkably, she stopped.

I also remember one day when she was in second grade. She came home from school, saying sadly, "I don't have any friends."

By the way, we paid for her to attend private Christian preschool, kindergarten, and the first grade. But then let her go to public school, starting from the second grade, thinking it would be good that she could also experience a different environment.

I prayed to God to grant her good friends. Within one week, she had two invitations to birthday parties. One of the classmates who invited her even became a close friend.

I also recall one lady, who had just accepted Jesus in my home evangelistic meeting, shared her prayer experience in a similar circumstance.

She was having a hard time potty-training her young son. She asked God for help. Then, soon after, she noticed her son watching a TV program in the living room. To her amazement, it was teaching little kids how to use the toilet.

After the show, he then walked to the restroom and started using it all by himself!

7 - A NOTE ON PRAYERS

What Kind of Prayers Would God Answer?

Prayers Asked According to His Will

Apostle John says,

"This is the confidence we have in approaching God: that if we ask anything according to his will, he hears us" (1 John 5:14).

It teaches that while we are sure that God will answer our prayers, we are not to assume that God is like a vending machine, that we can ask anything, and He will deliver. Instead, it must be according to His will. It means, for one, that whatever we pray for must be consistent with the moral principles He would like us to follow.

God's Moral Principles

LOVE GOD AND LOVE PEOPLE

Jesus was once asked,

"[28]... Of all the commandments, which is the most important?" He said, "[29] the most important one, answered Jesus, is this: 'Hear, O Israel: The Lord our God, the Lord is one. [30] Love the Lord your God with all your heart and with all your soul and with all your mind and with all your strength.' ³¹ The second is this: 'Love your neighbor as yourself.' There is no commandment greater than these" (Mark 12:28-31).

Before we pray, we need to ask if it is for loving God and for loving people as ourselves.
James 4:1-3 warns,

"¹ what causes fights and quarrels among you? Don't they come from your desires that battle within you? ...
³ When you ask, you do not receive, because you ask with wrong motives, that you may spend what you get on your pleasures."

I prayed to God for His wisdom to respond to that man yelling at me in the right way, so that I would not just impulsively yell back and confront him.
God's answer was to give him an apple because he must be thirsty by then. In retrospect, I think God was teaching me that what he actually needed was love and care. He apparently was feeling rejected and insecure for not getting financial aid.
I prayed to God to comfort my crying daughter, and also asked God that she would have good friends at school. I asked for these things because I wanted to be a good father who cared for his children's legitimate needs. God blesses requests such as these.
On the other hand, if the prayer request is for self-serving motives that harm others or are driven by hatred, it is certain that God, who is loving, just, and merciful, would not listen.

God's Moral Character

HE IS LOVE

Jesus says,

"For God so loved the world that he gave his one and only Son, that whoever believes in him shall not perish but have eternal life" (John 3:16).

HE IS JUST

God tells the Israelites,

"[15] When you spread out your hands in prayer, I hide my eyes from you; even when you offer many prayers, I am not listening. Your hands are full of blood!
 [16] Wash and make yourselves clean. Take your evil deeds out of my sight; stop doing wrong. [17] Learn to do right; seek justice. Defend the oppressed. Take up the cause of the fatherless; plead the case of the widow" (Isaiah 1:15-17).

HE IS MERCIFUL

"Be merciful, just as your Father is merciful" (Luke 6:36)."[8] The Lord is compassionate and gracious, slow to anger, abounding in love. [9] He will not always accuse, nor will he harbor his anger forever "(Psalm 103:8-9).

God's Specific Commandments

The fundamental principles mentioned above help guide us on what to pray. However, the Bible also includes specific and clear moral commandments for us to follow, such as not lying, committing adultery, or other sinful acts.

It is important to check ourselves, since some people may misinterpret the general principles and justify bad behavior, which is explicitly warned against and will not be heard by God, let alone be blessed.

Why Would God Not Answer Our Good Prayers Sometimes?

Having discussed the general moral principles of God, we might have come across situations, where we were confused as to why God did not answer our requests, although they were consistent with God's ethical character.

For example, it may trouble us that, despite our fervent prayers, God did not heal a faithful and loving person.
Generally speaking, God wants us to be free from sickness (James 5:13-16). That was why one of the central ministries Jesus did was healing the sick (Matthew 4:23). Even today, believers' prayers continue to result in many credible testimonies of miraculous healing.

IT IS FOR A GOOD PURPOSE

Nevertheless, if one is not healed, it is for a good purpose, although we may not understand.
Psalm 119:71 writes,

"It was good for me to be afflicted so that I might learn your decrees."

2 Corinthians 12:6-9 records Apostle Paul's willingness to accept affliction, so as to keep him humble:

"[6] Even if I should choose to boast, I would not be a fool, because I would be speaking the truth. But I refrain, *so no one will think more of me than is warranted* by what I do or say, [7] or because of these surpassingly great revelations.

Therefore, in order to keep me from becoming conceited, I was given a thorn in my flesh, a messenger of Satan, to torment me.

"⁸ Three times I pleaded with the Lord to take it away from me. ⁹ But he said to me, 'My grace is sufficient for you, for my power is made perfect in weakness.' Therefore I will boast all the more gladly about my weaknesses, so that Christ's power may rest on me."

That said, for a specific individual at a particular time, instead of perhaps for a good spiritual purpose while on Earth, it might be God's will to call them to heaven now. He is the author of life. He alone has the authority to decide the timing.

Again, while we may not understand God's will sometimes (Isaiah 55:8-9), we can be sure that God's will is good and benevolent for us.

In Jeremiah 29:11, God says,

"'For I know the plans I have for you,' declares the Lord, 'plans to prosper you and not to harm you, plans to give you hope and a future.'"

God gave this assurance when He was telling the Israelites, that even though they would be exiled to Babylon in captivity for disobedience, they would be brought back to Jerusalem in 70 years.

God's character is consistent, whether toward the Israelites or other people.

To Sum Up Regarding What Kind of Prayers God Would Answer

I will present my request to God, according to God's principles, but always add "Lord willing" in my prayer to ensure that if it is not His best will, I am okay with it. I trust that His choice is better than mine.

It works very well. I have peace with myself, knowing I have done what I can, and do not let doubts creep into my mind if the situation does not turn out how I prayed for it to.

Incidentally, I always end my prayer with "in Jesus' name," since it is because of Jesus (God the Son), and through Jesus, that we now have access to God (the Father). In addition, Jesus himself says, "And I will do whatever you ask *in my name*, so that the Father may be glorified in the Son" (John 14:13).

Therefore, my typical prayer looks like this: "Heavenly Father, < my request >, Lord willing, in Jesus' name."

THE LORD'S PRAYER

It is fitting that we conclude this section with the precious Lord's Prayer. It is how Jesus teaches his disciples to pray:

"[9] This, then, is how you should pray:

"'Our Father in heaven, hallowed be your name, [10] your kingdom come, your will be done, on earth as it is in heaven. [11] Give us today our daily bread. [12] And forgive us our debts, as we also have forgiven our debtors. [13] And lead us not into temptation, [a]

but deliver us from the evil one [b]'" (Matthew 6:9-13).
Footnotes
- a. The Greek for *temptation* can also mean *testing*.
- b. Or *from evil*; some late manuscripts *one, / for yours is the kingdom and the power and the glory forever. Amen.*

By the way, this prayer has been set to music many times; the one composed by Mr. Albert Hay Malotte in

1935 (entitled "The Lord's Prayer") remains a timeless classic. Many artists have recorded the song.

Do we need to do anything?

We Should Do Our Part

While we must be sure that what we pray for is according to biblical principles, so that God may hear our prayers, we should also be aware that it does not mean we do not need to do anything.

For my crying baby daughter, I made sure that I did everything I could and should have done for her, before asking for God's help.

When God told the Israelites fleeing Egypt, that He would provide food for them, He said,

"... I will rain down bread from heaven for you. The people are to go out each day and gather enough for that day. In this way I will test them and see whether they will follow my instructions" (Exodus 16:4).

Even when God literally provided food from heaven, it did not just come down directly to their dinner tables. The Israelites still had to go out and collect it as instructed by God.

However, this does not mean prayers should only be the last resort. My first prayer of the day usually is said sitting at the breakfast table. I pray that God guides me on how to cherish my life and the time of the day, and to do things that will glorify Him.

When I taught at college, before each class began, while standing before the students, I would say a silent prayer, "God, may you grant me your love and wisdom to teach my students." It helped me have the right attitude.

A Comment I Heard

I still can vividly recall a time at church, when snacks were served after Bible study. A person who was not just overweight but obese said, "If God wants me to have diabetes, so be it," while eating his donut.

Some might have misunderstood the concept of God's sovereignty, thinking they have no personal responsibility at all, because "everything is in God's control."

Unless we think humans were made like robots, I believe we do have free will, hence the responsibility to make good choices.

As a matter of fact, it was Adam and Eve's willful rejection of God's clear warning, that caused the downfall of humanity. (See Genesis Chapter 3 of the Bible, and more on this in Part Three of this book.)

Some may want to keep a healthy diet, but just could not resist the urge. Thankfully, as God's children, we now have the power of the Holy Spirit to enable us to overcome temptations. We *can* now learn to make good choices in our life.

Romans 8:1-4 assures us:

"[1] Therefore, there is now no condemnation for those who are in Christ Jesus, [2] because through Christ Jesus the law of the Spirit who gives life has *set you free from the law of sin and death*.

"[3] For what the law was powerless to do because it was weakened by the flesh, God did by sending his own Son in the likeness of sinful flesh to be a sin offering. And so he condemned sin in the flesh, [4] in order that the righteous requirement of the law might be fully met in us, *who do not live according to the flesh but according to the Spirit."*

How an Actor Quit His Smoking

I once read about a man's testimony about how he finally kicked his smoking habit. He was a famous actor in Taiwan named Sūn Yuè. Although his career was quite successful, he was really frustrated with his addiction. He wished he could quit doing it, knowing it was damaging his health.

He had tried many ways, but all failed. He would resolve every New Year, swearing he would finally stop it that year. Sadly, he failed again every time.

Then he became a born-again Christian.

One day, not long after he was saved, he woke up in the morning and suddenly wondered, "Why does my mouth smell so bad? It is disgusting!"

He quit smoking for good that day!

Yes, as a believer, God's power is available to us. If we seek His help, we no longer have to give in to temptation. But we must be willing to use it. That is our responsibility. Sūn Yuè apparently was still trying to quit smoking and did not just give up.

The difference this time was that now, with God's power, he succeeded!

In America, many people have heard about the popular AA programs (Alcoholics Anonymous) and its 12 Steps. It was actually founded on the Christian belief that attests to the spiritual power of God to overcome addiction.

Nonetheless, sadly, tens of thousands of people still die on the roads every year, because of drunken driving in the United States. However, as Christians, we can do effective things to avoid that tragedy.

When we drive, if we will apply God's spiritual power given to us, we can learn to resist the urge to drink, and to follow safety practices by buckling up and paying attention to traffic. That is our privilege and obligation.

But what if a crazy driver just hit me, even when I have taken all the safety precautions?

Do My Best, and Leave the Rest to God

The bottom-line lesson that I have learned about this is: Do my best, and leave the rest to God. That is to fulfill my part according to biblical principles, but leave things beyond my control to God.

With that in mind, I will focus on driving carefully, ensuring I have tightened my seat belt, and not doing anything distractive like talking or texting. I will leave the rest to God and not worry over those things I cannot control.

Taking Care of Our Health in a Balanced Way

Regarding my health, if I have done my best to take good care of my body: exercise regularly, choose healthy food, take medicines if called for, etc., yet still get diabetes, it is okay with me (not that I would like to have the disease).

I accept God's authority over people's lives since He is the author of life. Although I do pray that, Lord willing, I will not get it.

As we grow old, we all will typically die of some sickness. Despite that, with God's care and our willingness to do our part, we will increase the likelihood of being able to age well and have a good quality of life.

To Sum Up Regarding If We Need to Do Anything

By seeking God's powerful help to overcome addictions, but also doing what we can to drive safely, we certainly no longer have to die in a crash, thinking we are incapable of stopping drinking and driving.

Moreover, indeed, we no longer have to have diabetes, believing we cannot resist the temptation, and have to give in and indulge ourselves in tasty, yet unhealthy, food.

We now have a viable alternative. We *can* make good choices. Yes, God is in control, but it is His sovereign will that human beings should have free will to choose, and thus be held accountable for our decisions.

It is a balance of God's sovereignty and human being's responsibility.

It works beautifully!

In Conclusion

My experience from that pounding on my door tells me, that God promises believers that if we will pray to Him for help according to His will, He will answer our prayer. There is no need to be anxious about anything.

We no longer have to fight alone. We are His children, and He cares about us.

8 - "DON'T TELL HER!"

After graduating from the University of Texas, I accepted a job offer and went to Dallas to work. One day, not long after I was born again, a friend said that Chen (not his real name) was kicked out of his apartment and had no place to live. At that time, I was single and lived in an apartment.

I barely knew him; nonetheless, I felt I should offer him a temporary place to stay. He came by bicycle after I called him. I let him sleep on a couch in the living area.

Several days later, he told me, "I am going to kill Stephanie (not her real name), don't tell her!" I did not know Stephanie personally. I had only heard about her and that she was his younger sister.

I did not even know her official English name or where she lived, let alone how to contact her, but I said, "You should kill me too, because Christians should not lie." I then went to bed.

By the way, I had a tiny apartment. There was a divider wall between the living area and the sleeping space, but there was no door that I could close and lock.

The next day, while preparing to leave for work, I noticed he was deep in thought. I asked him, "Are you okay?" Without looking at me, he slowly and firmly said, "I do not think Stephanie is a real Christian. When I called her last night and said I was going to kill her, she was scared to death."

He left a couple of days later. I have not heard from him since.

Looking back, even though this happened just a short time after I was truly saved, I was not afraid to tell him, without any hesitation, that I would not lie, even at the risk of possibly being harmed too. I remember I slept quite well as usual that night.

Free From the Fear of Death

In retrospect, I was surprised how I could deal with it so calmly. Later on, when I studied the Bible, I found the reason:

"[14] Since the children have flesh and blood, he [Christ] too shared in their humanity so that by his death he might break the power of him who holds the power of death—that is, the devil— [15] and *free those who all their lives were held in slavery by their fear of death*" (Hebrews 2:14-15).

Yes, Jesus has conquered death so that we no longer have to be enslaved by the fear of death. We no longer need to feel powerless and have to give in to doing things we know are wrong and are against our conscience.

As Jesus says:

"Do not be afraid of those who kill the body but cannot kill the soul. Rather, be afraid of the One who can destroy both soul and body in hell" (Matthew 10:28).

The devil and his followers can kill our bodies; however, they cannot kill our souls. Only God can do so because He is the Creator of both body and soul.

All human beings, including believers, will die at least once.

Nevertheless, believers will not die a second time on the Day of Judgment. In fact, when believers die, their souls will be with God. Then, when the end of time comes, their bodies will be resurrected and transformed into glorious bodies, and they will live forever in heaven with Him.

As for those who rejected God's salvation, they will also be resurrected, but will be condemned to the eternal lake of fire, with both their souls and bodies, thus the "second death" (Daniel 12:13; 1 Thessalonians 4:13-18; Philippians 3:21; 1 Corinthians 15:50-55; Revelation 20:11-15. This subject will be explained in more detail in Part Three and Four).

"Great Cloud of Witnesses"

The book of Hebrews points out many people in the Old Testament times, from Noah, Abraham, Moses, to David, and many more others, who were not afraid of hardship and even death because of their faith in God, and calls them "great cloud of witnesses" (Hebrews 12:1; 11:1-39).

That bravery continues in the New Testament era, starting from those early Christians, like the *apostles*, who risked their lives rather than staying silent and not sharing the gospel in Jerusalem (Acts 4:18-20),

To those *martyrs*, who died in Rome's coliseums rather than submitting to the Roman Empire's religious oppression about two thousand years ago,

To those *missionaries*, such as Robert Morrison, the first Protestant missionary to China, who went there at the age of 25 in 1807 from England, and devoted all his life to translating the entire Bible into Chinese, while enduring fierce hostility toward him from the Chinese's government, and the Roman Catholic Church at Macau,

(We will cover the three major branches of Christianity: Roman Catholicism, Eastern Orthodoxy, and Protestantism in Part Three.)

And James Hudson Taylor, founder of the Chinese Inland Mission, who, along with his missionaries, continued to go back to China from England, even after many of them and their families, including children, were killed by the violent mobs in the Boxer Rebellion between 1899 and 1901,

To *my grandfather*, who chose to be jailed rather than be forced to bow down to a man-made deity in the early 20th century,

And to *those who have risked their lives, even today*, for their faith and ministry in communist China and some Muslim countries.

They all testified to the powerful truth that, for believers, the fear of death has been conquered and is replaced with bravery, love, and compassion!

My encounter with the threat of possible death certainly was not as severe as the threats faced by those courageous Christians. Nonetheless, God has let me taste what it is like to be free from the sting of death.

It is liberating!

9 - "WHY DOES SHE LOOK SO PARTICULARLY BEAUTIFUL TODAY?"

Ready to Start a Family

After working for about a year in Dallas, I was ready to start a family. As indicated in Part One, I felt strongly that I had to make sure my wife was a Christian and willing to be as committed to marriage as I was.

Moreover, I wanted to be certain that she would be okay with giving ten percent of our income to our church and other Christian organizations, too, because if she had a problem with that, we might be arguing about it from our very first Sunday at church.

While on the subject, in hindsight, the ten percent offering (as stated in the Old Testament's Leviticus 27:30) is only the basic starting point.

In the New Testament, it is noted that giving beyond that amount is even more pleasing to God, as demonstrated by the example of a poor widow, who was particularly complimented by Jesus (Mark 12:41-44).

Scripture also emphasizes that any offerings must be voluntary and from our heart: "Each of you should give what you have decided in your heart to give, not reluctantly or under compulsion, for God loves a cheerful giver" (2 Corinthians 9:7).

I am willing to give back what God has given me so abundantly, not just physically and intellectually, but also spiritually. A ten percent offering is just a token of my thanks to God. However, I wanted to ensure that my wife would be happy to do this as well.

When my older sister, Elizabeth, heard of what I was looking for, she shared it with an elder at a Chinese church in Los Angeles. He said there actually was such a member in his church, who had been actively engaged in evangelism and was practicing tithing herself. Her name is Margaret.

At the time, she had moved back to Michigan, where her parents lived, after graduating from a university in California. I flew up there to visit her and her family. After that, I called her often on the phone.

In fact, I spent at least a thousand dollars on long-distance calls. The cost in the early 1980s was not cheap; there was no such thing as unlimited calls with a low monthly fixed fee then!

When I visited her a second time later, I asked her what she thought about divorce. I said, "If there is no commitment to marriage, I would rather not get married at all, and I will remain single for all my life."

The next day, we drove from Lansing to Mackinac Island for a day trip. While I was driving, I happened to turn to look at her and thought she was really beautiful. She was not a bad-looking woman at all, but "Why does she look so particularly beautiful today?" I said to myself.

At that very moment, she said, "I thought about what you commented yesterday regarding marriage, I feel since there are Ten Commandments in the Bible, I don't see why the commitment to marriage cannot be a commandment too."

Spiritual Beauty

I was very happy and excited about what she had just said, and thought, "No wonder she looks so particularly pretty today. I am witnessing a phenomenon, that is there is *spiritual beauty* on top of good physical appearance!"

We had a great time on the island. When we were crossing a bridge heading back from Mackinac Island that evening, I turned and looked to my left, and saw spectacular and beautiful fireworks exploding in the night sky all over the island. It was for the Fourth of July celebration, yet it was like celebrating for us too.

We got married on Thanksgiving Day of that year in 1982. It has been 39 years since then!

10 - A NOTE ABOUT MARRIAGE

I am grateful that God impressed upon me the critical importance of making a commitment beforehand, so as to ensure a good chance of having a stable and successful marriage.

At that time, I had not finished reading all the Scriptures yet. Sometime later, I found that there are, in fact, definitive teachings on the subject of marriage and divorce.

Biblical Teachings about Divorce

From the Old Testament

Malachi 2:16 warns,

"'The man who hates and divorces his wife,' says the Lord, the God of Israel, 'does violence to the one he should protect,'[a] says the Lord Almighty. "So be on your guard, and do not be unfaithful."
> Footnotes
> a. Or *"I hate divorce," says the Lord, the God of Israel, "because the man who divorces his wife covers his garment with violence,"*

From the New Testament

Matthew 19:3-9 records Jesus' response to the question of divorce:

"³ Some Pharisees came to him to test him. They asked, 'Is it lawful for a man to divorce his wife for any and every reason?'

"⁴ 'Haven't you read,' he replied, 'that at the beginning the Creator 'made them male and female,' ⁵ and said, 'For this reason a man will leave his father and mother and be united to his wife, and the two will become one flesh'? ⁶ So they are no longer two, but one flesh. Therefore what God has joined together, let no one separate.'

"⁷ 'Why then,' they asked, 'did Moses command that a man give his wife a certificate of divorce and send her away?'

"⁸ Jesus replied, 'Moses permitted you to divorce your wives because your hearts were hard. But it was not this way from the beginning. ⁹ I tell you that anyone who divorces his wife, except for sexual immorality [or marital unfaithfulness to him], and marries another woman commits adultery.'"

It is evident that, from both the Old and the New Testaments, except for adultery, there is no excuse for divorce. It is a sacred union that God ordained.

By the way, some may think this only applies to believers. But Scripture explicitly teaches that in the case of a wife who is not a believer, the husband must not use it as a justification for divorcing her if she is willing to live with him. Nevertheless, if she wants to leave, he should let her go.

This is also applicable when the husband is the unbeliever. She, the believer, must not divorce him if he is willing to live with her (1 Corinthians 7:12-16).

In retrospect, as I referred to it in Part One, given so many divorces nowadays, even in the Christian communities, without that firm commitment, our marriage might not have withstood the ups and downs in our life.

Christians Can Still Make Mistakes, but There Is Hope

Christians still have the sinful nature, just like anybody else. It was due to the fall of Adam and Eve.

As mentioned, this inclination will not go away until believers are resurrected and transformed, when the end of the age comes (more on this subject in Part Three and Four).

The Empowering Holy Spirit in Us

However, as shared before, being born again does mean that with the Holy Spirit in us, we can learn to choose to overcome our sinful inclination in our daily life, if we will depend on the power of the Holy Spirit to overcome it (Romans 8:4).

But having said that, it is a growing process. Christians may still make mistakes. For example, behaving selfishly.

Marriage (or perhaps any human relationship) is like the weather. It will not be sunshine all the time. There will be cloudy days, there will be rainy days, and there may even be days of thunderstorms!

Indeed, there were times that I was furious and upset. Margaret also experienced those kinds of emotions sometimes. Nonetheless, if whenever we encounter some difficulties or disappointments, we would quit, then our marriage will not have a good chance of success.

With God's care and our commitment, marriage can be stable and overall joyful, despite the challenges we may face.

"Let Us Walk in the Light of His Love"

When I was designing our wedding invitation 39 years ago, somehow, I had this idea and had this sentence printed on the card, *"Let us walk in the light of His love."*

What do I mean by that?

There are two aspects:

FIRST, HE LOVES US.

He created us and ordained marriage. He cares about our marriage. He would not like to see a family broken apart.

We can pray to Him for help in times of need.

As the Bible declares in Romans 5:1-5, God will "pour out his love into our hearts," so we will have the hope that we can learn even to rejoice and triumph in the face of trials.

His loving care is like the light that shines brightly in the darkness of challenging times.

SECOND, WE CAN ALSO LEARN TO LOVE OUR SPOUSE WITH GOD'S LOVE GIVEN TO US, AS ROMANS 5:5 PROMISES, EVEN IN TRYING CIRCUMSTANCES

Perhaps I should say, *especially* in trying circumstances. Although I love my wife very much, human love is imperfect. On the other hand, God's love is perfect and everlasting.

Apostle John urges us,

"⁷ Dear friends, let us *love one another, for love comes from God*. Everyone who loves has been born of God and knows God... ¹¹ Dear friends, since God so loved us, we also ought to love one another. ¹² No one has ever seen God; but if we love one another, God lives in us and his love is made complete in us" (1 John 4:7; 11-12).

There are four types of love mentioned in the Bible in Greek:

- *Eros:* sexual and romantic love (the root word of the English "erotic")
- *Philia:* love of friends
- *Storge:* love of parents for children
- *Agape: (Greek: agapē)* love of God for mankind

We might associate *eros* with lust, but sexual love is certainly good and blessed in the marriage.

However, agape love is the highest form of love and is the type of love the Bible speaks about the most, over 200 times in the New Testament.

What does agape love look like? How do we love one another with agape love from God? What is Apostle John saying about the kind of love in the above passage?

Agape love

1 Corinthians 13:4-8 reveals,

"⁴ Love [*agape*] is patient, love is kind. It does not envy, it does not boast, it is not proud. ⁵ It does not dishonor others, it is not self-seeking, it is not easily angered, it keeps no record of wrongs. [6] Love does not delight in evil but rejoices with the truth. [7] It always protects, always trusts, always hopes, always perseveres. [8] Love never fails."

For instance, when we feel we are wronged, our human instinct is to get even and retaliate in kind.

While we should not tolerate or even encourage bad behavior (verse 6, "love does not delight in evil"), and need to seek God's wisdom on how to address it and stop it, two wrongs do not make it right (verse 5b, "it is not easily angered, it keeps no record of wrongs). It will just start a vicious cycle of bitterness and retaliation.

Apostle Paul encourages us,

"[17] Do not repay anyone evil for evil. Be careful to do what is right in the eyes of everyone. [18] If it is possible, as far as it depends on you, live at peace with everyone. [19] Do not take revenge, my dear friends, but leave room for God's wrath, for it is written: "It is mine to avenge; I will repay," [a] says the Lord. ...

"[21] Do not be overcome by evil, but *overcome evil with good*" (Romans 12:17-21).

Footnotes
    a.   Deut. 32:35

In retrospect, I experienced God's overwhelming agape love for me, when I realized He sent his beloved Son, Jesus, to die for my sins, as I shared in Part One.

Now, we are to love our spouse and other people with that kind of sacrificial love we have experienced from God.

My sister Elizabeth gave us a plaque inscribed with that Corinthians passage as one of her wedding gifts. It is a great reminder!

Incidentally, I later found a passage in the Scriptures that says, "Come, descendants of Jacob, let us walk in the light of the Lord" (Isaiah 2:5).

It is incredible that God, who through prophet Isaiah, urged Israelites to follow Him in their daily life thousands of years ago, has also, I feel, been encouraging all believers, including my wife Margaret and me, with the same calling, *to walk in His light*, even today!

My idea for the design of our wedding invitation was, I believe, an inspiration from God to walk in His light, just as He called the Israelites to do thousands of years ago.

I can now appreciate even more deeply, what Scripture exclaims in Revelation 4:8b, "'Holy, holy, holy is the Lord God Almighty,' [a] who *was*, and *is*, and *is to come*."

Footnotes
    a. Isaiah 6:3

Is God's Warning Outdated?

It Is for Our Own Good

Some may think that God's commands are too strict and are outdated in our modern times. However, it is for our own good that God created man and woman, established marriage, and commanded us to keep it.

God says in Genesis 2:18,

"It is not good for the man to be alone. I will make a helper suitable for him."

As I grow older, I appreciate my spouse's companionship more and more every day.

And not only that, but our marriage has also helped us become better people. While there is always room for improvement, and there have been tough times, our marriage has helped us become aware of our own shortcomings.

It has also reminded us to care for each other's needs, not just our own.

It is definitely a meaningful and rewarding experience to learn to walk together in the light of His love!

The Perils of Divorce

Extensive research has shown that loneliness is a major cause of stress and depression. Divorce, I believe, not only will bring the parents loneliness, but it may also force the children to make painful choices, being caught between dad and mom.

In a broken family, there are no winners.

I trust that since God created us, He knows what is best for us. Therefore, instead of treating divorce as an option, man should cherish and love his wife as he loves himself, even sacrificially (Ephesians 5:22-33).

I have no doubt that those who heed the warnings from God regarding marriage will get the most benefits, as it is divinely intended for us to receive from it.

Some may say it is easier said than done. I understand. Nobody wants to end a marriage with a divorce when they get married. Nonetheless, there is hope if we seek His assistance and learn to love our spouse with agape love. It can be done.

I am conscious that this is a sensitive subject, particularly in domestic violence. It is my personal opinion that, in such cases, a physical separation to ensure the safety of the spouse and the children while seeking counseling is prudent.

In Conclusion

God loves us. It is He who ordained marriage.

If we would follow His command to commit ourselves to marriage, and seek His help in times of need, God will enable us to learn to love our spouse with agape love from Him, and thus enjoy perhaps the most important human relationship in our life!

11 - PEACE FROM JESUS

The Fundamental Peace

As believers, we have that fundamental peace with God because, through Jesus, we have reconciled with our Creator, and are no longer condemned for our sins. We are now looking forward to that day, when the kingdom of heaven comes.

Peace in Times of Trouble

In the meantime, before that day comes, we can start to learn to depend on Jesus to have peace, while we are still in this present world of chaos and sufferings.

Jesus declares, "I have told you these things, so that *in me you may have peace*. In this world, you will have trouble. But take heart! I have overcome the world" (John 16:33).

He also affirms,

"Peace I leave with you; my peace I give you. I do not give to you as the world gives. Do not let your hearts be troubled and do not be afraid" (John 14:27).

One might ask, "How could believers have peace facing troubles?"

As commented before, when that violent man screamed at me, I prayed to God for wisdom to handle it; I did not feel scared and helpless. When I was told to be silent by a possible death threat in Dallas, I was able to be calm and not intimidated.

Two Particularly Assuring Promises

Many teachings and promises in the Bible assist believers in dealing with adversity. Among them, two have been particularly encouraging for me.

The First

1 Corinthians 10:13 assures us: "No temptation has overtaken you except what is common to mankind. And God is faithful; *he will not let you be tempted beyond what you can bear*. But when you are tempted, he will also provide a way out so that you can endure it."

Being God's children, He knows our limits; He will never allow things we cannot bear to happen to us. That is assuring.

The Second

Romans 8:28 affirms:

"And we know that in *all* things God works for the good of those who love him, who have been called according to his purpose."

The key here is that it applies to all things. And if we continue to trust and love God, it will turn out to be good for us.

In situations where it is apparent that we have done something wrong, it is easier to understand why we are getting the consequences. For example, we did not pay attention while driving, then had an accident, or were not honest with people. Now, we are receiving backlash from those who were lied to.

Scripture cautions,

"If you suffer, it should not be as a murderer or thief or any other kind of criminal, or even as a meddler" (1 Peter 4:15).

That said, for problems not due to our faults, we sometimes question why God allows it to happen.

But if we do not doubt God's goodness and continue to trust and love him, we will learn valuable spiritual lessons.

As a matter of fact, Romans 5:1-4 says that we can even rejoice facing suffering because we will grow spiritually:

"[1] Therefore, since we have been justified through faith, we have peace with God through our Lord Jesus Christ, [2] through whom we have gained access by faith into this grace in which we now stand. And we boast in the hope of the glory of God.

"[3] Not only so, but we also glory [or 'rejoice'] in our sufferings, because we know that *suffering produces perseverance;* [4] *perseverance, character; and character, hope.*"

Whenever I am in a difficult situation, I try to remind myself of those two promises. Yes, it will not be beyond what I can bear, and yes, it will be for the good of my spiritual growth.

Doing that helps calm me down, and I can deal with it with a positive and hopeful attitude.

By the Way, How Should Christians Deal with Mistakes?

In cases where a problematic situation happens to us because of our faults, how can we address it constructively?
1 John 1:9 advises us,

"If we confess our sins, he [God] is faithful and just and will forgive us our sins and purify us from all unrighteousness."

Proverbs 28:13 reminds us, "Whoever conceals their sins does not prosper, but the one who confesses and renounces them finds mercy."

Therefore, instead of denying it, covering it up, and letting it spiral out of control, we can ask God and the people affected by our mistakes to forgive us and seek to correct it. I will share more on this regard at the concluding note of this Part Two.

My Encounters that Testify to the Truthfulness of the Two Promises

A "Drifter"?

After I started working in Dallas and was born again, I lost my job five times in the next five years! It even caught the attention of a member of my church's fellowship group. I still remember he said, "Poor little George, he can write a book with the title 'Little George – The Drifter'."
While I did not appreciate his comment, I understood how people would perceive it. However, despite that kind of remark, somehow, throughout those five years, I did

not feel discouraged or panicked at all. My focus was to make sure that if I had done anything wrong, I would correct it and move on.

COMPANY-WIDE LAYOFF

The first job I lost was due to a massive company-wide layoff. It was a mid-sized electronic company that made memory chips for computers. Very few people survived the ax when it fell.

On that fateful Friday, as we walked out of our office building carrying our boxes, there were real estate agents standing at the door, handing out coupons for discounted realtor fees, asking if we would sell our houses.

Fortunately, my manager gave me an excellent reference letter at the exit interview. I found my second job quickly. It was with a major high-tech corporation in the area.

OUR WEDDING SEEMINGLY INTERRUPTED

The second job loss happened on the day when I was to pick up my fiancée Margaret.

We planned to select her wedding dress and make other preparations. I was with that high-tech firm for less than a year. We were to get married in about a week. I had just submitted my request to take some days off.

When I just sat down in my office that morning, I was called to the Human Resources Department. Then I was told I was laid off, effective immediately. No reason was given.

While driving home that day, I shouted, "No Way!" in the car, as if I were screaming at an opposing enemy. I was certain Margaret was the woman God wanted me to marry. This curveball definitely was not thrown at me by God.

I called my supervisor to ask him if I had done anything wrong. He said, "George, you had done everything I asked you to do. I kind of feel guilty."

Though I was sure about going forward with the wedding, I wanted to be sure that Margaret and her parents were okay with it, too. I called her and asked if she wanted to postpone until I secured a job.

Without hesitation, both she and her parents, who are devoted Christians too, affirmed that we should go ahead and get married.

After the wedding and the honeymoon in California, we took my mother, who came from Taiwan for our wedding, to Florida for sightseeing. During the trip there, I filled out a job application and mailed it.

As soon as we were back in Dallas, I got the job and started *the next day*. Not a day was wasted.

It was as if God had a perfect plan for me. Instead of letting our wedding be seemingly "interrupted," we had an entire month of celebration and vacationing.

If I had not been laid off, I would have had at most one week of leave, since I had yet to earn my two weeks annual vacation time off.

MOTHER'S FUNERAL

However, this latest position did not last long either. After working only six months there, my mother passed away. When I returned from Taiwan after the funeral, I was told I no longer had the job. Again, no reason was given.

I was quite surprised, because right before I left for Taiwan, my supervisor still said that I had performed well, and even finished all my assignments before the deadlines. He was very pleased with my work.

Later, the agent of the employment agency I used told me, "We checked with that company, and they said that it was due to personality conflict."

I did not know whom they were talking about, because I did not recall I had any personal issues with anyone there. In any case, I moved on and started looking for work again.

Thankfully, I found a job again not long after.

"ALTHOUGH TRIALS ARE NOT ENDING, BUT SO IS MY GRACE."

The fourth and fifth jobs I lost also happened without giving me any cause. I was just "laid off". Nevertheless, throughout these challenging ordeals, I never felt scared or depressed. Somehow, God gave me these crystal-clear words in my mind, *"although trials are not ending, but so is my grace."*

I felt hopeful and upbeat. I did not question why God let it happen. I just fixed my attention on improving anything I needed to and then looking for my next job.

Amazingly, in these five years, not only did I find work within about two months, or even sooner, but my salary also increased 57%! I still have my tax records to prove it. That was more than 10% a year. If I had stayed in the same company, I do not know I would have gotten that kind of annual raise, if at all.

A BLESSING IN DISGUISE

It was undoubtedly a blessing in disguise. After five years, my work was stable. It seemed that God allowed it to happen to let me experience his grace and, in the process, to strengthen my faith.

I did not tell anybody how I lost my jobs, nor did I mention the fact that I got a significant wage increase *every time*.

People in the church, who did not know what actually transpired, might think that I had done something terribly wrong, and that God was chastising me repeatedly. To unbelievers, it might have seemed that the God I believe in is not a good god at all.

However, for me, it was a precious spiritual experience. I later found this passage in the Bible:

"2 Consider it pure joy, my brothers and sisters, [a] whenever you face trials of many kinds, 3 because you know that *the testing of your faith* produces perseverance.

"4 Let perseverance finish its work so that you may be mature and complete, not lacking anything.

"12 Blessed is the one who perseveres under trial because, having stood the test, that person will receive the crown of life that the Lord has promised to those who love him" (James 1:2-4, 12).

Footnotes
  a. The Greek word for *brothers and sisters* (*adelphoi*) refers here to believers, both men and women, as part of God's family; also in verses 16 and 19; and in 2:1, 5, 14; 3:10, 12; 4:11; 5:7, 9, 10, 12, 19.

Looking back, the severities of my adversity were minimal, compared to those who even lost their lives because of their faith. God just let me appreciate what it was like to be His Children facing troubles.

It is undeniably true, that a hard situation will not be beyond what I can bear, and that it will be for the good of me.

"Why Are You So Happy?"

After that first five years, I started to work at a computer data processing company, which was affiliated with a group of financial institutions. It had been a stable job. However, after several years, the company decided to close the Dallas shop and move to another state.

All employees would lose their jobs.

In the months leading to the scheduled closure, people were feeling anxious about it. As for me, while I was a bit disappointed, since I had been working there for three years, I remained positive and just focused on looking for new opportunities.

Then, one day, while walking past a colleague's cubical, he turned his head and asked me from inside his office, "Why are you so happy?" He was a senior staff member, very capable, and seemed to be smoking all the time.

Surprised, I asked, "Do you really want to know my honest answer?" He looked at me, nodding, but seemed unsure what I would say. "It is because I believe in Jesus." He responded quickly, "Well, I rejected him long time ago."

He was a nice guy, always willing to help. I liked him. I just wished he had also accepted Jesus, so he would not have to worry so much. For some reason, after so many years, I still vividly remember his question and facial expression that day.

Days before we were to leave, we all received a big, fat severance check, which I had never had before. For me, it was more than ten thousand dollars, and that was the dollar in the year of 1988.

The company had promised that if we agreed to stay on for a few more months to support the transition, we would get several months of severance pay. I promptly deposited it and kept it as our family's emergency fund.

As for my next job, I got it even before the company closed. Again, I was hired with a good increase of pay. The new job's location was even closer to home; it was only a 15-minute drive.

"Do You Really Think I Can Do It in One Week?"

This company was a Fortune 500 corporation. My job there was stable, and I received good annual evaluations and raises, too.

But after about five years, the company decided to outsource most of its computer department operations. That meant most employees in the department would be without a job soon.

The working atmosphere once again (as in my previous job when a layoff was announced) was tense and uncertain for many people. There had been several rounds of layoff. I survived a few times, but it seemed that the company then adopted a policy to encourage people to quit, so that they would not need to pay severance.

I say that because one day, my manager suddenly told me to write two new computer programs from scratch in just one week, without any of the specifications defined. It was clearly unrealistic. I had never been assigned such a project before.

I still worked as hard as I could, but I did not panic and was still able to sleep at night because I thought, if God would never give me something I could not bear, how could a human being think he could do that?

A couple of days later, when I went to the restroom, my manager happened to come in too, and stood at the stall right next to mine. It was not exactly a great place for any conversations, let alone with your boss.

Nonetheless, I asked him (calmly, not accusingly), "Do you really think I can do it in one week?" He said, "Sure." But then, a little bit later, one of my co-workers came to me and said that our boss had just sent him to support me with the project.

God is faithful!

When the scheduled outsourcing came, I was called to my manager's office. I said, "Okay, give it to me," and happily (because I believed God would open another door for me again) accepted the exit notice. I then calmly and sincerely asked him if he would write me a reference letter.

Thankfully, I received a good recommendation from him. Sure enough, I secured another job at another Fortune 500 company. And yes, with increased pay again, and this time, even at a higher position with four weeks of annual vacation (usually, it was two weeks for most professional jobs).

My Last Job before Attending Dallas Theological Seminary

This final job lasted about one and a half years. However, this time, it was not because I was let go but because I quit. I was going to attend seminary full-time.

Though it was such a well-paying job, I felt strongly that it was time. It seemed that God had completed training me through all these uncertainties in the world, and that it was time for me to be further equipped in a seminary setting.

By the way, when I was dating Margaret, I asked her, "If God would call me to full-time ministry in the future, would that be fine with you?" She said, "YES," without any hesitation.

I enrolled in 1996 at the age of 46.

"I Am So Tired of Being Sick."

After graduating with a master's degree in theology, I started working as a pastor and, later, as an adjunct professor at local colleges.

Then, in 2006, I had a heart attack.

As spoken of in Part One, my father died of a heart attack when he was 59. My mother also passed away from either a heart attack or a stroke. I learned later that, in America, people between 55 and 58 are the prime age group for having heart attacks, and many of them do not survive the first one.

I was right in the middle of that age group, although I did not smoke or drink. I was not overweight, generally ate healthy food, and exercised regularly.

I am grateful that, according to the doctor's description, it was a "small" attack. I survived and had two stents inserted.

However, after the procedure, I still felt some chest pain almost every afternoon. I did not know if I needed to call 911 or if I could just tough it out. The doctors did not give me clear instructions on how to cope with it either.

In the following summer, when I felt the pain, I would call an emergency ambulance and be checked into the hospital. Then, I would be discharged without any treatment, saying my arteries were not blocked.

But when I got home, I would still feel the pain. I was in and out of the hospital so often during the summer that one day, I told Margaret, "I am so tired of being sick!"

I felt I could not take it anymore. Margret was exhausted, too, from caring for and worrying about me.

AN UNEXPECTED CALL

Soon afterward, a lady from the church I previously pastored called and left a message. I baptized her in that church. She attended the church regularly but had never called me before, and did not call me again after that either. She said, "Pastor Chiou, please take good care of your health."

When I called back, her husband answered. He started to say that he had exactly the same situation as mine, having chest pain. Still, it was not severe enough to require surgery. It was due to a blockage of a small vessel that would *not* trigger a heart attack.

I finally realized that it was the answer to my dilemma! I did not need to worry about it after all!

I forgot the spiritual lesson I learned before: I do not have to be anxious when facing troubles. Even though I did not blame God for my situation, I became very upset and frustrated by how the hospitals and the doctors had treated my illness.

But once again, God is so faithful that He apparently moved her to call me and relieve the deep concern and anxiety that was about to overwhelm me.

I have since exercised more often (from three times a week to six) and kept an even stricter diet (limited red meat but allowed more vegetables). I have not felt frequent chest pains anymore and have not had to go to the hospital since that summer. It has been 16 years. In some way, I am even healthier than before!

Again, just as Scripture says in 1 Corinthians 10:13,

"No temptation has overtaken you except what is common to mankind. And God is faithful; he will not let you be tempted beyond what you can bear. But when you are tempted, he will also provide a way out so that you can endure it."

In Conclusion

Yes, after all these years of personal challenges, big and small, I can testify that the peace Jesus gives his believers is not as the world gives. Yes, we can have peace despite troubles in this world.

    We need not be afraid!

    Incidentally, I found a truly touching and beautiful song by Maranatha! Music entitled "*My Peace*." Search YouTube for "My Peace – Maranatha Singers" and enjoy!

12 - WHAT IS THE PURPOSE OF OUR LIFE?

WHAT BRINGS REAL HAPPINESS?

These are big questions many people contemplate. Some may instinctively think of being rich and famous. But do these things bring real meaning and happiness to us?

About Getting Rich

Is the purpose of getting wealthy to be able to afford all the expensive gourmet food, like a second even a third steak? We may be able to afford it; the irony is that it also can block our arteries (due to the harmful effects of high cholesterol).

Or is it for a bigger car, a larger house, a huge boat, or a quarter-million-dollar ride (the price as reported in 2021) for a few minutes of thrill in weightlessness near the edge of space?

All these material things or physical excitements that money can buy do bring a temporary high. However, shortly after that, people will feel low again. Some may even indulge in drugs or alcohol, which may end up costing them their lives.

GEORGE S. CHIOU

How Much Happiness Can Money Buy?

DANIEL KAHNEMAN'S STUDY

Daniel Kahneman, a researcher at Princeton University and a Nobel Prize winner for economics in 2002, published a report with Angus Deaton on this subject:

"Recent research has begun to distinguish two aspects of subjective well-being. Emotional well-being refers to the emotional quality of an individual's everyday experience—the frequency and intensity of experiences of joy, stress, sadness, anger, and affection that make one's life pleasant or unpleasant. Life evaluation refers to the thoughts that people have about their life when they think about it.

"We raise the question of *whether money buys happiness*, separately for these two aspects of well-being. We report an analysis of more than 450,000 responses to the Gallup-Healthways Well-Being Index, a daily survey of 1,000 US residents conducted by the Gallup Organization.

"... When plotted against log income, life evaluation rises steadily. *Emotional well-being also rises with log income, but there is no further progress beyond an annual income of ~$75,000.*"

(Daniel Kahneman and Angus Deaton, research article, *"High income improves evaluation of life but not emotional well-being,"* The Proceedings of the National Academy of Sciences of the United States of America (PNAS), September 21, 2010, 107 (38) 16489-16493; https://doi.org/10.1073/pnas.1011492107, used by permission.)

Incidentally, Mr. Kahneman was awarded the Nobel Prize for Economics "for having integrated insights from psychological research into economic science, especially concerning human judgment and decision-making under uncertainty."

(Press release by the Nobel Prize Organization, https://www.nobelprize.org/prizes/economic-sciences/2002/press-release/)

THE FINDING

The study indicates that the emotional satisfaction money can buy stops increasing beyond $75,000 a year. This was the figure the researchers concluded around 2008 and 2009; it may be adjusted for inflation for today's dollars.

According to the Bureau of Labor Statistics consumer price index, using its CPI Inflation Calculator, $75,000 in January 2008 is equivalent, in purchasing power, to about $96,000 in June 2021.

The point is that it is still a finite, relatively small amount compared to the notion that, perhaps, one must be really wealthy, like a millionaire, to be happy.

Why Is the Amount of Happiness Money Can Buy So Limited?

WE ARE NOT JUST PHYSICAL BEINGS

Genesis 2:7 records, when God created man,

"... the Lord God formed a man from the dust of the ground and breathed into his nostrils *the breath of life*, and the man became a living being [literally, a living soul]."

Ecclesiastes 12:7 says, when man dies,

"... the dust returns to the ground it came from, and the spirit returns to God who gave it."

Jesus remarks in Matthew 16:26,

"What good will it be for someone to gain the whole world, yet forfeit their soul? Or what can anyone give in exchange for their soul? "

Jesus cautions us that even if a person is the richest in the world, it will not satisfy his or her soul. It is a vacuum that cannot be filled with physical wealth.

We cannot feel peaceful and truly happy without getting right with God, who created us and gave us our soul. Our soul must be connected to God in order to feel true happiness.

A NOTE ON THE SOUL AND THE SPIRIT

The Bible speaks of human beings as spirit, soul, and body:

"May God himself, the God of peace, sanctify you through and through. May your whole spirit, soul and body be kept blameless at the coming of our Lord Jesus Christ" (1 Thessalonians 5:23).

In the context of the above passage, the spirit is man's highest part, which enables him to communicate with God (John 4:24, "God is spirit, and his worshipers must worship in the Spirit and in truth").

The soul is the sentient part: our will, emotions, and self-consciousness. And the body is the physical part.

However, elsewhere in the Scriptures, in many instances, only body and spirit (Ecclesiastes 12:7; 2 Corinthian 7:1; and James 2:26), or body and soul (Genesis 2:7 and Matthew 10:28), are mentioned.

It is probable that in these passages, the terms "soul" and "spirit" are interchangeable. Either the soul or the spirit denotes the immaterial part of man, as contrasted to the material part (the body).

In this book, if only the soul or the spirit is mentioned, it is used interchangeably also.

How, Then, Should We Take Good Care of Our Soul?

1 Peter 2:24-25 states,

"[24] He himself [Jesus] bore our sins' in his body on the cross, so that we might die to sins and live for righteousness; 'by his wounds you have been healed.' [25] For 'you were like sheep going astray,' but now you have returned to the Shepherd and Overseer of your souls.'"

Human souls are separated from God because of sins. By believing in Jesus and receiving the forgiveness of sins, believers' souls are returned to being under His loving care. We are like sheep; once, we were wandering and going astray, but now we have come home to our shepherd's safety and care.

Believers will no longer feel lost in this chaotic world. We are no longer trapped in the vicious cycle of seeking physical pleasure, feeling down and empty again, trying to find our next fix, and then suffering emptiness again.

SOUL FIRMLY ANCHORED IN HIS CARE

Not only that, but our soul is also now firmly anchored in His care. We will not be cast away again.

Hebrews 6:19-20 assures us that,

"[19] We have this hope [the assurance of salvation through Jesus] as an *anchor* for the soul, firm and secure. It enters the inner sanctuary behind the curtain, [20] where our forerunner, Jesus, has entered on our behalf. He has become a high priest forever …"

The "inner sanctuary behind the curtain" uses imagery from Old Testament times, when the high priest would enter the Most Holy Place of the Tabernacle through a curtain, and make atonement for sins on behalf of the Israelites.

But now, with Jesus being the eternal high priest for all people, not just for Jews, all who believe can access God's atonement for sins and saving grace, once for all and permanently.

Jesus also encourages believers to:

"Love the Lord your God *with all your heart and with all your soul and with all your mind and with all your strength*" (Mark 12:30).

After we got right with God through Jesus, and now, as God's children, we are in loving fellowship with our Creator with our body and soul. It is a balanced, complete, and enduring peace and happiness.

We are made whole again!

Incidentally, I found an especially moving song that sums up the point of this section well. Its title is, *"Oh, let the Son of God enfold you"* (written by John Wimber, produced by Maranatha! Music). Check it out on YouTube and be encouraged!

So, Is Making a Lot of Money Not Good for Us?

Not at all. Money itself is neutral. It is how we see it, how we earn it, and how we use it that makes the critical difference.

The Perils of Not Managing Wealth Wisely

As discussed above, if we view wealth as the goal of our life, we will not find enduring happiness. We will always try to earn just one more dollar.

The Bible warns:

"For the love of money is a root of all kinds of evil. Some people, eager for money, have wandered from the faith and pierced themselves with many griefs" (1 Timothy 6:10).

While we are chasing after wealth, at the same time, our soul is screaming for help. Consequently, we will still feel empty inside, yet wonder why.

Moreover, if we do not use the money the right way, it can even be a curse rather than a blessing.

GOLD-PLATED HUB CAPS

I once came across a news report about a person in Dallas who, after installing gold-plated hub caps on his car, was robbed and killed. It was tragic and ironic for such a thing to happen.

LOTTERY PRIZE

Reporter Abigail Hess of CNBC (Consumer News and Business Channel – A division of NBCUniversal) wrote in the article, *"Here's why lottery winners go broke,"* on August 25, 2017:

"Lottery winners are more likely to declare bankruptcy within three to five years than the average American. What's more, studies have shown that winning the lottery does not necessarily make you happier or healthier."

She further states, "Jack Whittaker, who won $315 million in a lottery in West Virginia in 2002, tells Time, 'I wish that we had torn the ticket up.'

"Since winning, Whittaker's daughter and granddaughter died due to drug overdoses. Just eight months after winning, he was robbed of $545,000. 'I just don't like Jack Whittaker. I don't like the hard heart I've got,' he said. 'I don't like what I've become.'"

How Do Christians See Money?

If we regard it not as the end, but as the means to do what God wants us to do, we will feel genuine happiness, since our spirit will be right with God on this. God does bless some people with opportunities to make a lot of money. However, as elaborated below, it is to glorify God and assist people in need.

How Do Christians Use Money?

Ezekiel 16:49-50 in the Old Testament cautions,

"[49] 'Now this was the sin of your sister Sodom: She and her daughters were arrogant, overfed and unconcerned; they did not help the poor and needy. [50] They were haughty and did detestable things before me. Therefore I did away with them as you have seen.'"

Galatians 2:10 in the New Testament states,

"All they asked was that we should continue to remember the poor, the very thing I had been eager to do all along."

2 Corinthians 9:9 encourages us,

"As it is written: 'They have freely scattered their gifts to the poor; their righteousness endures forever.' [a] "
Footnotes
    a.   Psalm 112:9

Both the Old and the New Testaments stress the critical importance of generosity and aiding the poor. The Bible calls for us to use the money not to indulge in our own luxurious lifestyle, but to do the good deeds God wants us to do, especially helping the less fortunate and the needy.

HOW MUCH MONEY SHOULD WE SPEND FOR OURSELVES THEN?

It is quite interesting that the Scripture also has unambiguous advice on this.
Apostle Paul writes,

"[14] At the present time your plenty will supply what they need, so that in turn their plenty will supply what you need. The goal is equality, [15] as it is written: "The one who gathered much did not have too much, and the one who gathered little did not have too little" (2 Corinthians 8:14-15).

I believe it is teaching us to live a middle-class lifestyle.
By the way, what is the middle-class income in America?
Mr. Rakesh Kochhar, a senior researcher at Pew Research Center, Washington, D.C., writes in an article entitled, *"Through an American lens, Western Europe's middle classes appear smaller,"* that "...In 2010, middle-class households in the U.S. had incomes ranging from $35,294 to $105,881."
(6-5-2017, https://www.pewresearch.org/fact-tank/2017/06/05/through-an-american-lens-western-

europes-middle-classes-appear-smaller/, accessed 7-12-2021)

(Disclaimer: Pew Research Center bears no responsibility for the analyses or interpretations of the data presented here. The opinions expressed herein, including any implications for policy, are those of the author and not of Pew Research Center.)

The midpoint of that range is about $70,000. Incredibly, that is close to the amount of $75,000 found in the research I just referred to, regarding the limit money can buy us happiness.

Furthermore, it is common knowledge that if a society has extreme poverty and extreme wealth, but only has a relatively small middle class, it is inherently politically unstable. Crimes and social unrest follow.

God not only tells us the limitation of happiness money can buy for us as individuals, but also what is good for a happy and peaceful community. And it was written almost 2,000 years ago.

THE PITFALLS OF HOARDING WEALTH

In Luke 12:16-21, Jesus uses a parable to warn about the dangers and the foolishness of hoarding wealth:

"... [20] But God said to him, 'You fool! This very night your life will be demanded from you. Then who will get what you have prepared for yourself?'

"[21] This is how it will be with whoever stores up things for themselves but is not rich toward God."

We will never be able to bring a single penny to heaven with us. On the other hand, all the good deeds we did for God on Earth, including those done with our wealth, will be remembered and rewarded in heaven (Hebrews 6:10; Revelation 14:13).

One caution, though, is that this is not about salvation. Salvation is a free gift from God (Ephesians 2:8); nonetheless, after we are saved, God expects us to be a good steward of whatever He blesses us with and to use it to serve people (Ephesians 2:10).

How Do Christians Earn Money?

The Bible calls for us to earn it not just legally, but also ethically and morally. It also calls for us specifically to make it honestly and fairly.

Proverbs 21:6 cautions:

"A fortune made by a lying tongue is a fleeting vapor and a deadly snare."

Jesus reserves one of the most severe condemnations for lying, saying that liars are children of the devil:

"You belong to your father, the devil, and you want to carry out your father's desires. He was a murderer from the beginning, not holding to the truth, for there is no truth in him. When he lies, he speaks his native language, for he is a liar and the father of lies" (John 8:44).

Lying is the direct opposite of who God is.

He is the truth (Isaiah 45:19; John 14:6). No matter what we do, including making money, we must be honest. That means, as a worker, being truthful to our employer, or as a business owner, being honest to our employees and customers, for instance.

As for being fair in making money, we should pay workers fair wages and not exploit their labor, for example.

James 5:1-5 warns rich people sternly:

"[1] now listen, you rich people, weep and wail because of the misery that is coming on you.
"... [4] Look! The wages you failed to pay the workers who mowed your fields are crying out against you. The cries of the harvesters have reached the ears of the Lord Almighty. [5] You have lived on earth in luxury and self-indulgence. You have fattened yourselves in the day of slaughter."

A CASE TO PONDER IN DALLAS

I still can recall reading a Dallas newspaper one day in the 1980s on the divorce rate of company employees in the city. One of the top businesses with a high divorce rate was a well-known software corporation.

The article reported that the company's CEO told their employees they might not be able to go home for *the next three months* until the project was finished, but he would give them a big gift to take home for their spouses afterward.

I just shook my head in disbelief. After three months of absence, they might not even have a wife or husband still at home, let alone be there to accept the gift.

I was working in the computer industry then, and I knew that particular company was known to demand a lot of overtime work from its employees. Besides, since a typical software developer is a salaried job, the company is not legally required to pay overtime.

The more hours those staff with fixed salaries worked, the more profit the company made. That owner was a wealthy man. Nevertheless, it is not a good example of how Christians should make money.

In addition, even for non-believers, biblical principles actually make business sense, as the following instance tells us.

AN EXAMPLE TO LEARN FROM IN LOS ANGELES

Many can recall the tragic incident in South Los Angeles in April 1992. It was the mayhem of the Rodney King Riots. Violence erupted after a jury acquitted four white police officers in the beating of black motorist Rodney King.

The riots lasted more than five days, leaving more than 50 people dead and over 2,000 injured. More than 1,000 buildings were damaged. The entire city blocks were looted and burned.

However, according to a book, one grocery store stood intact.

It turned out that the store's white owner had been very kind to the community. He paid his employees well and did not charge his customers higher prices, even though it was in the inner-city area (for details, refer to the book by Bill Clinton, *My Life* (New York: Vintage Books, 2005), p. 409).

I do not know if that businessman is a Christian, but paying workers fair wages and charging customers reasonable prices are certainly consistent with biblical principles.

His good way of conducting business saved his store.

Treating employees right and not ripping off customers, indeed, makes excellent business sense in the long run. The morale of the staff will be high, the turnover rate will be low, and customers will be satisfied and come back repeatedly to the smiling, happy employees who greet them.

To Sum Up Regarding Getting Rich

The consequence of not managing wealth right can be devastating. Instead of a blessing, it can become a curse. On the other hand, if we see wealth as a vehicle to do good deeds and not as the end itself, and earn it in a godly way, it will contribute to the enduring happiness and meaning of our life!

About Being Famous

I once heard someone say, "If I cannot be a great good guy, I would like to be a big bad gangster."

For some people, fame seems to be the goal, regardless of what it is known for.

However, even if the fame is not gained from illegal activities, will it bring us real happiness?

We all have read about sad stories of suicides by celebrities and well-known people. While we might not know the exact reasons for these tragedies, and some could be due to illness that caused people not to think normally, many had indulged in drugs and alcohol, and apparently had not been quite satisfied with their life when they committed suicide.

What we can conclude is that fame does not guarantee happiness. In fact, if one is not prepared to handle it, it can be overwhelming and problematic.

Fame Itself Is Not Bad

Just like being wealthy in itself is not bad, fame in itself in not either. It is how we see it, how we earn it, and how we use it that makes the critical difference.

If we view it not as the end but as the means to help people and earn it appropriately, then it can be deeply rewarding.

However, for those who regard fame as the end goal of life for themselves, it will not satisfy their soul. They will still feel hollow. It is a void that cannot be filled with fame.

In fact, it is at the time when we achieve a certain level of prominence and still find ourselves unhappy, that serious problems really arise.

What Can I Do to Possibly Top What I Just Did?

"What is the next target of my life?" "What can I do to possibly top what I just did?" Severe feelings of loss and desperation may set in. Some may try alcohol, some may try drugs, or some may even try to divorce their spouse of many years, hoping somehow it would give them a "new start."

13 - WHAT IS THE CHRISTIANS' OBJECTIVE OF LIFE?

So if wealth and fame in themselves cannot bring enduring happiness, and since, if they are not managed wisely, they can even be detrimental to us, then what should it be? What is the Christians' objective of life?

First, I will discuss life's priorities, and then I will share what the goal should be. Because if we get our priorities right, we will see the correct objective.

Christians' Priorities of Life

In Chapter 1 of the Book of Genesis, Scripture describes how God created the world. God first made the Earth, sky, plants, and animals. Then He made humans:

> "… so that they may rule over the fish in the sea and the birds in the sky, over the livestock and all the wild animals, and over all the creatures that move along the ground" (1:26).

From the above passage, and from Jesus' answer to the question of what the most important commandments are (that is, to love God and love people), it is definitive what the biblical view of our priorities is.

God is first, humans second, and all other creations, such as animals, plants, and physical matter, third (God > Humans > All other creations).

God over Humans

This priority is manifested from the fact that so many Christians in the early church era continued to spread the good news of Jesus, despite the explicit warnings and the subsequent persecutions by the then Roman government and the religious authorities in Jerusalem.

Apostle Peter and John said, in response to such threats,

"[19] 'Which is right in God's eyes: to listen to you, or to him [God]? You be the judges! [20] As for us, we cannot help speaking about what we have seen and heard'" (Acts 4:19-20).

Acts 5:29 records,

"Peter and the other apostles replied: "We must obey God rather than human beings!"

What does it mean to Christians today?

When someone asks us to do things against God's principles, we should not just give in.

When I was teaching at a private college, I followed all the school's policies. And I had received good evaluations from the students.

Nevertheless, toward the end of the semester, my immediate supervisor told me that, in effect, I must let a student pass even though the student did not turn in the required assignments.

I refused to comply. The school apparently was more interested in retaining students than providing a quality education. I knew I was risking offending my supervisor and possibly losing my job. However, I chose to keep a clear conscience and be able to sleep well in the night.

Some may say, "I cannot afford to do that." I understand the worry; still, I believe that if we do the right thing in God's eyes, He will take care of our needs. (More on this kind of concern later.)

Humans over All Other Creations

This means we value the well-being of humans more than anything else in the world. For example, in pursuit of wealth or fame, some may work so hard that they pay little attention to their own health, or their spouse's and children's emotional needs. Such a person is even called a "workaholic," like having a disease.

HOW I HANDLED MY JOBS

I worked in the computer field for 15 years. Throughout this period, I would ensure that the company with which I accepted the offer would not require employees to work excessive overtime, although the salary might be higher.

I would make sure that I had time for rest and exercise for myself, and above all, for taking care of my wife and children, too. Although we could not afford expensive trips, I would take the family for an annual vacation and spend time together.

HOW WE RAISED OUR CHILDREN

In addition, before our first child was born, we agreed that she would stay home for the first three years and be a full-time mom to our newborn infant. We felt that a baby needed a parent's full attention during that critical period.

After the first three years, a young child would begin wanting to play with other kids; then, we would let her attend half-day preschool. That was what we did for both of our daughters. We paid their private school tuition until they attended public school in the second grade.

For several hundred dollars a month, it amounted to public college tuition at that time in the early 1980s and '90s. With only my paycheck to support the family (I worked full time until I attended seminary in 1996), we probably were driving one of the oldest cars among our church members or my colleagues at work.

Indeed, we had been driving used cars until our first daughter was in college, and the second one was in middle school when I bought my wife our very first new car.

As for my car, when I sold it in 2015, it was 26 years old (a 1989 sedan I bought in 1992). I had been changing the car's engine oil myself regularly with quality oil and filter. Amazingly, it was still running well, except for an issue of leaking power steering fluid when I sold it for 1,000 dollars!

Sometimes, people frowned at my old vehicle, yet it was all worth it. Both of my daughters had a good foundation physically and academically. They seldom were sick, and they would get up every morning on time themselves, go to school, and study diligently without us having to worry much about it.

While many factors affect how a child will grow up, especially how they make their own choices, as far as parents' responsibilities go, I believe our extra money spent in their early childhood made a positive contribution.

Yes, people are definitely more important than a nicer car or more money in the bank.

HOW MY WIFE MARGARET DEALT WITH HER JOB'S DEMANDS

Regarding my wife Margaret, after our second daughter was in middle school, she started working full-time as a math teacher.

The first school she taught at was known to be a particularly tough one, because of the students' behavior issues there. It was incredibly stressful every day. She said one teacher even suffered a heart attack in the classroom and later died.

Sometimes, when she came back from school in the afternoon, I would jokingly, but actually a bit worriedly, say, "Today, you went to hell and back!"

After about six years (in retrospect, it was remarkable that she could survive that long), one day, when she came home from school, she looked exhausted. I checked her pulse; it was pounding. I said, "You must resign. This cannot continue. Your life is at risk. "

Even though we needed her paycheck (at the time, I was teaching part-time at a college while trying to plant a church), our belief on what must be done was clear. She left in two months at the end of the school year.

Fortunately, we had made sure that we did not live beyond our means (we still do so now) and, therefore, had some savings. With my part-time job, we should be okay for a while. Even without them, the choice was in no doubt: her health is more important than money.

After working temporary jobs for about a year, she found a much better school (in terms of the stress level) to teach. We were very thankful!

"SEEK FIRST HIS KINGDOM AND HIS RIGHTEOUSNESS"

It reminded me of what Jesus says in Matthew 6:31-33,

"^{31} So do not worry, saying, 'What shall we eat?' or 'What shall we drink?' or 'What shall we wear?' ^{32} For the pagans run after all these things, and your heavenly Father knows that you need them. ^{33} But seek first his kingdom and his righteousness, and all these things will be given to you as well."

If we follow God's principle of prioritizing people over money, He will provide for our physical needs.

By the way, some may argue that since Scripture teaches that humans are superior to animals, it is okay to do whatever we want to them.

On the contrary, the Bible requires that we be good stewards of whatever God created for humans. We are to manage them well. That means to protect them (unless some are dangerous to us). This goes for the environment, too. Christians should be at the forefront of keeping our air clean, and our drinking water safe.

To Sum Up Regarding Christians' Priorities of Life

Yes, if we set our priorities right: God first, people second, and all other creations third, all things will fall into their proper places. It will enable us to make the right decision at the critical junctures of our lives.

Psalm 111:10 reveals,

"The fear of the Lord is the beginning of wisdom; all who follow his precepts have good understanding. To him belongs eternal praise."

He is the source of all wisdom!

Are Christians' Priorities Not Burdensome?

Incidentally, besides the biblical priorities discussed above, some may be troubled by so many do's and don'ts in the Scriptures. People want to do whatever they want, believing that is what freedom is about.

Nevertheless, is it real freedom for us? For instance, it may seem inconvenient, if we choose to be home when kids are home, so that we can supervise and assist them. However, being parents, it certainly is real freedom from having to worry about our children in the long run.

I once witnessed a mother crying loudly at the open house of our daughter's high school in front of the principal and many parents in the room, asking for help for her son's drug addiction. I felt sad seeing that she was so hopeless and broken-hearted.

I do not know her situation. Although this school is in a wealthy neighborhood with a low crime rate, I understand that there can be many reasons a kid gets into problems. And there are things that parents simply cannot control. She might have done all she could.

Yet, if what we do may help our children become less likely to be situated in a tempting environment, while it might be inconvenient, or even cost some opportunities for our career, I believe, in the end, this creates real freedom for both the kids and the parents.

HOW I AND MARGARET MADE OUR CAREER CHOICES

For both of our daughters, while in K to 12 schools, we ensured that at least one of us was at home when they came back from school, not just during the semester, but also throughout the summer and winter breaks when they were in the house.

That was one of the reasons why Margaret chose to be a teacher, so that she would be with them during their school breaks.

This priority limited our options for jobs and careers. However, we felt that at least that was what we could do to support them by providing a stable and secure environment.

Some may think that the biblical principles are sound, but they are just hard to follow. However, I often felt a strong conviction and the desire to do so. On top of that, God's power will enable us to overcome our weakness or selfishness.

Yes, it can be hard to let go of our self-centered inclination; however, I do feel it is a worthy and achievable goal.

"YOUR WORD IS A LAMP FOR MY FEET, A LIGHT ON MY PATH" (PSALM 119:105)

As attested by the prophet Isaiah,

"We all, like sheep, have gone astray, each of us has turned to our own way" (Isaiah 53:6).

Those do's and don'ts are like streetlights shining in the dark road, illuminating the safe way for us to take, and the unsafe spots to avoid!

Jesus urges us,

"[28] Come to me, all you who are weary and burdened, and I will give you rest. [29] Take my yoke upon you and learn from me, for I am gentle and humble in heart, and you will find rest for your souls. [30] For my yoke is easy and my burden is light" (Matthew 11:28-30).

What God wants from us is our willingness to seek His wisdom and care; the rest is relatively easy. On the other hand, the consequence of just relying on ourselves and doing it our own way is feeling confused, lost, and heavy-laden.

Christians are not exempt from life's adversities, just like anybody else. However, with a clear sense of security, direction, and purpose God provides, life can be a challenging but truly joyful ride indeed!

Yes, instead of feeling burdensome, choosing to follow biblical priorities and its teachings is a liberating experience!

The Christians' Objective of Life

There are two aspects of it: personal and professional.

Personal: To Grow Spiritually and Become More and More like Jesus

It can be achieved by practicing loving God and loving people as ourselves.

The husband-wife and parent-child relationships are great areas to start. As shared before, I believe our marriage has helped us become better people.

There are no perfect couples, including Christians. However, if we see our spouse and our children as our opportunity to learn to love people, instead of just for our own selfish gratification, then we will have more positive attitude towards marriage and children.

Sometimes, when I was upset about something, I would feel a lot better if I reminded myself about that. Of course, the goal is to progress to love people from outside our home as well.

WHAT DOES IT LOOK LIKE TO BE "LIKE JESUS"?

The passage of 2 Peter 1:3-8 shows us the promises, and how and what it is like to grow spiritually after we are born again:

"[3] His divine power has given us everything we need for a godly life ... so that through them you may *participate in the divine nature*, having escaped the corruption in the world caused by evil desires.

"[5] For this very reason, make every effort to add to your faith goodness; and to goodness, knowledge; [6] and to knowledge, self-control; and to self-control, perseverance; and to perseverance, godliness; [7] and to godliness, mutual affection; and to mutual affection, love.

"[8] For if you possess these qualities in increasing measure, they will keep you from being ineffective and unproductive in your knowledge of our Lord Jesus Christ."

Please note that this is about growing in our faith after we are saved. It is not about salvation. Salvation is a free gift from God, as pointed out before (more discussion in Part Four); it is not obtained by merit.

Nevertheless, after we are saved, God would like us to start learning and experiencing a divine and joyful life, away from the corrupting influence of the past.

It is like a spiritual baby growing up to maturity. Theologically, we call this stage *sanctification*.

THE FRUIT OF THE SPIRIT

Another especially precious Scripture on spiritual growth is in Galatians 5:16-23,

"[16] So I say, walk by the Spirit, and you will not gratify the desires of the flesh [sinful nature].

"... [19] The acts of the flesh are obvious: sexual immorality, impurity and debauchery; [20] idolatry and witchcraft; hatred, discord, jealousy, fits of rage, selfish ambition, dissensions, factions [21] and envy; drunkenness, orgies, and the like. I warn you, as I did before, that those who live like this will not inherit the kingdom of God.

"[22] But *the fruit of the Spirit* is love, joy, peace, forbearance, kindness, goodness, faithfulness, [23] gentleness and self-control. Against such things there is no law. "

God points out to us a beautiful and encouraging path. But having said that, we must know that it is a work-in-progress process until Jesus comes again.

CHRISTIANS STILL CAN SIN IF WE CHOOSE TO IGNORE HIS TEACHINGS

As I have touched on sinful nature in Part One, under "Follow Christ Earnestly," Christians still have this inclination. It will not go away until we are resurrected and transformed to glorious bodies at the end times. The theological term for this last stage of a Christian life on Earth is called *glorification*.

Thus, the three stages of the renewal of a Christian's life are:

- *Salvation* (when we put our trust in Jesus and are no longer condemned)

- *Sanctification* (when we grow spiritually)
- *Glorification* (when we are resurrected and transformed with no more sinful nature, the full redemption of our bodies (Romans 8:23))

However, until then, we still can sin.

"DO NOT GIVE THE DEVIL A FOOTHOLD"

Ephesians 4:26-27 reminds us, "[26] In your anger do not sin" [a]: Do not let the sun go down while you are still angry, [27] and do not give the devil a foothold."

> Footnotes
> a. Psalm 4:4 (see Septuagint)

Anger is not a sin if it is for a righteous reason. Yet, even for a moral purpose, we must resolve it quickly, lest we allow the devil an opportunity to tempt us.

Dr. Warren Wiersbe says it well:

"According to Jesus, anger is the first step toward murder (Matt. 5:21-26), because anger gives the devil a foothold in our lives, and Satan is a murderer (John 8:44). Satan hates God and God's people, and when he finds a believer with the sparks of anger in his heart, he fans those sparks, adds fuel to the fire..."

(Warren W. Wiersbe, *Be Rich (Ephesians) – Are you losing the things that money can't buy?* (Wheaton, Illinois: Victor Books, 1976), p. 113. Used by permission of David C. Cook. May not be further reproduced. All rights reserved.)

The case of King David

Although King David's story was not about handling anger, it was a case of how we can give Satan a foothold in other aspects of our lives.

King David was a God-fearing man God anointed as the King of Israel. Nevertheless, the Bible records this unfortunate incident:

"[1] In the spring, at the time when kings go off to war, David sent Joab out with the king's men and the whole Israelite army. They destroyed the Ammonites and besieged Rabbah. But David remained in Jerusalem.
"[2] One evening David got up from his bed and walked around on the roof of the palace. From the roof he saw a woman bathing. The woman was very beautiful..."

King David then slept with her and had her husband killed (2 Samuel 11:1-15).

The consequences were severe; among them were:

"... [11] This is what the Lord says: 'Out of your own household I am going to bring calamity on you. Before your very eyes I will take your wives and give them to one who is close to you, and he will sleep with your wives in broad daylight'" (2 Samuel 12:9-11).

I think King David gave the devil a foothold by not going out with his army. He had nothing to do, and then saw a woman bathing. He then committed adultery and murder.

We must be particularly mindful of this historical tragedy, because if someone as devoted as King David can commit such a serious crime, how easily we can too.

The lesson to learn is that we must avoid the environments or opportunities that might be tempting. Billy Graham is an excellent contemporary example for us today.

An excellent example set by Billy Graham

Rev. Billy Graham was a well-known evangelist. He founded The Billy Graham Evangelistic Association in 1950.

David Masci and Gregory A. Smith, at Pew Research Center, write:

"The Rev. Billy Graham, who recently died at age 99, was one of the most influential and important evangelical Christian leaders of the 20th century. From humble beginnings in rural North Carolina, Graham went on to become a world-famous evangelist who drew huge crowds while, at the same time, developing close relationships with several U.S. presidents.

"Graham is probably best known for the nearly six decades he spent traveling the world, preaching and evangelizing to millions in his stadium crusades… Finally, Graham will be remembered as the "pastor to presidents;" he befriended and advised presidents from *both* parties, including Dwight Eisenhower, Lyndon Johnson, Richard Nixon and Bill Clinton."

(David Masci and Gregory A. Smith, *"5 facts about U.S. evangelical Protestants,"* Pew Research Center, Washington, D.C. (March 1, 2018), URL.https://www.pewresearch.org/fact-tank/2018/03/01/5-facts-about-u-s-evangelical-protestants/, accessed 8-10-2021.)

(Disclaimer: Pew Research Center bears no responsibility for the analyses or interpretations of the data presented here. The opinions expressed herein, including any implications for policy, are those of the author and not of Pew Research Center.)

I have long admired the character of Dr. Graham, because I had not heard of any scandal from his vast organization while he was in charge. He had been focused on the core message of Jesus' love for humankind and had largely avoided partisan politics.

By reading his biography (Billy Graham, *Just as I am: the autobiography of Billy Graham. – 1st Ed* (New York, NY: HarperCollins Worldwide, 1997)), I noticed that it was not a coincidence that he had been able to maintain the reputation of his organization and also himself.

< He avoided the temptation of money >

To ensure his organization would not succumb to the temptation of greed, he helped set up the Evangelical Council for Financial Accountability. This independent agency serves as an outside auditor for monitoring the financial integrity of its member organizations.

As for his own compensation, he limited it to a fixed salary comparable to a typical minister in any average large-city church.

< He prevented sexual immorality >

To prevent sexual immorality, He committed to not travel, meet, or eat alone with a woman other than his wife.

Some might think Dr. Graham's approach was too rigid. Yet, I totally agree with him. I would rather be safe than sorry. Besides, if he had failed, the damage would have been enormous, given his worldwide ministry.

Even for people like me, it is also worthwhile as well, because being faithful to my wife definitely is more important than a temporary sinful pleasure. Moreover, it will be a good example for my children, too.

< However, his son Franklin Graham is controversial >

I must point out that I have mixed feelings about the Billy Graham Evangelistic Association nowadays, because I do not know for sure the spiritual status of this organization under his son now.

For instance, there was a report on his son's high compensation, which is contrary to his father's principle of only accepting an average salary. (Christine Wicker, "*Why Franklin Graham's salary raises eyebrows among Christian nonprofits,*" Washington Post, August 18, 2015.)

In addition, I wonder if his son has heeded his father's warning of partisan politics. (Laurie Goodstein, "*Billy Graham warned against embracing a President. His son has gone another way,*" New York Times, February 26, 2018.)

Christianity Today, the evangelical magazine started by Billy Graham in 1956, which rarely involves itself in politics, strongly opposed the nominated Republican presidential candidate in 2016. (Andy Crouch, executive editor, "*Speak Truth to Trump,*" Christianity Today, October 10, 2016.)

However, even given such a stern warning by a generally apolitical Christianity Today, which his father founded, Franklin Graham apparently still chose to get involved and support the problematic candidate, as one can see based on the following article from Time magazine.

Elizabeth Dias published the article in 2016, "*Go inside Franklin Graham's 'Party Bus' in this 360-Degree Video*" (Time, February 22, 2016, 11:36 AM EST.)

Though Graham said in the rallies that he was not telling them whom to vote for, by singling out the issue of abortion, he was obviously endorsing Republican candidates.

At the end of Part Three, under the question, "Why would some Christians vote for an apparently amoral political candidate? " I will comment on the subject of abortion, and share my thoughts on how Christians can best handle politics.

MY UNFORGETTABLE IMPRESSION OF SOME OF THE MATURE CHRISTIANS I MET

Mrs. Glass

The first Christian that comes to mind is Mrs. Glass. She was a missionary at our college (Chung Yuan Christian University in Taiwan). Mrs. Glass was in charge of the English club on campus. We would gather in her residence and practice speaking English.

The most enduring impression she made upon me was her constant smile. To this day, her peaceful, kind, and friendly demeanor never escape my memory. Looking back, now I know that was the fruit of the Holy Spirit!

Dr. John F. Walvoord

The next one I can vividly recall was the late Chancellor of Dallas Theological Seminary, Dr. John F. Walvoord. He was still teaching at the seminary when I attended the school there. Unfortunately, I did not have a chance to take his class. Nevertheless, I could not forget his humble manners whenever I saw him on campus.

He was a well-established educator, author, and scholar, yet he was so humble. I think that is why God so blessed him.

A missionary of Overseas Mission Fellowship

The last one I cannot ever forget was a missionary of OMF (formerly China Inland Mission). He visited our church in

Dallas many years ago. At the time, I was still working in the computer industry, and had not gone to seminary yet.

He was in his 60s or 70s, a white man who spoke excellent Mandarin. If I am not mistaken, he had gone to China for some time and did not leave until after the Communists took over the country.

I recall when I looked at him, standing at the front of the room, something suddenly brought tears to my eyes. I was not sure what it was; perhaps it was his devotion to serving Chinese people, his genuine love and care for people, and, yes, maybe his Christ-like character.

He reminded me of the moment when I first read this passage written by Apostle Paul, "I served the Lord *with great humility and with tears* and in the midst of severe testing by the plots of my Jewish opponents" (Acts 20:19). I was deeply touched by Paul's humbleness and compassion.

At that very instant, in the church before me, I witnessed what a godly, spiritual person looked like.

TO SUM UP REGARDING CHRISTIANS' PERSONAL OBJECTIVE OF LIFE

Christians must be aware that we still can sin. Still, by taking precautions like Billy Graham, and also depending on the Holy Spirit to resist temptation, we will sin less and less. We will then begin to bear the fruit of the Spirit.

That means, hopefully, when people see us, they will sense the humility, love, joy, peace, and kindness from the Holy Spirit in us, and not the arrogance, selfishness, rage, factions, and hatred from our sinful nature.

Professional: To Be a Good and Faithful Servant of God

We are encouraged to use whatever talents, gifts, and opportunities God bestows us to serve others and glorify God (1 Peter 4:10; Ephesians 2:10).

WHAT KIND OF GIFTS DOES GOD GIVE THE BELIEVERS?

I will list two of the related Scriptures here.
Romans 12:6-8 writes,

"⁶ We have different gifts, according to the grace given to each of us. If your gift is prophesying, then prophesy in accordance with your[a] faith;
"⁷ if it is serving, then serve; if it is teaching, then teach; ⁸ if it is to encourage, then give encouragement; if it is giving, then give generously; if it is to lead,[b] do it diligently; if it is to show mercy, do it cheerfully."
Footnotes
   a. Or *the*
   b. Or *to provide for others*

Apostle Paul says in 1 Corinthians 12:28-30,

"²⁸ And God has placed in the church first of all apostles, second prophets, third teachers, then miracles, then gifts of healing, of helping, of guidance, and of different kinds of tongues.
"²⁹ Are all apostles? Are all prophets? Are all teachers? Do all work miracles? ³⁰ Do all have gifts of healing? Do all speak in tongues[a]? Do all interpret?"
Footnotes
   a. Or *other languages*

IS GOD FAIR? SINCE SOME GIFTS SEEM MORE IMPORTANT THAN OTHERS

The purpose of our gifts is to serve others

A gift from God is not something we boast about; instead, it is for us to use it to glorify God and help people.

Eph. 4:11-12 points out,

"¹¹ So Christ himself gave the apostles, the prophets, the evangelists, the pastors and teachers, ¹² to equip his people for works of service, so that the body of Christ may be built up."

When Jesus' apostles were arguing about who should be sitting beside Him in the coming Kingdom of God, he said:

"²⁶ ... whoever wants to become great among you must be your servant, ²⁷ and whoever wants to be first must be your slave—
"²⁸ *just as the Son of Man [Jesus] did not come to be served, but to serve,* and to give his life as a ransom for many" (Matthew 20:26-28).

It is astonishing to hear that Jesus, who is God and came in the flesh, is saying his power is for serving people, not himself, and even sacrificially. And that was said two thousand years ago.

More will be asked from those who receive more

Luke 12:48 writes,

"... From everyone who has been given much, much will be demanded; and from the one who has been entrusted with much, much more will be asked."

Jesus tells a story about what a good and faithful servant is that clearly explains this principle.

< What is a good and faithful servant? >

"... ¹⁴ Again, it will be like a man going on a journey, who called his servants and entrusted his wealth to them. ¹⁵ To one he gave five bags of gold, to another two bags, and to another one bag,[a] each according to his ability. Then he went on his journey.

"¹⁶ The man who had received five bags of gold went at once and put his money to work and gained five bags more. ¹⁷ So also, the one with two bags of gold gained two more. ¹⁸ But the man who had received one bag went off, dug a hole in the ground and hid his master's money..." (Matthew 25:14-30).

   Footnotes
      a. Greek *five talents ... two talents ... one talent*; also throughout this parable; a talent was worth about 20 years of a day laborer's wage.

In the rest of this long passage, Jesus commended both the man who earned five bags, and the man who gained two bags for being a "good and faithful servant," while calling the one who did nothing to the gold he received wicked and lazy.

It shows what constitutes a good and faithful servant in God's eyes.

Again, more will be asked from those who receive more. The one who received five bags is expected to earn more than two.

In fact, it is not about how much money we receive, but the *percentage* of the money we make from it.

Have we fully utilized what God has given us? If so, the one who received only two bags of gold is considered just as good and faithful, as the one who was given five bags of gold. All have achieved 100% of what they were entrusted with.

< A kind school bus driver >

I once read an article about a Christian bus driver for a public school.

"Wayne Price has been driving a school bus for five years, but his faith is what really drives him to do everything in his life.

"During the early morning of December 11, the last week before schools in Montevallo, Alabama, closed for winter break, Price got a phone call that his school would be opening 2 hours later due to bad weather, including icy conditions and fog.

"For many children in other cities, school delays and closures are a cause for celebration. But a delayed opening in Montevallo also means that many children will not be able to get breakfast at the school cafeteria — or any morning meal at all...

"... After hanging up the phone... Before hitting his usual route, he headed to a local McDonald's to get himself a biscuit ... and one for every kid on the bus...

"... In addition to his morning and afternoon pickups to and from school, Price is a mentor to youth groups and organizes teen and college-aged student trips to volunteer on Navajo reservations.

"... Fifty McDonald's biscuits and a lot of full bellies later, Price continues to be grateful for *'where God has [him] right now* caring for them.' ..."

(Erica Chayes Wida, *"School bus driver hailed as a hero after buying breakfast for 50 students during ice storm,"* TODAY, December 18, 2018, 11:48 AM EST, *https://www.today.com/food/alabama-school-bus-drive-buys-mcdonald-s-50-kids-t145322.*)

What a beautiful story of serving others with Jesus' love! It also shows that no matter how small a position we hold, like Mr. Price, we certainly can be as good and faithful a servant as those holding higher positions, such as the principal of the school.

On the other hand, if the principal is a Christian, yet does not *fully* utilize their power and opportunities to serve the students, then the school driver ironically will get much more reward than the principal when the end of time comes.

Believers Will Be Rewarded for a Job Well Done

Apostle Paul writes for Christians,

"For we must all appear before the judgment seat of Christ, so that each of us may receive what is due us for the things done while in the body, whether good or bad" (2 Corinthians 5:10).

He also says,

"¹⁰ By the grace God has given me, I laid a foundation as a wise builder, and someone else is building on it. But each one should build with care. ¹¹ For no one can lay any foundation other than the one already laid, which is Jesus Christ.

"¹² If anyone builds on this foundation using gold, silver, costly stones, wood, hay or straw, ¹³ their work will be shown for what it is, because the Day will bring it to light. It will be revealed with fire, and the fire *will test the quality of each person's work.*

"¹⁴ If what has been built survives, the builder will receive a reward. ¹⁵ If it is burned up, the builder will suffer loss but yet will be saved—even though only as one escaping through the flames" (1 Corinthians 3:10-15).

When Jesus comes again at the end of the world, Christ will judge all, including Christians. However, for believers, it is not about life and death (a question of salvation), but about what we have done with our new life (a matter of reward).

Those who have done a good job will be awarded, while those who have not will suffer loss but will still be saved.

Therefore, the questions Christians might want to ask themselves are, "Have I used God's given gifts and opportunities to glorify God and love people as myself, the best I can?", "Have I been a good and faithful servant of God?"

Incidents Encountered When I Served Others

"YOU SHOULD GRAB IT!"

As remarked in Part One, I went to Dallas to work after graduating from the University of Texas. I also volunteered to help the Indochinese refugees with an inter-church evangelistic fellowship.

One day, the fellowship leader asked me if I would like to be the group leader for the following year. I said, "I just had a terrible quarrel with my wife Margaret, I do not think I am qualified."

At the time, we were married for less than a year. He said that for Christians, it was a growing process and encouraged me to accept the offer. I said I needed to think about it.

Then a brother of the fellowship called me and said, "George, it is a position many people will be so eager to get, you should grab it!" urging me to take it.

I did not call to accept the position right away. Instead, I prayed to God, "If you want me to take it, please let me and my wife be reconciled and be fine again."

Thank God, we were okay again. I then took the offer. I thank God for impressing upon me that character is fundamental in order to serve Him, and it starts from my own home.

I later learned that Scripture does have specific teaching on the qualifications for church leaders:

"(If anyone does not know how to manage his own family, how can he take care of God's church?) "(1 Timothy 3:5)

It is amazing to see how God has often led me to do the right thing, and then later on, I would discover that the Bible indeed teaches it. This happened when I was thinking about marriage and now, again, about church ministry.

It has been a pleasant and encouraging confirmation.

"YOU SHOULD BE A DEACON OR ELDER BY NOW!"

Sometime later, another similar situation happened at the church. One day, a brother walking by me suddenly said, "People like you should be a deacon or elder by now!"

I was quite puzzled by his comment. I did not know what to make of it. I never consider positions or titles a goal, like climbing a ladder in the church hierarchy. My attention has always been to ensuring I do the best I can in the work entrusted to me by God at a given time.

At the time, I was teaching children and adults Sunday schools. In addition, as a co-worker in the mission department, as referred to in Part One, I led an annual church evangelistic crusade that hundreds of people attended and where many were saved.

Perhaps that was why he said that. Nonetheless, I was sure If I did a good job, God would open new opportunities and responsibilities for me, whether they were a "higher" and more "important" position or not.

Therefore, whether the church rewarded me with a position of deacon or elder did not even cross my mind.

My Calling from God

My calling from God has always been to share the good news of Jesus to as many people as possible, and to teach them the precious words of God from the Bible. It turns out that it is exactly what Jesus tells his followers to do in Matthew 28:16-20, often called "The Great Commission"!

After I graduated from seminary, I had several opportunities for more stable and better-paid jobs. However, I did not take them, since it would distract me from my primary mission.

MANDARIN CHINESE?

One of them was a full-time, salaried, well-paid job with good benefits. It was to teach Mandarin Chinese at a prestigious private academy.

Nonetheless, I did not accept it, and instead, chose to continue to teach as a part-time adjunct professor in world religions, at a community college with low hourly pay and zero benefits (yes, it is zero. no sick pay, no vacation pay, let alone health insurance).

WORLD RELIGIONS!

I was, in fact, carrying a full-time load of four or even five classes each semester with nearly 200 students. It often required a waiver signed by the senior officer of the college, since it exceeded the load a part-time staff was allowed to teach.

Yet since I was classified as an adjunct faculty, I was basically working full-time with part-time pay (about half of what I would have earned, counting the benefits), if I were treated as a full-time employee.

However, teaching world religions helped me to be more knowledgeable about other faiths. It has enabled me to connect better and explain Christianity's beliefs to people of different religious backgrounds. It also helped me author this book for the section regarding other religions in Part Three.

GOD LEADS ALL ALONG THE WAY

I am very thankful that throughout the 40 years since I was truly saved, I have been experiencing God's leading and encouragement all along the way, from reading the Bible systematically, starting a family, raising our children, serving in the church, attending seminary, pastoring churches, to teaching at colleges, and now writing about God's grace and love in my life.

Hopefully, when it is time for me to be with Christ, I will be considered one of those "good and faithful servants" of God, someone who is not just saved, but has served Him and others well with the talents and the opportunities He bestowed upon me.

It is exciting to look forward to that day! This is also my wish for all the born-again Christians that we can all celebrate together for a job well done!

14 - CONCLUDING THOUGHTS FOR PART TWO

From the personal experiences in my life, I can conclude, without any doubt, that what it is like to be saved is as follows:

A New Creation

Apostle Paul proclaims in 2 Corinthians 5:17,

"Therefore, if anyone is in Christ, the new creation has come: The old has gone, *the new is here!*"

It was at that apartment in Dallas 40 years ago, that I clearly sensed a brand-new life was born in me!

The heavy burden of our past sins is removed from our shoulders! We are no longer condemned to eternal death. Having been cleansed of guilt, God's love is now poured into our hearts through the Holy Spirit He gave us (Romans 5:5).

A fresh new life, *freed* from sin's damnation, *empowered* by the indwelling Holy Spirit, and *filled* with God's love in our heart, has begun!

No Longer Alone

All believers are now God's children (1 John 3:1). We no longer have to fight alone.

As referred to before, Jesus assures us, "I have told you these things, so that *in me you may have peace*. In this world, you will have trouble. But take heart! I have overcome the world" (John 16:33).

Jesus Is Our High Priest before God

Hebrews 4:14-16 states:

"[14] Therefore, since we have a great high priest who has ascended into heaven, Jesus the Son of God, let us hold firmly to the faith we profess.

"[15] For we do not have a high priest who is unable to empathize with our weaknesses, but we have one who has been tempted in every way, just as we are—yet he did not sin.

"[16] *Let us then approach God's throne of grace with confidence*, so that we may receive mercy and find grace to help us *in our time of need*."

Jesus is with us all the time. He is our high priest before God the Father. He is our advocate. We are not alone anymore.

Christ is God who came in the flesh. He has been tempted as human, yet did not sin, thus He understands our weakness, and is able to help us overcome it.

We can now pray to God for help, in the name of Jesus Christ, in our time of need.

The Holy Spirit Is Here to Assist Us Too

Furthermore, not only is Jesus with us, but the Holy Spirit is also here to assist us.

Romans 8:26 promises,

"In the same way, the Spirit helps us in our weakness. We do not know what we ought to pray for, but *the Spirit himself intercedes for us* through wordless groans. "

Sometimes, we may be so discouraged that we do not even know what to pray, yet the Spirit understands our weaknesses and needs and will pray for us.

There have been times that I just asked the Holy Spirit to pray for me, because I was so frustrated and upset.

In short, with God's care, we need not be afraid. We can face the challenges of our life with confidence. We will have peace from Jesus, knowing we are not alone and helpless anymore.

By the way, at this point, you may be a bit confused about God, Jesus, and the Holy Spirit. Matthew 28:19 writes, "Therefore go and make disciples of all nations, baptizing them in the name of the Father [God the Father] and of the Son [Jesus] and of the Holy Spirit."

It is the concept of the Trinity (not three gods, but one God in three persons). We will explain it in Chapter 30 regarding Christianity.

Common Promises

Once one puts his or her faith in Jesus, although God gives his children different talents, opportunities, responsibilities, and problems in life, big or small, all of us will receive common promises.

For example, as shared before, we can all count on him to answer our prayers if we do so according to his will.

In addition, we can all count on him that whatever comes up against us in life, it will not be beyond what we can bear, and it will be beneficial for our spiritual growth.

It Is Not Too Late

Some might have regrets after reading about my experiences in marriage and raising children, etc.; nonetheless, I hope they are helpful and encouraging insights about life.

God is merciful. If you wish you could have done something differently, it is not too late to take corrective and positive measures.

As cited earlier, 1 John 1:9 promises,

"If we confess our sins, he is faithful and just and will forgive us our sins and purify us from all unrighteousness."

Although I believe I have done good things for our children, I am far from perfect. There were actually quite a few issues I wish I had addressed differently.

The way I dealt with it was that I would apologize to them when I became aware of it, and would ask God to forgive me. I would continue to seek ways to improve going forward, but not let it pressure me to become too discouraged.

Already divorced and remarried? It would be good to seek commitment from each other for the current marriage. Moreover, it would help to sincerely express our regrets to our children from a prior marriage, if we have hurt them. I believe a sincere apology would go a long way toward healing emotional wounds.

It Is a Maturing Process

For believers, it is a maturing process. While we must be mindful that God's forgiveness of sins is not for us to sin again (Romans 6:1-2), we need not feel too sad when we make mistakes (1 John 1:8-10; 2:1-2; Hebrews 4:14-16).

We should acknowledge our fault, but feel encouraged and seek to do better in the future.

A Purposeful, Joyful, and Hopeful New Life Ahead

Each Christian's life journey may be different. Nonetheless, under our Creator's guidance and unchanging, loving care, all can learn to live a purposeful, joyful, and hopeful new life, _despite_ any chaos, sicknesses, or troubles we may face.

Time after time, I have sensed clear direction and comfort from God. That firm conviction of purpose and meaning in life has never left me. As a matter of fact, it has grown even stronger, ever since those brilliant stars in the night sky in Taiwan caught my attention more than 50 years ago.

The New Life Begins Now

Yes, in Christ, not only do you have the hope of having eternal life in heaven in the future, but you can also _begin_ to learn to live the new life, with the body, mind, and soul to the full, while still in this world, *the minute you put your trust in Jesus.*

PART THREE - Questions You Might Be Asking

15 - INTRODUCTION

You are perhaps interested in what I have shared so far. But there may be some questions that keep you from believing. I totally understand.

Jesus did not just command us to trust him. He took the time to answer many questions people asked.

Keep in mind, though, that one need not know all the answers to all the questions in order to believe. At some point, the evidence will be so convincing and clear that many will feel compelled to put faith in Him.

While I do not have the answer to all the questions, and even the responses I provide here might not be the best, fortunately, many excellent books are available (usually under the category of "Christian Apologetics"). Search any online bookstore, such as Amazon, and you will find many valuable resources.

For instance, the book by Norman L. Geisler, *When Skeptics Ask – A Handbook on Christian Evidences* (Grand Rapids, Michigan: Baker Books, 1999, Third printing) is excellent.

Some parts of the book perhaps are a bit difficult to grasp, but overall, it is a great work. In addition to Baker Books, publications from publishers, for instance, the Zondervan Corporation and InterVarsity Press, are good sources, too.

The following are some questions that people might ask, and my understanding of the issues that can benefit the discussions.

16 - QUESTIONS ABOUT SCIENCE AND OTHER RELATED ISSUES

Hasn't Science Disproved the Existence of Any God?

Some may be troubled that we are even talking about any religions in the 21st century. However, science as we know it today is extremely limited, compared to the science of the vast universe, which we have yet to learn.

I once came across a story about a Russian cosmonaut. At that time, Russia was ruled by the Communist Party of the Soviet Union, a country officially being an atheist state. He, upon circling the Earth for the first time and not seeing any deity, declared that God does not exist.

The story may be just a joke, yet it makes a critical point.

We know so far that there are at least more than 100 billion stars just in our own galaxy (the Milky Way). On top of that, there are an estimated 10 trillion galaxies in the universe.

That means there are, as Elizabeth Howell writes:

"1,000,000,000,000,000,000,000,000 stars, or a "1" with 24 zeros after it (1 septillion in the American numbering system; 1 quadrillion in the European system).

"Kornreich emphasized that number is likely a gross underestimation, as more detailed looks at the universe will show even more galaxies."

(Elizabeth Howell, *How Many Stars Are in the Universe?*" published May 18, 2017, Science & Astronomy, Space.com.)

There is a Chinese saying that says a person with limited vision is like "the frog at the bottom of the well" (井底之蛙, jǐng dǐ zhī wā – this is the Mandarin pronunciation according to the Chinese Pinyin system). He is like a frog, sitting at the bottom of a well, declaring that the width of the sky is only as wide as the well's opening.

It is not to tease or criticize people who believe in science. It is simply to point out that while we have learned a lot about our environment on Earth, and as much as we can from looking as far as we can at outer space, when compared with what is out there, what we know is only like a drop in the bucket.

Indeed, a believer in science would humbly acknowledge the reality that we still do not know very much.

If, With Our Limited Knowledge, We Cannot Prove that God Does Not Exist (Agnostic, Unknowable), Then How Do We Know God Exists? Is It Knowable?

What We Cannot Know, God Can Tell Us about It

It is called *revelation* in theological terms. It is knowable in that sense. In fact, the last book of the Bible is named the Book of Revelation.

When our daughters were little, I used to play hide-and-seek with them. I would count to ten and try to find where she hid. Often, it was easy for me to find her.

However, when it was her turn, it was not so easy. Sometimes, she would become so frustrated that I would jump out of my hiding place and say, "I am here!"

God is the alpha and the omega (the Greek alphabet's first and last letters).

According to Revelation 22:13,

"I am the Alpha and the Omega, the First and the Last, the Beginning and the End."

This passage tells us that God is the source of all creation and history. Moreover, it goes without saying that in order to be able to do that, God is also the source of all knowledge.

Humans may know A and B, and seek to discover C. On the contrary, God is A and Z. He is the ultimate.

From the first book of the Bible, which tells us how this world began ("In the beginning God created the heavens and the earth" (Genesis 1:1)), to the last book, which reveals to us how this world will end and usher in a new era ("Then I saw a new heaven and a new earth, for the first heaven and the first earth had passed away, and there was no longer any sea" (Revelation 21:1)), the Bible tells a complete story.

How Does God Reveal Himself to Us?

God reveals himself through the world He created, direct communications, and the sacred texts.

THE CREATED WORLD

Psalm 19:1 declares:

"The heavens declare the glory of God; the skies proclaim the work of his hands."
Footnotes
  a. Psalm 19:1 In Hebrew texts 19:1-14 is numbered 19:2-15.

As I wrote in Part One, it was those glittering stars in the night sky on that summer evening that convinced me of the existence of God.

Others may be touched by other beautiful creations, for example, the magnificent sunrise and sunset, the bright colorful flowers, the deep green trees, and the great majestic mountains!

DIRECT COMMUNICATIONS AND THE SACRED TEXTS

God also revealed himself more specifically by speaking directly to the prophets, whom He raised in the Old Testament times, and through Jesus, who spoke to the apostles in the New Testament period.

Those prophets and the apostles then wrote down what they were told and what they personally witnessed, regarding what God and Jesus did for them and others.

Most importantly, what was done through Jesus was most critical.

As Hebrews 1:1-2 states,

"[1] In the past God spoke to our ancestors through the prophets at many times and in various ways, [2] but in these last days he has spoken to us by his Son [Jesus], whom he appointed heir of all things, and through whom also he made the universe."

Jesus spent about three years traveling all over Israel, personally explaining, teaching, and answering questions regarding what the Israelites had been reading about Moses and other prophets, and what to do in order to enter the coming kingdom of heaven.

Yes, it is knowable from the Bible, which was inspired by God (2 Timothy 3:16), written by the prophets and the apostles, and passed down to us.

Some may wonder, "But is the Bible reliable and trustworthy as recorded and passed along to us? Could there be transmission errors?" I will share my thoughts on this question later in Chapter 30.

What Is This Debate Between Evolutionists and Creationists over the Origin of Life?

There are many valuable resources on this subject. Searching for "creationism" or "intelligent design" online will yield plenty of them that supply evidence supporting creationism.

I will share my own take on it.

A Painting

I thought about when people visit a museum and marvel at a beautiful painting, they would typically wonder, "who painted it?" Nobody would say that the artwork just painted itself naturally, claiming that given enough time, those different colors would eventually learn to find themselves the right spots on the canvas.

A Baby

I then pondered over how a baby is born. We know now that every human cell has a complete set of chromosomes (46 in total), except for our reproductive ones, i.e., a male's sperm and a female's egg; each has 23.

When these two unique types of cells, each with half of the total number of chromosomes, are combined during fertilization, it becomes a complete set of chromosomes.

After about 30 hours, the fertilized egg starts to split according to the genetic information *encoded in this DNA*, and then the process begins to accelerate.

From *one cell* to two, two to four, four to eight, eight to sixteen, and in nine months, a baby made of *trillions of cells* is born. He or she can cry, laugh, think, look at you, and learn to call you mom or dad. And later on, would ask you, "Mom, where did I come from?" and even wonder, "What is the meaning of life?"

It is breathtaking!

According to Chelsea Toledo and Kirstie Saltsman's article, *"Genetics by the Numbers,"* regarding the genetic information encoded in *each* of our body's cell's DNA:

"3.2 billion - That's how many base pairs—or sets of genetic "letters" [DNA codes that tell the cell how to make a specific protein] —make up the human genome.

To list all those letters, a person must type 60 words per minute, 8 hours a day, for about 50 years!

"6 - That's how many feet long the DNA from one of your cells would be if you uncoiled each strand and placed them end to end. Do this for all your DNA [in all the trillions of cells of your body], and the resulting strand would be 67 billion miles long—the same as about 150,000 round trips to the Moon."

(Posted June 12, 2012, on The National Institute of General Medical Sciences (NIGMS), https://www.nigms.nih.gov/education/Inside-Life-

Science/Pages/genetics-by-the-numbers.aspx, accessed 12-20-2021)

You might wonder how this could be possible. Can the length of my body's DNA in each cell combined reach the Moon and back 150,000 times? It is possible because the width of the strand is only 50 trillionths of an inch.

That is a gigantic amount of microbiological encoding for just one human being!

I believe that, if a painting calls for a painter, a baby certainly demands a creator.

By the way, when I was a little kid, I did ask my mother where I came from. She jokingly said, "Oh, I picked you up from a garbage dump!"

Although I did not understand her answer at all at the time, I did remember very well that was what she said.

About Sex

I still can recall clearly that one day in the 1980s, I was watching a PBS TV series, *Cosmos: A Personal Voyage*, hosted by the well-known professor of astronomy, Carl Sagan.

He said that the reason we have men and women today was that some time long ago, nature "*stumbled upon* sex," so we have sex.

I was astonished and speechless. I could not believe what I just heard. It suggests that evolutionists actually place a great deal of faith (yes, faith) in what nature and its supposed random acts can do.

To make sure my recollection is correct for writing this book, I researched to find out if the program had been published. I found it. In that video, he said:

"... one day, *quite by accident*, a molecule arose which was able to make a crude copy of itself... this was the ancestor of DNA...

"... plants have evolved... a number of one cell plants joined together the first multi-cellular organism, equally important, was the invention, not made until early November [Sagan's cosmic year], of sex, it was *stumbled upon* by the microbes...."

(*COSMOS – Ultimate Edition*, ©2000 Cosmos Studios, Inc., Disc One, Episode 2, "*One Voice in the Cosmos Fugue*")

I appreciate Dr. Sagan's films, which introduce the magnificent universe to millions of people worldwide, but regarding the origin of life, I must respectfully disagree.

I believe we can soundly conclude that:

Given the extremely complex structures of life, manifested in not just ourselves, as shown in the programming of our DNA, but also in the lives all around us, like the beautiful trees, flowers, birds, and dogs (yes, human's best friend), to claim that this extraordinary intelligence is just the result of some random "accidents," occurred in the natural world by themselves, is highly unlikely and inadequate.

Why Is There So Much Suffering in the World?

Many of us are troubled by the situation that there are so many pains and afflictions like wars, diseases, deaths, natural disasters, violence, deceptions, greed, hatred, and chaos in the world.

In Terms of Wars

Human history, sadly, has been largely a history of violent conflicts. Moreover, with the advancement of technology, ironically, we are getting frighteningly good at killing each other, too, in both the scope and the speed.

In World War I (1914-1918), almost 7 million civilians and 10 million military personnel were killed. Of them, more than 100,000 American soldiers perished.

World War II broke out merely 21 years later (1939-1945). An estimated 70–85 million people lost their lives, more than four times over the first one. Civilian deaths totaled 50 to 55 million. Military deaths totaled 21–25 million. Among them, more than 400,000 were American soldiers, who did not come home.

This horrendous carnage did not end until two atomic bombs exploded in two massive fireballs, reaching the sky at two Japanese cities and killing more than 150,000 people instantly. In addition, hundreds of thousands more died of slow and painful effects from radiation exposure later.

I concur with the view that there are just wars when we must defend our freedom, especially when attacked. Nonetheless, it is sad that we, human beings, have had to fight so hard and so violently against each other to end it.

Not only that, but since then, we humans have made more than 10,000 nuclear warheads (as of 2022); each is even more destructive than the one before. Hydrogen bombs can be 1,000 times more deadly than the atomic bombs dropped on Japan.

Only one such device can wipe out an entire city.

Furthermore, a single ICBM (Inter Continental Ballistic Missile), each capable of carrying several nuclear warheads and targeting different cities simultaneously, can reach many U.S. population centers from Russia (or from China and North Korea) in *less than 30 minutes*, and vice versa.

With thousands of these monstrous weapons deployed and operational today, we are pointing them at each other, threatening to wipe ourselves out of existence at the push of a button.

The current "peace" between nuclear-armed countries is precariously held by the so-called MADD (Mutually Assured Destruction Deterrent).

It is pure madness.

Many religions have different answers. I will lay out some of the responses offered by the major ones after we discuss a couple of questions first.

Incidentally, Carl Sagan also saw the perils of mankind's misuse of technology. But, being an atheist, he did not offer a spiritual reason for humanity's problem, yet it is interesting to note that he was really worried, and even warned in a seemingly religious tone:

"It is as if there were God who said to us, 'I set before you two ways, you can use your technology to destroy yourself [about the possibility of nuclear wars] or to carry you to the planets and the stars. It is up to you'" (Scene 12, *Cosmos XIII, "Who speaks for earth?"* Cosmos Studios Inc., 2000).

Why Do We Need Anything Other than Science to Solve Our Problems?

As the dilemma mentioned above shows, science is like a two-edged sword; it cuts both ways.

For example, it can assist us in producing abundant crops. But on the other hand, now we realize that it can also enable us to build nuclear weapons that threaten our very own existence.

Even when we are using technology benevolently, like producing more food, ironically, we still face worldwide hunger.

According to the report *"The state of food insecurity of the world"* by the Food and Agriculture Organization of the United Nations (Rome, 2010), there were 925 million undernourished people in the world in 2010.

Undernourishment exists when caloric intake is below the minimum dietary energy requirement (MDER). The report points out that despite good harvests, hunger was still prevalent due to wars and corruption.

Escaping to Mars will not solve our predicament either. If we cannot get along with each other here on Earth, there is little assurance we can do so on Mars. We may simply bring our problems to another planet.

The real root cause lies in our hearts. Technology cannot solve our heart problems. That is what religion addresses.

17 - ARE SCIENCE AND RELIGION COMPATIBLE?

Some think religion and science are incompatible, claiming that science describes all the reality, and that only science can answer all the questions about life.

Science and Religion Are Complementary

Not only are science and religion compatible, but they are, in fact, complementary. We need both to comprehend all reality.

Because science primarily deals with only the physical realm, while religion may include physical dimensions, it is not limited by it; it also addresses the spiritual domain of reality.

As a matter of fact, in this sense, science is just a subset of all reality.

In other words, science seeks to understand the natural world; nonetheless, it does not and cannot answer questions such as the meaning of life.

For example, science can describe the force of gravity between any two masses with a precise mathematical formula:

$F = (G * m1 * m2)/r^2$

F: the force of gravity

G: the universal gravitational constant (6.67 *10^11)
m1: the mass of the first object
m2: the mass of the second object
r: the distance between the centers of the two objects

On the other hand, science will be at a loss to "measure" the depth of love or hate between two people. Can we measure love with a unit of weight, like a "ton" of love?

Our problems as human beings are fundamentally spiritual, not physical.

Why can we not live peacefully with each other? Why do we lie, hate, and even kill people? Why do we hoard millions, even billions of dollars of wealth, yet still not be satisfied and happy? Is the huge sum of money not enough to buy what we need?

Christianity talks about science but covers more than that.

It tells us how we came to exist (a physical question); furthermore, it primarily focuses on why we are here, how we can overcome animosity towards each other, even love each other, and enjoy a meaningful life (a spiritual pursuit). We will discuss it in more detail later in the section on Christianity.

What about the Trial and Condemnation of Galileo Galilei by the Roman Catholic Inquisition in 1633?

Some may say, "But what about the Catholic Church which insisted that the Earth is the center of the universe and that the sun is circling the Earth, and persecuted Galileo Galilei who discovered that it is not the case?"

First of all, Scripture does not say that the Earth is the center of the universe. Secondly, it was wrong for the Catholic Church to use force on religious matters, especially when the Church misinterpreted the Scriptures.

(Regarding the use of force by the Catholic Church, refer to the discussion on the issue of church and state later in this book, regarding the religion of Islam, under the question, "What are the differences between the major religions in the world?")

Some argue that science and religion are incompatible, claiming that science relies on testable empirical evidence and observations, while religion relies on subjective belief.

But as mentioned before, it is like the Chinese saying about "the frog at the bottom of the well." Our ability to observe is so limited that a believer in science would humbly acknowledge the reality that we still do not know very much, and thus should not make premature conclusions.

I believe the Bible speaks the truth in both science and spiritual matters; therefore, there is no need to force others to accept it, because the truth will speak for itself.

Christians should be, and many have been, quite open to the evidence of science, because it was God who created the physical world in the first place.

I will explain this under the subtitle "How do I know that the Bible is telling the truth?" in Chapter 30, "Questions about Christianity."

Many Renowned Scientists Are Also Devoted Christians

Indeed, there have been many well-known scientists who are also devoted Christians.

Galileo Galilei himself was a devout Christian who "... saw not a divorce of religion and science but only *a healthy marriage*: 'God is known by nature in his works, and by doctrine in his revealed word,'

"... Galileo contended that proper interpretation of Scripture would agree with observed fact. The 'Book of Nature,' written in the language of mathematics, would agree with the 'Book of Scripture,' written in the everyday language of the people. Besides, the 'Bible teaches men how to go to heaven, not how the heavens go'."

(From the article: *Galileo Galilei – Misjudged Astronomer*, Christianity Today, https://www.christianitytoday.com/history/people/scholarsandscientists/galileo-galilei.html, accessed 9-29-2020.)

Many other distinguished scientists are also earnest Christians, like Isaac Newton, Johannes Kepler, Robert Boyle, Michael Faraday, William Thomson, and Arthur Holly Compton (awarded the Nobel Prize in Physics), to name a few.

Are Scientists Automatically Qualified as Experts on Spiritual Matters?

While science and religion are complementary, it is critical to note that they are two hugely distinct aspects of reality.

It is troubling that some scientists would appear on TV programs, author books, and hold seminars to declare that there is no morality, no purpose of life, and no free will in our universe, as if they were also the experts in the spiritual realm, seemingly because of their knowledge of the physical world.

Brian Greene

In the article, "*String theorist Brian Greene wants to help you understand the cold, cruel universe*" (Jeffrey Kluger, TIME magazine, March 2-9, 2020, p. 22), regarding if human beings have free will, Brian Greene, a theoretical physicist, claims:

"Sorry, not a chance. Your particles are just obeying their quantum mechanical marching orders; you have no ability to intercede in that quantum mechanical unfolding. None whatsoever."

To him, we are just "particles." It seems that everything is only purely physical. We are like robots.

Dennis Overbye raises a valid question in his review of Greene's book (*UNTIL THE END OF TIME: Mind, Matter, and Our Search for Meaning in an Evolving Universe*):

"Can physics explain not just how the mind — neurons and electrochemical impulses — works but also explain the feeling of *having* a mind, that is to say consciousness? Greene is cautiously hopeful it can. …But he's not always sure."

("*Just a Few Billion Years Left to Go*," New York Times Book Review, Published February 17, 2020, Updated March 4, 2020.)

Nowadays, it appears that just because a person is good at physical science, they are also a master regarding the spiritual domain.

It is problematic.

Einstein

I admire Einstein as an outstanding physicist, but he reportedly encountered serious issues in human relationships.

SPIRITUAL MATTERS ARE INDEED ABOUT RELATIONSHIPS

Some may question why I am talking about people's personal relationships. They do not seem to be the problem here. I understand the perception. However, the spiritual aspect of life is indeed about relationships.

It is about how we should treat each other, namely our parents, spouses, children, and other human beings. Above all, if indeed we were created, how we should relate to our Creator.

As a matter of fact, the core of the whole Bible is about relationships. From the very first book of Genesis to the last book of Revelations, it talks about the love relationship between God and His created humans. It touches on how we should treat and love other people, and how to take good care of our families.

EINSTEIN'S WAY OF RESOLVING MARITAL CONFLICTS

It was reported that he tried to resolve the conflict by writing a letter (like a contract) to his wife, which spelled out her specific behavior acceptable to him, such as when she was allowed to talk to him.

Reporter Dinitia Smith wrote regarding that letter,

"The stipulations were as cold and precise as any of his mathematical equations. In July 1914, Albert Einstein wrote to his first wife, Mileva Maric, the mother of his two sons, laying down a series of conditions under which he would agree to continue their marriage ..."

Please refer to the article for the detailed conditions stipulated:

"Dark Side of Einstein Emerges in His Letters" (New York Times, November 6, 1996, Section C, p. 1).

It seems that Einstein tried to use a physical formula to solve the problem of one of the most important human relationships.

EINSTEIN'S RELIGIOUS BELIEFS

Some thought Einstein was a believer in God, but according to the article, *"Einstein found the Bible 'primitive, childish'*:

"... His vague language on God had long been interpreted by the faithful that Einstein was a fellow believer. But, in a letter being auctioned in England, Einstein was quite critical of religion and the Jewish people, of which he was a proud member..."

(Christianity Today, https://www.christianitytoday.com/news/2008/may/einstein-found-bible-primitive-childish.htmll, accessed 8-14-21.)

Regarding the auctioned letter written by Einstein, see the news report by the Guardian, *"Childish superstition: Einstein's letter makes view of religion relatively clear: Scientist's reply to sell for up to £8,000, and stoke debate over his beliefs."*

(https://www.theguardian.com/science/2008/may/12/peopleinscience.religion, accessed 8-14-21)

Although Einstein did have his own view on religious matters, and would respond when asked about his thoughts on this subject, fortunately, Einstein did not seem to presume himself also to be a scholar in fields other than physics.

Nevertheless, besides Brian Greene, others do.

Stephen Hawking

Stephen Hawking was an excellent astrophysicist. His perseverance and effort to overcome disability were commendable, too.

However, he was also eager to play an expert role in spiritual matters beyond his field of studies. He wrote books, gave speeches around the world, and advocated his opinions on the questions regarding the existence of God, and the way we should live our lives.

HIS CLAIMS

He claimed, "... I have shown the laws of nature suggest there is no need for a creator or God. The universe just came into existence all by itself... It spontaneously created itself in the big bang... "

He declared, "... Since I believe there is no afterlife, I think it is important to realize we only have a short time alive and should make the best of it."

(*"Hawking: the remarkable story of a beautiful mind,"* directed, filmed, and produced by Stephen Finnigan; written by Stephen Hawking, Stephen Finnigan, and Ben Bowie; Darlow Smithson Production Ltd., 2013; PBS Distribution, 2014.)

He mocked those people who still seek a divine solution to counter the theories of some physicists, saying, "What was God doing before the divine creation? Was he preparing hell for people who asked such questions?" (Rod Pyle, *"Big Bang Didn't Need God, Stephen Hawking Says,"* Space.com, April 17, 2013).

ON THE QUESTION OF AFTERLIFE

It is fine to want to make the best of our lives on Earth. Christians believe firmly in it, too. But "What is the underlying motivation?" and "What is the best way to live it?"

Some may think that since there is no afterlife, and there is no God to hold us accountable for our actions on Earth, therefore, making the best of our life means we should do whatever we want as long as we can get away with it.

This kind of thinking can induce people to act irresponsibly and even dangerously.

Hawking did not do anything dangerous physically, but others have taken this line of thought to the extreme.

The late Chinese Communist Party's chairman, Mao Tse-tung, reportedly proudly said, "I am like a monk holding an open umbrella - no hair, and no sky."

Searching online for "和尚打傘，無法無天," (hé shang dǎ sǎn, wú fǎ wú tiān), one will find many references regarding Mao's use of this expression.

What does it mean?

A Buddhist monk has a shaved head; thus, he has "no hair." The Chinese pronunciation of "hair" is the same as "law".

And since he is holding an open umbrella, he does not see the sky either. In Chinese, the "sky" is the same word as "heaven," which, according to Chinese traditional religion, is the term for the revered heavenly deity.

Thus, it means "No law, No God."

Many believe that Mao was, in effect, saying, "I am proud to be lawless and godless. I am accountable to no one."

While it is not certain if he did say it or meant it that way, since there are opposing views, his actions were indeed consistent with that kind of mentality.

History has recorded that because of his constant cruel and violent persecutions of perceived political enemies and religious believers, including the horrendous ten-year-long so-called Cultural Revolution, tens of millions of Chinese, perhaps even more, died of brutal death.

Many were subject to so-called "public trial" (公審 gōng shěn) by mobs without due process. It was literally "no law". This carnage, starting in 1949, did not end until he died almost 30 years later in 1976. It was a catastrophic human tragedy.

During the Cultural Revolution, Mao was practically worshiped like a deity. It was known as "the god-making movement" (造神運動 zào shén yùn dòng).

The communist party even published the so-called "Little Red Book" (Quotations from Mao), and demanded that it be regarded as the supreme guidance for all. Thus, not only did he not believe there was a god in heaven, ironically, but he also behaved as if he himself were a deity.

Some may think people just invent a God in heaven and the afterlife to scare us.

But whether a creator exists in the universe is an objective question about reality. It demands our serious consideration, since it entails critical behavioral consequences.

Does a higher power really exist? Will we be held accountable to such power or not? This subject will be discussed in Chapter 18, under the question, "Are all religions not the same?"

ON THE EXISTENCE OF A CREATOR

Hawking's view resembles Carl Sagan's: "nature just stumbled upon sex." All just happened naturally and accidentally "without the need of a creator," except that I must say that Sagan was aware of human weakness, and warned about the danger of self-destruction.

As remarked before, our knowledge about this vast universe is extremely limited. It is like a tiny grain of sand on a vast beach. To declare that there is no God or no need of God, from our finite human understanding, is overhasty, to put it mildly.

Furthermore, our awareness keeps changing and revising as we continue observing and learning about the cosmos. In fact, Hawking's views have been challenged by new discoveries. Check the article "*Stephen Hawking Was Wrong. Black Holes Are Bald"* by Rafi Letzter for details (Space.com, September 18, 2019).

ON THE REALM OF SPIRITUAL MATTERS

While we recognize that he did have some good knowledge of the physical world, although it was limited and fallible, did he also understand the spiritual aspects, for example, love, human relationships, and the right way we should live?

In human relationships, it is uninspiring and troublesome that he divorced his wife of many years, Jane, and married his assistant.

Jane not only saved his life (when he was critically ill in Switzerland, Jane insisted that he not be taken off life support and be transported back to England), but also had been instrumental in helping him achieve his fame. She had been constantly by his side, caring for him and their children for 30 years.

He and his assistant later ended up divorcing as well.

Jane's remarks

Jane said later in an interview, that she felt that she and their three children were left behind following Hawking's attained fame, according to an article written by the reporter Ian Burrell:

"The former wife of Stephen Hawking has described how she and their three children were 'left behind' after the cosmologist was surrounded by 'sycophantic' admirers following the publication of his landmark work *A Brief History of Time*.

"In an interview to coincide with the release this week of the Hawking biopic *The Theory of Everything*, the physicist's ex-wife Jane said their life became 'very complicated' after her husband achieved fame.

"'I rather felt that the family had been left behind,' she told *Radio Times*. 'To me, Stephen was my husband and the father of my children; one does not say to one's husband, 'Oh, you're so clever! I must worship the ground under your feet, or in this case, wheels.'

"'I found this kind of sycophantic attitude – the attitude adopted by so many people around Stephen – exceptionally frustrating and, of course, it grew a lot worse when we finally had to engage carers.'"

(Courtesy of © Ian Burrell/The Independent, "*Stephen Hawking's wife Jane Wilde on their marriage breakdown: 'The family were left behind',*" Tuesday, December 30, 2014, 10:54.)

Hawking's autobiographer's comments

His autobiographer, Kitty Ferguson, commenting on Hawking and Jane's marriage, said:

"He [Hawking] wanted this worldwide celebrity... He enjoyed this... Celebrity was fun. He embraced it and in a way that was not necessarily very good for the family, the children. So this was further real problems in the marriage" ("*Hawking: the remarkable story of a beautiful mind*").

Jane said, "... We were engulfed and swept away by this great wave of fame and fortune, and I have to say really it all got rather too much for me to cope with. I suppose that's when we ceased to be as happy as we had been. And then the marriage broke up.

"I felt as if a rug not just had been pulled out from under my feet, but opened up and swallowed up… it took me quite a little while to recover my sense of my own entity" (Ibid.)

TO SUM UP REGARDING HAWKING

I feel that although Hawking was an extinguished physicist, he did not appear to be a master of spiritual matters, and neither was he a good example of how we should live our life.

I am not sure he is a good model of how we should handle our marriage and treat our children, either. His children might have been okay with it, but divorces have forced many kids to choose between mom and dad.

Dysfunctional marriages and broken families have caused tremendous pain in our human society, which could have been avoided, or at least lessened, if we had paid attention to the spiritual aspect of life.

Neither was he an encouraging example of how we should manage fame and wealth, as distressingly experienced by his first wife, Jane.

It seems ironic that Hawking might know how the black holes worked, millions of light-years away from him in space. And yet, he did not seem to understand how to appreciate and love his spouse, who had been diligently supporting him, and to love his children, who depended upon him to care for them, in his own house, right next to him, and here on Earth.

Some may think I am too critical of Hawking, especially for the fact that he was a severely disabled person. However, this is not about his disability, but about his seemingly using his fame to advocate for his godless, no-afterlife-and-enjoy-now-for-myself lifestyle.

While he has passed, his books and films still speak to millions. He had every right to champion his views on spiritual matters. Nevertheless, his fame in physics does not mean he was also qualified to comment on the spiritual realm.

People deserve a chance to consider, I believe, a better alternative regarding how we can live the best of our life. It compels us to have a serious conversation.

Johannes Kepler

While Johannes Kepler did not shy away from talking about spiritual topics, he was not just schooled in science, but also in theology.

HIS ACCOMPLISHMENTS

Johannes Kepler was one of the most accomplished scientists in modern science.

"Kepler's efforts produced their most famous fruit in his first two laws of planetary motion, published in his 1609 masterpiece, The New Astronomy, and his third law of planetary motion, discovered in 1618.

"These laws set the stage for the emerging scientific revolution. Fifty years later, Isaac Newton's search for an underlying explanation for Kepler's laws led him to formulate his own law of universal gravitation."

He was "schooled not only in mathematics and astronomy but also in theology, Kepler initially intended to serve as a minister [in Protestant Lutheran Church]."

(Joseph L. Spradley, *"Luminous Wonder, Heavy Cross - A sense of cosmic awe sustained Johannes Kepler through deep sorrow*," Christianity Today, https://www.christianitytoday.com/history/issues/issue-76/luminous-wonder-heavy-cross.html., accessed 11-18-2020.)

Kepler not only contributed to the study of astronomy, but also mathematics, and Christianity. NASA (National Aeronautics and Space Administration of the United States) lists many "firsts" attributed to him, among them:

- First to correctly explain planetary motion, thereby becoming the founder of celestial mechanics and the first "natural laws" in the modern sense, being universal, verifiable, and precise.

- His book *Stereometrica Doliorum* formed the basis of integral calculus.

- First to derive the birth year of Christ, which is now universally accepted.

(From the article: *Johannes Kepler: His Life, His Laws, and Times*, NASA, https://www.nasa.gov/kepler/education/johannes#articles, accessed 11-17-2020.)

HIS FERVENT RELIGIOUS CONVICTION FROM STUDYING THE COSMOS

"Kepler mastered, like the best scientists, the most complicated technical issues, especially in astronomy, but he always emphasized his philosophical, even theological, approach to the questions he dealt with:

"God manifests himself not only in the words of the Scriptures but also in the wonderful arrangement of the universe and in its conformity with the human intellect.

Thus, astronomy represents for Kepler, if done philosophically, the best path to God."

(Di Liscia, Daniel A., "*Johannes Kepler,*" The Stanford Encyclopedia of Philosophy (Fall 2019 Edition), Edward N. Zalta (ed.), URL = https://plato.stanford.edu/archives/fall2019/entries/kepler/, accessed 11-17-2020.)

KEPLER'S OWN WORDS

Kepler was a devoted Lutheran Protestant Christian, who personally saw the carnage of the war of the Roman Catholic Church's Counter-Reformation against Protestant Christians.

He strongly opposed the Catholic Church's use of the state power to silence the opposition, and hoped people would come to their senses, so that peace would eventually come. In his book, he pleaded:

"*The more anyone falls in love with mathematics, the more fervent will be his dedication to God*, and the more he himself will make every effort to practice gratitude, the crown of virtue,

"So that he will join me in prayer to the merciful God that much more sincerely: let him crush the warlike confusion, eliminate devastation, snuff out hatred, and venture forth to discover that golden harmony once again."

("*Epitome Astronomiae Copernicanae,*" GW vii, 9:10-12, cited by James A. Connor in his book, *"Kepler's Witch: An Astronomer's Discovery of Cosmic Order Amid Religious War, Political Intrigue, and the Heresy Trial of His Mother,"* (New York, New York: HarperCollins, 2004), p. 335.)

Why Did Stephen Hawking and Johannes Kepler, Who Were Both Brilliant Physicists, Draw Drastically Opposite Conclusions, When Looking at the Same Universe?

As referred to before, in Psalm 19:1 of the Bible, the writer exclaims:

"The heavens declare the glory of God; the skies proclaim the work of his hands."
Footnotes
   a. Psalm 19:1 In Hebrew texts 19:1-14 is numbered 19:2-15.

However, people like Stephen Hawking did not have the same reaction as physicists like Kepler did. They were all distinguished, intelligent scientists.

What is the reason?

A case told by Jesus, I believe, answers such a question:

A RICH MAN AND A BEGGAR CALLED LAZARUS

"[19] There was a rich man who was dressed in purple and fine linen and lived in luxury every day. [20] At his gate was laid a beggar named Lazarus, covered with sores [21] and longing to eat what fell from the rich man's table. Even the dogs came and licked his sores.

"[22] The time came when the beggar died and the angels carried him to Abraham's side.

"The rich man also died and was buried. [23] In Hades [the Greek word often translated "hell"], where he was in torment, he looked up and saw Abraham far away, with Lazarus by his side.

"²⁴ So he called to him, 'Father Abraham, have pity on me and send Lazarus to dip the tip of his finger in water and cool my tongue, because I am in agony in this fire.'

"²⁵ But Abraham replied, 'Son, remember that in your lifetime you received your good things, while Lazarus received bad things, but now he is comforted here and you are in agony.

"²⁶ And besides all this, between us and you a great chasm has been set in place, so that those who want to go from here to you cannot, nor can anyone cross over from there to us.'

"²⁷ He answered, 'Then I beg you, father, send Lazarus to my family, ²⁸ for I have five brothers. Let him warn them, so that they will not also come to this place of torment.'

"²⁹ Abraham replied, 'They have Moses and the Prophets; let them listen to them.'

"³⁰ 'No, father Abraham,' he said, 'but if someone from the dead goes to them, they will repent.'

"³¹ He said to him, *'If they do not listen to Moses and the Prophets, they will not be convinced even if someone rises from the dead'*" (Luke 16:19-31).

This case demonstrates a critical aspect of human nature: If a person chooses not to accept clear evidence, more proof will not convince them. For such an individual, to put it plainly, it is not a head issue; it is a heart issue.

In Conclusion

Science and religion are not only compatible but are also complementary. Both are part of reality. In fact, science is just a tiny subset of all reality.

With a humble heart, we should be able to see God's existence and the magnificence of his creation by observing the wonder of the cosmos (the theological term for it is *"general revelation"*).

That said, we must be careful not to draw conclusions on the specific details of spiritual matters, such as morality, free will, love, relationships between humans, and between humanity and the creator, by merely basing our limited knowledge in the finite physical domain.

Therefore, scientists are not automatically qualified as experts on the spiritual realm.

These particular spiritual questions are primarily answered through the inspired word of God in the Bible (called the *"special revelation"*) and not through the physical universe.

There is a Chinese saying, "緣木求魚" (yuán mù qiú yú). It literally means, "Climb up a tree to catch fish." One will not find free will, morality, or relationships of love, by just looking at the physical stars.

No wonder Brian Greene does not see any of them up there in the sky, because it is in the Bible where they are made known. That is where the "fish" are.

It is where Johannes Kepler is different from Brian Greene and Stephen Hawking. He not only observed the physical world, but also humbly and diligently read and studied the Scriptures that the Creator inspired.

Greene and Hawking might have read the Scriptures, but apparently, they dismissed it, while Kepler took it seriously.

As Apostle Paul points out in 2 Timothy 3:16,

"All Scripture is God-breathed [inspired] and is useful for teaching, rebuking, correcting and training in righteousness,"

Thus, with a humble heart eager to seek all truth, Kepler was able to see and marvel at the complete picture of all reality.

18 - ARE ALL RELIGIONS NOT THE SAME?

THEY ALL WANT TO HELP US GET OUT OF SUFFERING, RIGHT?

It Is an Objective Pursuit of the Truth

Some may think that to claim a particular faith as the only correct answer is too narrow-minded, even arrogant. I understand the perceptions.

However, in the search for the answers to the big questions about life, like: "where did we come from?", "Why are we here?", and "Where are we going?" it is not about being "open minded" or wanting to be nice and not offending anybody.

It is a matter of finding the truth about life. It is an objective pursuit.

On the Question of God

THERE CAN BE ONLY ONE ACCURATE ANSWER

For instance, on the question of where we came from, and thus whether there is a creator god or not, there are three possible main answers: No god (atheism), One God (monotheism), or Many gods (polytheism). Only one answer can be true.

They are mutually exclusive.

There may be some varieties out of these three possible responses, for instance, the view that there are many gods, but one is dominant; nonetheless, this can be classified as polytheism.

IT IS A PRACTICAL MATTER

To find out the truth about god actually is to face reality and be pragmatic and wise.

Just for the sake of discussion, imagine that there is no god at all; how much time and effort we would have wasted venerating a non-existent being!

On the other hand, if there is only one God, who has created the world, including mankind, who is in control of the universe and loves us, how much we would have missed, if we ignored such a mighty and caring Creator!

Conversely, if there are many gods, yet we only worship one, how many other deities would we have overlooked and perhaps offended because of our ignorance?

Moreover, back to the one god scenario, if there are not many gods but only one, how seriously wrong and how severe a consequence might we suffer for such a foolish act of bowing down to all kinds of perceived deities, and not to the only one true God?

A Chance Encounter with a Buddhist

I recently met a very sincere Buddhist on a flight to Los Angeles. He just lost his beloved wife to cancer after three years of exceedingly painful and torturous treatments. He was brokenhearted.

While showing me many pictures of her, he started talking about religion. He said that all religions are good. He probably just wanted to be polite because I am not a Buddhist.

I asked him if he would be upset, if his doctor knew that there was only one particular medicine that could cure his wife's cancer, but he did not tell him and simply said, "Don't worry, all drugs are good, and you need to be open-minded."

He said, "Yes! I would be really angry."

I then answered his questions about Christianity and shared some of my thoughts regarding my faith. We had an hour-long, quite pleasant, meaningful conversation and parted ways. I sincerely hope he will consider what I shared with him and find peace and comfort in Christ's love.

In Summary

It is a fundamental question concerning life. When only one is true and effective in solving our troubles, we cannot afford to ignore it. We must be serious about it and try to ascertain what that correct answer exactly is.

Again, it is about finding the truth, an objective pursuit of reality.

19 - WHAT ARE THE DIFFERENCES BETWEEN MAJOR RELIGIONS IN THE WORLD?

Some may say, "Okay, but why do you believe that Christianity is the correct answer? How about other faiths? What are the differences?" I will briefly lay out some of the main contrasts by using Professor Young's analytical framework for comparing different religions (Young, p. 13; see below for the book he wrote):

- What is the sacred? (In other words, what is the perceived ultimacy, an impersonal force, a personal god, many gods, or other ultimacies?)

- What is the basic human problem that needs transformation?

- What is the cause of the problem?

- What is the end or goal of transformation?

- What are the means of transformation?

We will discuss those faiths that originated from the Middle East (Judaism, Christianity, and Islam) first. Then, the beliefs that started in Asia (Hinduism, Buddhism, Confucianism, and Taoism) will be analyzed.

The primary source of information on these differences is from the book written by Professor William A. Young, *The World's Religions – World Views and Contemporary Issues, Third Edition* (Upper Saddle River, NJ: Prentice Hall, ©2011, Reprinted by permission of Pearson Education Inc.).

If material from Young's book is used, I will quote his words directly or summarize the author's points. To indicate such a usage of the author's work, a smaller font size (size 10) is applied.

If you see words in the regular font size (size 12, typically in a parenthesis), in the midst of the quoted smaller sized text, they are my words to further explain Young's content, or to add additional information for you.

I will also add extra paragraphs for additional explanations, or insert subtitles and subheadings (all in regular size 12) to organize the quoted text.

Young's book is a comprehensive work with over 400 pages. The extract here is a small part of it. For further interest, please consult the text or other sources regarding world religions.

Another book I find valuable is written by Michael Molloy (*Experiencing the World's Religions – Tradition, Challenge, and Change*, Fifth Edition (New York, NY: McGraw-Hill, 2010)).

At the end of each religion, I will then share my thoughts regarding that particular faith.

By the way, a significant amount of royalties was paid for using Young's materials. But I feel that giving readers an overall view of a religion first before I share my thoughts, will provide a good general context of that faith.

20 - JUDAISM

Judaism is the shared history of the Jewish people, who, by birth or by conscious decision and action, identify themselves with the heritage and continuing experience of the Jewish people.

The Hebrew Bible and the History of the Jewish People

(Note: The subtitle above and the subheadings below, such as "**Torah**" and "**HOW THE WORLD CAME TO EXIST**," are added by me to organize the quoted text better.)

The history of the Jews is recorded in the Hebrew Bible called *Tanak*. It consists of three sections: *Torah* ("Law, instruction"), *Nevi'im* ("Prophets"), and *Kethuvi'im* ("Writings").

Torah

HOW THE WORLD CAME TO EXIST

The first book of *the Torah*, Genesis, recounts the creation of the universe, including humans, by the one true God (Jehovah). Next comes the primal history of mankind: the first man (Adam) and woman (Eve) in the Garden of Eden, their expulsion from paradise because of their disobedience.

THE ABRAHAMIC COVENANT

Then, the story focuses on the relationship between God and the one nation God chose to play a special role in history. The narrative of the ancestors of Israel, and the special covenant God entered into with Abraham and his descendants is recounted.

Abraham is promised by God that his descendants will become a great nation in a land of their own as well as a source of blessing to other nations. (Refer to Genesis 12:1-3 for details regarding the promise received by Abraham.) (Note: The reference in the parentheses is my extra information for you.)

MOSES' TEN COMMANDMENTS

Later on, at the mountain of Sinai, God appears to Moses and gives him the Ten Commandments and other laws, as the basis of a new covenant relationship with the people of Israel. God promises that he will protect them if the people will agree to follow the laws. (Refer to Exodus 20:1-17.)

Nevi'im

In the next section of the Tanak, the prophetic books, the story of the history of the people of Israel continues. The rise and fall of ancient Israel, and the roles of kings and prophets are recounted.

The Book of Joshua, Judges, 1st and 2nd Kings, Isaiah, Jeremiah, Amos, and others are among the Scriptures in this section.

During this period, God sent prophets repeatedly to warn the Israelites to repent, stop idolizing false gods, and follow His laws lest they suffer dire consequences. Yet, oftentimes, God's prophets were ignored.

(Note: the above two paragraphs and all paragraphs below, in regular font size 12, starting from "The Diaspora," are contents I added for you.)

Kethuvi'im

The last section of the Tanak, the Writings, contains a variety of types of literature. Included are the narrative books that parallel and extend the story told in the prophetic books, such as the First and Second

Chronicles. A unique work is the Book of Daniel. It is an apocalyptic writing that reveals the end of history and the beginning of a new age.

The other books of the Writings are largely poetic. They include a collection of hymns associated with worship in the Jerusalem temple and other poems (Psalms), wisdom books (Proverbs, Jobs, Ecclesiastes), and a collection of poems of sorrow occasioned by the destruction of Jerusalem by the Babylonians (Lamentations).

The Diaspora

The Jewish diaspora (or exile) is the dispersion of Jews out of their homeland and later settlements in many parts of the globe.

The first exile was the Assyrian Captivity, the expulsion of the people of the Kingdom of Israel (Samaria, in the northern part of Israel) to Assyria, by the king of Assyria in 722 B.C. (2 Kings 17:23).

As for the surviving Kingdom of Judah (Jerusalem, in the southern part of Israel), the destruction of Jerusalem by the Babylonians and the deportation of the population to Babylon in 586 B.C. marked the start of the second exile.

These were the direct consequences of many Jewish kings' repeated disobedience of God's laws and the persistent disregard of God's warnings.

Below are the records of the last king of Judah, Zedekiah, before Jews were expelled to Babylon.

The Disobedience

"[11] Zedekiah was twenty-one years old when he became king, and he reigned in Jerusalem eleven years. [12] He did evil in the eyes of the Lord his God and did not humble himself before Jeremiah the prophet, who spoke the word of the Lord.

"¹³ He also rebelled against King Nebuchadnezzar, who had made him take an oath in God's name. He became stiff-necked and hardened his heart and would not turn to the Lord, the God of Israel.

"¹⁴ Furthermore, all the leaders of the priests and the people became more and more unfaithful, following all the detestable practices of the nations and defiling the temple of the Lord, which he had consecrated in Jerusalem" (2 Chronicles 36: 11-14).

The Warnings and the Consequences

"¹⁵ The Lord, the God of their ancestors, sent word to them through his messengers again and again, because he had pity on his people and on his dwelling place.

"¹⁶ But they mocked God's messengers, despised his words and scoffed at his prophets until the wrath of the Lord was aroused against his people and there was no remedy.

"¹⁷ He brought up against them the king of the Babylonians,[a] who killed their young men with the sword in the sanctuary, and did not spare young men or young women, the elderly or the infirm. God gave them all into the hands of Nebuchadnezzar.

"²⁰ He [King Nebuchadnezzar] carried into exile to Babylon the remnant, who escaped from the sword, and they became servants to him and his successors until the kingdom of Persia came to power" (2 Chronicles 36:15-17, 20-21).

Footnotes
 a. Or *Chaldeans*

God Is Fulfilling His Promises

Although Jews would be dispersed and even persecuted, God promises to bring them back to Jerusalem from all over the world one day in the future:

"⁶ This is what the Lord Almighty says: 'It may seem marvelous to the remnant of this people at that time, but will it seem marvelous to me?' declares the Lord Almighty.
"⁷ This is what the Lord Almighty says: 'I will save my people from the countries of the east and the west. ⁸ I will bring them back to live in Jerusalem; they will be my people, and I will be faithful and righteous to them as their God'" (Zechariah 8:6-8).

It is remarkable that in 1948, the nation of Israel was restored in Jerusalem after more than 2000 years.
Today, Jewish people continue to move back to Israel from around the world. And the day when the complete restoration of the relationship between the nation of Israel and God will come at the end of time, as prophesized.
Regarding the city of Jerusalem,

"It will be inhabited; never again will it be destroyed. Jerusalem will be secure" (Zechariah 14:11); "On that day holy to the Lord will be inscribed on the bells of the horses, and the cooking pots in the Lord's house will be like the sacred bowls in front of the altar" (Zechariah 14:20).

The Sacred

The Great "I Am": Monotheism, at the heart of Judaism, is the oft-repeated *Shema* (a liturgical prayer), which begins: "Hear, O Israel! The Lord is our God, the Lord alone!"
There is only one God, who is a personal God, who is the sole source of all life and who has no equals. God is all-powerful and all-knowing. God is personal in the sense that God relates to the creation and to humans, with characteristics such as love and anger.

The Basic Human Problem

Missing the Mark: All branches of Judaism agree that humans have the freedom to decide whether to follow the will of God or to rebel against it. Classical Judaism speaks of two contrasting tendencies (*yezers*) that are at war in each human's nature: a good impulse and an evil impulse. Those who choose to follow the "evil impulse" inevitably engage in deeds that "miss the mark".

The Cause of The Problem

Disobedience: Traditional Judaism teaches that God has revealed the way people are to live. Our choice is whether to obey God and follow the path (in Judaism, the halakha) or disobey God.

The Goal of Transformation

Next Year in Jerusalem: According to the Pharisaic view, at some time in the future – at a time known only to God – a human descendant of King David anointed by God (the Messiah) will appear and enter Jerusalem. The Messiah will restore the nation of Israel, with Jerusalem at the center. This belief is expressed in the toast that is part of the Passover liturgy, as the participants look with anticipation and hope to the coming of the Messiah: "Next year in Jerusalem!"

When the Messiah comes, a new age, the "age to come," will begin, bringing universal peace, harmony, and justice for all nations. Those who have died before the coming of this age will be raised from their graves to be judged. Those Jews, who have been obedient to the Torah, and those Gentiles (non-Jews) who have followed the minimal commandments given by God to all humanity after the Flood, will enter into this new Kingdom of God.

The Means of Transformation

The Way of Torah: At the heart of all branches of Judaism (Orthodox, Conservative, and Reform) is the Torah, the instruction from God on how to live obediently, which includes both the written and the oral Torah. What it means to follow the way of Torah in the modern world is a subject of much disagreement. However Torah is interpreted, there is consensus that following the way of Torah is not a burden but a joy.

Please note that the above-quoted views are mostly held by Orthodox Judaism. As for the Conservative and Reform branches, they are typically more flexible and take Scripture more symbolically than literally.

My Thoughts

Is Judaism Just About Jewish People?

The Abrahamic Covenant states,

> "² I [God, Jehovah] will make you into a great nation, and I will bless you; I will make your name great, and you will be a blessing.[a] ³ I will bless those who bless you, and whoever curses you I will curse; and all peoples on earth will be blessed through you" [b] (Genesis 12:2-3).
> Footnotes
>   a. Or *be seen as blessed.*
>   b. Or *earth / will use your name in blessings* (see 48:20)

Prophet Isaiah declares, "³ Let no foreigner who is bound to the Lord [God] say, 'The Lord will surely exclude me from his people.' ...

"...⁶ 'And foreigners who bind themselves to the Lord to minister to him, to love the name of the Lord, and to be his servants, all who keep the Sabbath without desecrating it and who hold fast to my covenant—

"⁷ these I will bring to my holy mountain and give them joy in my house of prayer. Their burnt offerings and sacrifices will be accepted on my altar; for my house will be called a house of prayer for all nations'" (Isaiah 56:3-7).

From the Hebrew Bible itself, it is abundantly clear that Judaism is not just about Jewish people. Instead, it is about all humanity.

Why Did God Choose to Make Covenants with the Jews?

Some may ask why God seems to favor a particular group of people. Are they superior?

Nowhere in the Scriptures does it say that Jews, as a people, were chosen because they were superior in any sense. In fact, "they are a stiff-necked people":

"^{9} 'I have seen these people,' the Lord said to Moses, 'and they are a stiff-necked people'" (Exodus 32:9);

"Understand, then, that it is not because of your righteousness that the Lord your God is giving you this good land to possess, for you are a stiff-necked people" (Deuteronomy 9:6);

"^{51} 'You stiff-necked people! Your hearts and ears are still uncircumcised. You are just like your ancestors: You always resist the Holy Spirit! ^{52} Was there ever a prophet your ancestors did not persecute? They even killed those who predicted the coming of the Righteous One [Jesus]. And now you have betrayed and murdered him [Jesus] "(Acts 7:51-52).

There was a pattern of blessings and curses by God throughout Israel's early history, as recorded in the Hebrew Bible.

God would bless the Israelites, and they would become complacent, arrogant, and forget about God's law. They would worship idols and many pagan gods, which would draw His anger and wrath. They would repent; God would then have mercy on them. Then, they would become disobedient again.

So why did God choose them? I think God chose Jewish people to be an example of the relationship between God and his created human beings.

In God's eyes, all are created and loved by him. United States Declaration of Independence, which says, *"All men are created equal,"* is truly biblical.

We are all the descendants of Adam and Eve, whom God created.

We are all of one race, which is the human race. And we are all part of the fallen humanity.

In fact, Apostle Paul, himself being a Jew, says,

"What shall we conclude then? Do we [Israelites] have any advantage? Not at all! For we have already made the charge that Jews and Gentiles [non-Jews] alike are all under the power of sin" (Romans 3:9).

In short, Jews are no better than any other people, and we are no better than Jews. All have sinned. All are stiff-necked people, and all need salvation.

That said, while it is due to God's providential care, it should be noted that Jews have diligently preserved and safeguarded God's words, as written in the Tanak, for thousands of years!

Furthermore, even after severe suffering, like the Holocaust in the Second World War, many Jews still hold firm to their faith in God.

What Is the Main Difference Between Judaism and Christianity?

Judaism is still waiting for the coming Messiah, while Christianity believes that Jesus is the one prophesized in the Hebrew Bible. His first coming was fulfilled about 2,000 years ago, and He will come again at the end of time.

WHY IS JESUS THE PROMISED MESSIAH?

The following passages from the Hebrew Bible and the New Testament support that conclusion:

From the Hebrew texts

Isaiah 7:14 declares,

"Therefore the Lord himself will give you[a] a sign: The virgin[b] will conceive and give birth to a son, and[c] will call him Immanuel. [d]"
    Footnotes
        a. The Hebrew is plural.
        b. Or *young woman*
        c. Masoretic Text; Dead Sea Scrolls *son, and he* or *son, and they*
        d. *Immanuel* means *God with us.*

Micah 5:2 prophesizes where he would be born,

"But you, Bethlehem Ephrathah, though you are small among the clans[a] of Judah, out of you will come for me one who will be ruler over Israel, whose origins are from of old, from ancient times."
    Footnotes:
        a. Or *rulers*

Isaiah 9:6-7 proclaims,

"⁶ For to us a child is born, to us a son is given, and the government will be on his shoulders. And he will be called Wonderful Counselor, Mighty God, Everlasting Father, Prince of Peace.

"⁷ Of the greatness of his government and peace there will be no end.

He will reign on David's throne and over his kingdom, establishing and upholding it with justice and righteousness from that time on and forever. The zeal of the Lord Almighty will accomplish this. "

Isaiah 53:4-5 says he will suffer for our sins,

"⁴ Surely he took up our pain and bore our suffering, yet we considered him punished by God, stricken by him, and afflicted. ⁵ But he was pierced for our transgressions, he was crushed for our iniquities; the punishment that brought us peace was on him, and by his wounds we are healed."

<u>From the New Testament</u>

Matthew 1:20-23 records,

"²⁰ But after he [Joseph] had considered this, an angel of the Lord appeared to him in a dream and said, 'Joseph son of David, do not be afraid to take Mary home as your wife, because what is conceived in her is from the Holy Spirit. ²¹ She will give birth to a son, and you are to give him the name Jesus, [a] because he will save his people from their sins.'

"²² All this took place to fulfill what the Lord had said through the prophet: ²³ 'The virgin will conceive and give

birth to a son, and they will call him Immanuel' [b] (which means "God with us").
> Footnotes
> a. *Jesus* is the Greek form of *Joshua,* which means *the Lord saves.*
> b. Isaiah 7:14

We can see that Mathew 1:22 says explicitly that Jesus is the fulfillment of the prophecy of Isaiah 7:14.

One of the very first actions Jesus did when he started ministering, was to go into the synagogue of Nazareth, his hometown, on the Sabbath day, and personally quoted from the Book of Isaiah:

"[17] and the scroll of the prophet Isaiah was handed to him. Unrolling it, he found the place where it is written: [18] 'The Spirit of the Lord is on me, because he has anointed me to proclaim good news to the poor. He has sent me to proclaim freedom for the prisoners and recovery of sight for the blind, to set the oppressed free, [19] to proclaim the year of the Lord's favor.'[a]

"[20] Then he rolled up the scroll, gave it back to the attendant and sat down. The eyes of everyone in the synagogue were fastened on him. [21] He began by saying to them, *'Today this scripture is fulfilled in your hearing'*" (Luke 4:17-21).
> Footnotes
> a. Isaiah 61:1,2 (see Septuagint); Isaiah 58:6

Some may say, "Jesus claimed to be the Messiah, but how do I know he was telling the truth? " I will answer this question under "Why is the belief in Jesus not a blind faith?" later in Chapter 30.

How Can Jews Be Saved?

God made a covenant with Jews as a nation. Israel, as a country, will be completely restored and blessed in the end, as said before.

However, even under Judaism, I believe an individual Jew will not be saved just because they are Jew. They must have faith in God for salvation.

FROM THE HEBREW TEXTS

Genesis 15:6 states,

> "Abram believed the Lord, and he credited it to him as righteousness."

Habakkuk 2:4 declares:

> "4 'See, the enemy is puffed up; his desires are not upright—but the righteous person will live by his faithfulness[b]—"
> Footnotes
> Or *Though he linger, wait for him; / he*
> Or *faith*

The New Testament also echoes that and enumerates all the many people who acted in faith in God during the Old Testament times and, thus, were saved (Hebrews 11: 1-40).

FROM THE NEW TESTAMENT

It is clear that an individual Jew will not be saved for simply being a Jewish descendant.

When John the Baptist saw many of the Pharisees and Sadducees (the two major Jewish religious sects at the time) coming to where he was baptizing, he said to them,

"⁷... 'You brood of vipers! Who warned you to flee from the coming wrath? ⁸ Produce fruit in keeping with repentance. ⁹ And do not think you can say to yourselves, 'We have Abraham as our father.'

"I tell you that out of these stones God can raise up children for Abraham. ¹⁰ The ax is already at the root of the trees, and every tree that does not produce good fruit will be cut down and thrown into the fire..." (Matthew 3:7-12).

Romans 10:12-13 sums it up well,

"¹² For there is no difference between Jew and Gentile—the same Lord is Lord of all and richly blesses all who call on him, ¹³ for, 'Everyone who calls on the name of the Lord will be saved.'[a]"

Footnotes
    a. Joel 2:32

Note that verse 13 is a quote from the Book of Joel in the Hebrew Bible.

In short, every individual, whether Jewish or not, need to repent of their sins, and have faith in Jesus to be saved.

Having said that, again, as a nation, God will keep his promise to restore the state of Israel completely, when the end of times comes.

Are Jews Not against Christianity?

Some may think that Jews have been against Christianity. It was Jews who demanded the crucifixion of Jesus, after all. Sadly, People might have persecuted or discriminated against Jewish people for this unfair accusation.

Yes, it was the Jews who demanded that Jesus should be crucified, but they did not represent all the Jewish people at the time. Let alone the Jewish people of today.

Jesus was himself Jewish, and all twelve apostles he called to follow him were Jews.

Furthermore, many Jews believed in Jesus, and played a key role in establishing the church in Jerusalem and spreading his teachings across the Roman Empire.

For instance, at one of the major miraculous events in the early church era, many Jews came from all over the Roman Empire to Jerusalem to attend the Pentecost, a Jewish festival celebrated on the fiftieth day after Passover.

In just one single day, about three thousand repented and accepted Jesus as their Savior, after hearing the apostles share the good news of Christ (Acts 2: 1-41).

Moreover, even today, there are still many Jews who believe that Jesus is the promised Messiah. For example, *Jews for Jesus*, was started by Moishe Rosen in 1970 in the United States. It is a well-established movement and has branch offices around the world.

These believers identify themselves as *Messianic Jews*.

There are other similar movements, like the *Messianic Jewish Alliance of America*. Although they are not like other Jewish believers who attend Christian churches, and still maintain their own congregations that keep Jewish customs and observe Jewish holidays, they do believe that Jesus is the promised Savior.

21 - CHRISTIANITY

Professor Young writes a concise description of the founder, Jesus:

"Jesus of Nazareth was a Jewish rabbi from the region of Galilee in the first century C.E., who attracted a small band of followers through his ministry of healing and teaching. After a short ministry, he was executed by Roman authorities.

"Historians would have paid him little notice, but his followers made the astounding claim that Jesus had been raised by God from the dead. They kept alive his teachings and the stories of his life and eventually wrote them down in different versions. [The four books of Matthew, Mark, Luke, and John, record in detail regarding Jesus' birth and ministry]

"They proclaimed the message that through the death and resurrection of Jesus, God had made a new covenant with humanity, and that, through Jesus, God offered redemption to all" (Young, pp. 201-202).

Note that Professor Young says Jesus "attracted a small band of followers." He might be talking about the twelve disciples Jesus called to minister with him, because when Jesus was ministering in the region, many people followed him. As a matter of fact, at just one event, there were five thousand men, not even counting the women and children, who came to listen to him and seek his healing (Matthew 14:21).

As mentioned before, Judaism is still waiting for the coming Messiah, while Christianity believes that Jesus is the one who was prophesized in the Hebrew Bible, that He fulfilled the prophecy about 2,000 years ago, and that He will come again at the end of the world.

Christianity accepts Judaism's Hebrew Bible as part of its Scripture and calls it the Old Testament. As for the texts written by Jesus' followers, they are called the New Testament. Both the Old and New Testament are integral components of Christianity's holy writings.

In a sense, Christianity truly is the continuation and the fulfillment of Judaism, if one would accept that Jesus is the promised Messiah.

I would save detailed discussions regarding the answers to the questions of the sacred, the problem, the goal, the means, and a lot more additional information, including my thoughts, later in Chapter 30, "Questions about Christianity."

22 - ISLAM

Islam is a religion that is relatively later than other monotheistic faiths that originated in the Middle East. It started around the 7th century A.D., as compared to Judaism (around 1800 B.C.) and Christianity (1st century A.D.).

Its scriptures (the Qur'an) referred to Abraham, Moses, and Jesus, who are prominent figures in Judaism's Hebrew Bible and Christianity's New Testament, over two hundred times combined (search results on *www.clearquran.com, accessed 4-9-2020*).

Author Michael Molloy writes, "... Indeed, there are numerous similarities between Islam and other religions [i.e., Judaism, Christianity, and Zoroastrianism] ... However, Muslims hold that Muhammad's religious ideas came directly from God (Michael Molloy, *Experiencing the World's Religions – Tradition, Challenge, and Change*, Fifth Edition, New York, NY: McGraw Hill, ©2010, p. 431).

> Muhammad was born in 570 or 571 A.D. in Mecca. He was orphaned when he was little and was adopted by his uncle. He had no formal education and remained illiterate throughout his life. At 25, he married a wealthy 40-year-old widow.
>
> Muhammad spent time meditating and had become convinced of the coming judgment that Zoroastrianism, Judaism, and Christianity describe and agonized over the fate of those who worshiped idols.
>
> While he was meditating during the month of Ramadan, an angel appeared and spoke to him. He memorized what he heard and had it written down by others. It became the Muslim sacred text, the Qur'an.

In 630 A.D., he led a force that conquered Mecca. He destroyed the idols in the Kaaba, leaving only the black meteoric stone and its enclosure intact, and instituted the new "nation of Islam".

He was the undisputed political as well as religious leader of Arabia, and united the desert tribes of the peninsula into an awesome fighting force. After he died, the Muslim armies continued to move beyond Arabia.

The Sacred

There is no God but Allah: Monolithic, Allah is heralded as the only God. Allah is personal; He alone is supreme. Allah is the transcendent, omnipotent creator, who rules and judges overall.

Muslims believe that Allah is the same God who spoke to Zoroastrians, Jews, and Christians. Although the prophets Allah chose to speak to these peoples fulfilled their roles, those who wrote down and transmitted the words have distorted Allah's truth. For example, the Christian idea of the Trinity is blasphemous, for it creates three gods instead of the one true God.

The Basic Human Problem

Rejecting Allah's Guidance: The basic problem to be overcome is idolatry, the human tendency to worship the creation rather the creator.

The Cause of the Problem

Distraction: Humans are distracted from the path Allah has revealed by jinn, the evil spirits, who appeal to the earthly nature of humans, causing them to forget what their higher soul (which is aware of Allah) is telling them to do.

The Goal of Transformation

Paradise and the "House of Islam": The Qur'an points to a Day of Judgment, when people will be judged on the basis of their deeds recorded in a heavenly book, and be led either to heaven or hell.

Islam also paints a picture of the goal toward which societies are oriented. The *dar al-islam* ("house of Islam or peace") is the ideal society that can be achieved before the end of time. The conservative interpretation of dar al-islam is that Sharia should be the only law in society.

Another important and related Muslim principle is *umma* ("people"). It is the ideal of a single, worldwide Muslim community. Extremists like Osama bin Laden have attempted to appeal to the concept of the umma to enlist the global Muslim community in their terrorist campaigns.

The Means of Transformation

A life of Submission: The Qur'an speaks of the righteous life on almost every page, with its commitment to personal piety and social justice. For the individual, the *five pillars* constitute the foundation of living. These are the obligations all Muslims recognize.

The five pillars are:

1. Repetition of the creed "There is no God but Allah; and Muhammad is His messenger [or prophet]" daily.

2. Daily prayer, which Muslims are required to perform five times a day.

3. Almsgiving. This is, in effect, a tax on certain kinds of property, paid at the end of each year.

4. Fasting during the entire month of Ramadan.

5. Pilgrimage to Mecca. The Qur'an requires every Muslim man and woman to make the journey to the holiest city of Islam, Mecca, at least once in a lifetime.

My Thoughts

Do Christians Worship Multiple Gods?

Probably one of the most pressing questions a Muslim might ask is, "Do Christians worship multiple gods?", since you hear this "God the Father, God the Son, God the Holy Spirit" from Christians.

The short answer is no. It is not about multiple deities (polytheism), but about one God in three persons (Trinity). I understand it isn't easy to comprehend. The following mathematical illustration may help.

As Dr. Geisler puts it,

"Does not 1+1+1 = 3? It certainly does if you *add* them, but Christians insist that the triunity of God is more like 1x1x1 = 1. God is triune, not triplex. His one essence has multiple centers of personhood. Thus, there is no more mathematical problem in conceiving the Trinity than there is in understanding 1 cubed (1^3)."

(Norman L. Geisler, *Baker Encyclopedia of Christian Apologetics* (Grand Rapids, Michigan: Baker Books, 1999), p. 732. Used by permission of Baker Academic, a division of Baker Publishing Group)

We will elaborate on this concept further, later in the chapter about Christianity.

Were the Texts of Judaism and Christianity "Corrupted" During Transmission?

Professor Young states that Muslims recognize the legitimacy of the Scriptures of Jews and Christians, but claim they were corrupted during transmission (Young, p. 228).

However, the discovery of the Dead Sea Scrolls provides one of the most potent and fascinating pieces of evidence, which testifies to the integrity and the preservation of God's words by the Jewish people. (More on the Dead Sea Scrolls in Chapter 30, "Questions about Christianity".)

When Were the Prophecies About Things to Come Fully Revealed?

Islam claims that Mohammed is the last and the greatest prophet (Ibid, Michael Molloy, p. 431).

Therefore, a critical question one would ask is, "When were the prophecies about things to come fully revealed?"

To Islam, it might hold that it was at the time of Mohammed, in the seventh century A.D., since he was the last and the greatest prophet.

But for Christianity, it was after Jesus told Apostle John directly and through angels. John wrote them down in the last book of the Bible, the Book of Revelation, in the first century A.D.

Indeed, on what is to come, both Judaism and Christianity clearly believe that the Messiah/Christ is the ultimate prophet, the final authority, and the fulfillment of any prophecies.

FOR JUDAISM

In Deuteronomy 18:18-20, God told Moses:

"[18] I will raise up for them a prophet like you from among their fellow Israelites, and I will put my words in his mouth. He will tell them everything I command him.

"[19] I myself will call to account anyone who does not listen to my words that the prophet speaks in my name. [20] But a prophet who presumes to speak in my name anything I have not commanded, or a prophet who speaks in the name of other gods, is to be put to death."

In Isaiah 7:14, it declares:

"¹⁴ Therefore the Lord [Jehovah] himself will give you[a] a sign: The virgin[b] will conceive and give birth to a son, and[c] will call him Immanuel. [d])
>
> Foot Notes:
> a. The Hebrew is plural.
> b. Or *young woman*
> c. Masoretic Text; Dead Sea Scrolls *son, and he* or *son, and they*
> d. *Immanuel* means *God with us.*

FOR CHRISTIANITY

Apostle Peter says, referring to the prophecy recorded in Deut. 18 of the Old Testament as quoted above, that Jesus was that prophet promised by God:

"²² For Moses said, 'The Lord your God will raise up for you a prophet like me from among your own people; you must listen to everything he tells you. ²³ Anyone who does not listen to him will be completely cut off from their people' [a]" (Acts 3:22-23).
>
> Footnotes
> a. Deut. 18:15,18,19

In the Book of Revelation, it records that Jesus Christ personally appeared to Apostle John and told him what is to come:

"¹⁷ When I [Apostle John] saw him [Jesus], I fell at his feet as though dead. Then he placed his right hand on me and said: "Do not be afraid. *I am the First and the Last*. ¹⁸ I am the Living One; I was dead, and now look, I am alive for ever and ever! And I hold the keys of death and Hades.¹⁹ "Write, therefore, what you have seen, *what is now and what will take place later*" (Revelation 1:17-19).

At the very end of the book, Jesus personally and specifically warns:

"*18* I warn everyone who hears the words of the prophecy of this scroll: If anyone *adds anything* to them, God will add to that person the plagues described in this scroll.
"*19* And if anyone *takes words away from* this scroll of prophecy, God will take away from that person any share in the tree of life and in the Holy City, which are described in this scroll" (Revelation 22:18-19).

It is a stern warning, since the consequence is eternal death.

To both Judaism and Christianity, it is evident that Christ is the ultimate, last prophet. For Judaism, Christ is yet to come. For Christianity, Christ, who is Jesus, has come, and will come again.

In short, for prophecies, after Jesus revealed them to Apostle John directly and through angels, John wrote them down in the Book of Revelation in the first century A.D., and the revelation on the future was completed.

Nothing is allowed to be added or changed after that. It is final. There are no more prophets or prophecies regarding what will take place in the future.

It is a critical difference between Islam and Judaism/Christianity.

How Can One Be Saved According to Islam?

When I was working as a computer specialist, I met a Muslim coworker. He is an African American, a sincere and friendly man. I once asked him, "Are you sure you will go to heaven when you die?" His answer was, "I do not know."

I think one of the critical differences between Christianity and Islam is that salvation is free by faith under Christianity, while according to Islam, one cannot seem to be sure if they have done enough good deeds to be saved.

Professor Young writes that, as stated by the Qur'an, on the Day of Judgment, people will be judged based on their deeds, and be led either to heaven or hell, per Surah 39.68-7 (Young, p. 242).

I must point out that some branches of Christianity have added work merits to the condition for salvation as well; nonetheless, the Scriptures do not support it.

More on this will be examined under the question, "What are the differences between the three major branches of Christianity?" in this Part Three, and under the subheading, "How you can truly be saved" in Part Four.

On the Issue of Church and State

In my observation, another major difference between Christianity and Islam is the issue of church and state. Should the government mandate, by force, a particular religion to which its citizens must pledge allegiance?

HOW CHRISTIANITY WAS FOUNDED IN THE FIRST CENTURY

Jesus and his followers did not use force to spread their faith. On the contrary, they used love and care, even to the point of sacrificing their own lives.

In the about three years of Jesus' ministry, "Jesus went throughout Galilee, teaching in their synagogues, proclaiming the good news of the kingdom, and healing every disease and sickness among the people" (Matthew 4:23).

Not only did Jesus heal the sick, but He also fed the hungry (Matthew 14:13-21), and in the end, even willingly died on the cross, so as to fulfill God's promise of sending the Savior to suffer for the consequences of humanity's sins.

When the armed crowd came to arrest him, sent by the chief priests and the elders, He refused to use force to defend himself, telling his follower who drew the sword:

"[52] 'Put your sword back in its place,' Jesus said to him, *'for all who draw the sword will die by the sword.* [53] *Do you think I cannot call on my Father* [God the Father], *and he will at once put at my disposal more than twelve legions of angels?* [54] *But how then would the Scriptures be fulfilled that say it must happen in this way?'"* (Matthew 26:52-54).

When Jesus sent his followers to spread the good news of the heavenly kingdom, He told them to love and help people:

"Heal the sick, raise the dead, cleanse those who have leprosy, [a] drive out demons. Freely you have received; freely give" (Matthew 10:8).

Footnotes
  a. The Greek word traditionally translated *leprosy* was used for various diseases affecting the skin.

In Matthew 10:17-36, Jesus told his followers that they would be persecuted, even by their own family (v. 35-36), and could even be killed for sharing the good news.

However, they were not to use force to confront them, "When you are persecuted in one place, flee to another..." (v. 23), and instead, be prepared to die for the gospel, just as Christ died for them.

THE CORRUPTION OF THE PAPACY

For nearly three hundred years, despite the Roman Empire's constant oppression, the early Christians persevered and continued to preach the gospel fearlessly but peacefully, and the faith continued to grow throughout the empire.

In fact, the Roman emperor Theodosius declared Christianity the empire's *official* religion in the fourth century.

It might sound good for Christianity. However, I believe the opposite happened.

Christianity, under the Bishop of Rome, who was *both a political and religious power*, instead of continuing Jesus' ministry of "to serve and not to be served" (Matthew 20:28), became a vicious tool of political dominance, exploitation, and oppression.

The Pope was even above the kings. The clergies enjoyed sole authority and wealth without any accountability.

The Roman Catholic Church brutally put down any challenges to its rule. For example, in 1415, John Huss, a Czech theologian and philosopher, who spoke out against the Church's corruption (such as the sale of indulgences), was condemned as a heretic and burned at the stake.

THE PROTESTANT REFORMATION

Martin Luther

It was not until the early sixteenth century that the Reformation movement, under Martin Luther (1483-1546), a German Catholic priest and college professor, seriously disputed the absolute power of the Roman Catholic Church and opposed its abuse.

Other reformers quickly emerged, like John Calvin (1509 – 1564).

Another group also sparked the Anabaptist movement:

"Among them were Jacob Hutter (d. 1536) and Menno Simons (ca. 1494-1561) [a Dutch Catholic priest], the founder of the Mennonites.

"The name *Anabaptist* ('baptism for a second time') comes from the practice of baptizing people as adults rather than as infants (as was the case not only in the Roman Catholic Church but also the other branches of the Protestant Reformation).

[Note: Anabaptists believe that baptism must be a personal, voluntary decision, which could only be possible as an adult exercising free will.]

"Anabaptists are perhaps best known for their advocacy of pacifism and the strict *separation of church and state*. Many Anabaptists groups have been persecuted for their beliefs" (Young, p. 207).

Fighting for religious freedom from the dictate of the Papacy ensued. Countless people died. In the Thirty Years' War (1618-1648) fought on the continental Europe, over 8 million perished, including 20% to 30% of the German population.

It was a horrendous tragedy. People had to fight so hard and even die for their freedom of faith.

Fortunately, with determined resistance against the Catholic Church, many Protestants in Germany and other parts of Europe eventually gained their liberation. They restored what it should be in the first place, as in the early church era: To freely worship God truly from our hearts without coercion.

As Jesus says, "Yet a time is coming and has now come when the true worshipers will worship the Father *in the*

Spirit and in truth, for they are the kind of worshipers the Father seeks" (John 4:23).

The Puritans

Although many Protestants gained freedom in Europe, the struggle continued in England. However, this time it was not against the dictate of the Roman Catholic Church, but the oppression of the Anglican Church of England.

On December 18, 1620, a small group of Puritans (the Pilgrims), arrived in the British ship the Mayflower and settled in the town called Plymouth Colony in the New World, led by Governor William Bradford.

In November of 1623, Governor Bradford issued the very first proclamation of Thanksgiving in America:

"To all ye Pilgrims: In as much as the great Father has given us this year an abundant harvest of Indian corn, wheat peas, beans, squashes, and garden vegetable, and has made the forest to abound with game and the sea with fish and clams,

"and inasmuch as he has protected us from the ravages of the savages, has spared us from pestilence and disease, has granted us freedom to worship God *according to the dictates of our own conscience.*

"Now I, your magistrate, do proclaim that all ye Pilgrims, with your wives and ye little ones, do gather at ye meeting house, on ye hill,

"between the hours of 9 and 12 in the daytime, on Thursday, November 29th, of the year of our Lord one thousand six hundred and twenty-three, and the third year since ye Pilgrims landed on Pilgrim Rock, there to listen to ye pastor and render thanksgiving to ye Almighty God for all His blessings."

By the way, it is worth noting that Governor Bradford mentioned being protected from "the ravages of the savages". God did not just protect them; providentially, He also sent an Indian, who could speak English, to help them and also taught them how to plant corn and survive:

"... Squanto, a local Indian who had been kidnapped and taken to England nearly a decade before, served as an interpreter with the local tribes. Squanto taught the Pilgrims to fertilize the soil with dried fish remains to produce a stellar corn crop.

"Massasoit, the chief of the nearby Wampanoags, signed a treaty of alliance with the Pilgrims in the summer. In exchange for assistance with defense against the feared Narragansett tribe, Massasoit supplemented the food supply of the Pilgrims for the first few years.

"... By autumn of 1621, the Pilgrims had much for which to be thankful. After the harvest, Massasoit and about ninety other Indians joined the Pilgrims for the great English tradition of Harvest Festival.

"The participants celebrated for several days, dining on venison, goose, duck, turkey, fish, and of course, cornbread, the result of a bountiful corn harvest. This tradition was repeated at harvest time in the following years."

(Author: ushistory.org, Title of Page: William Bradford and the First Thanksgiving, Title of Program: *U.S. History Online Textbook,* URL of Page: //www.ushistory.org/us/3b.asp, Date of Access: Thursday, July 22, 2021, Copyright: 2021.)

Roger Williams

Even though the Puritans were able to worship God according to their conscience, nevertheless, some other groups of Puritans seemed to make the same mistake of their oppressors in England: using force to control religious matters.

For instance, under Governor John Winthrop, Anne Hutchinson was arrested for being a heretic and banished from Massachusetts Bay in 1637.

Fortunately, Roger Williams, among others, continued to carry the torch of reformation by:

"First, he preached separation of church and state. He believed in complete religious freedom, so no single church should be supported by tax dollars. Massachusetts Puritans believed they had the one true faith; therefore such talk was intolerable.

"Second, Williams claimed taking land from the Native Americans without proper payment was unfair.

"Massachusetts wasted no time in banishing the minister.

"In 1636, he purchased land from the Narragansett Indians and founded the colony of Rhode Island. Here there would be *complete religious freedom*. Dissenters from the English New World came here seeking refuge."

(Author: ushistory.org, Title of Page: Dissent in Massachusetts Bay, Title of Program: *U.S. History Online Textbook,* URL of Page: //www.ushistory.org/us/3e.asp, Date of Access: Tuesday, September 08, 2020, Copyright: 2020.)

The First Amendment to the United States Constitution

The fight against government-mandated Christianity or any religion was not over in America until The First Amendment to the United States Constitution was enacted in 1791, guaranteeing the right to freedom of religion for all Americans:

"Congress shall make no law respecting an establishment of religion, or prohibiting the free exercise thereof; or abridging the freedom of speech, or of the press; or the right of the people peaceably to assemble, and to petition the Government for a redress of grievances."

Despite the fact that it was mostly Protestants who founded the United States, the founders ensured that they would not repeat the tragic mistake of forced religion made by the Roman Catholic Church and the Anglican Church of England.

The government would no longer be used to compel its citizens to accept a particular faith.

Even after the terrorist attack on September 11, 2001, when thousands of innocent American civilians, including children, were killed, while there might have been a backlash from some people, Muslims in America are still protected by the Constitution and can continue to worship freely.

In fact, the United States and other democratic Christian countries have spoken out against the Chinese Communist Party's reported oppression of the Uyghur Muslim minority in the Xinjiang province of China.

Today, all democratic Christian countries besides the United States, such as Germany and many other European nations, allow freedom of religion to be one of the fundamental human rights—no more government-mandated belief.

I will elaborate in more detail on the Reformation movement, particularly regarding the theological aspect, in the chapter about Christianity.

HOW ISLAM WAS ESTABLISHED

In contrast to Jesus and his followers' founding Christianity without the use of force, Mohamad was both the religious and the political leader if Islam. He led the charge to invade other nations, and established Islam on the lands he conquered.

"... Muhammad led a force that conquered Mecca... Muhammad was the undisputed *political as well as religious leader* of Arabia. Tribal leaders swore their loyalty to Muhammad, and he began to invite other nations to join the new 'nation of Islam'" (Young, p. 227).

Even today, while some countries with large Muslim populations allow other faiths, for instance, Indonesia, others still make Islam the only lawful religion. In such states, the public practice of any belief other than Islam is illegal, as is an intention to convert others.

MANDATED RELIGION IS SELF-DEFEATING

I believe dictating a faith is self-defeating. It is true for Christianity, Islam, or any other religion. While some people may have no problem accepting a particular belief as required by the government, for others, it makes faith a forced doctrine. It cannot really be called a faith, which should only be believed voluntarily from the heart.

THE TRUTH SHOULD AND WILL SPEAK FOR ITSELF

Furthermore, I have no doubt that the truth will speak for itself, and it will prevail. No force is needed for those who are seeking it. No force is necessary to coerce people to accept it. No force can change the truth.

There have been cases, even today, where some Muslims resorted to violence against people who made fun of their faith. I understand the anger. One should respect others' faith. It is never right to insult other religions.

But violent retaliation is not the solution.

For Christians, if somebody openly questions or ridicules our beliefs, we can peacefully debate and explain the issues raised. That is the essence of freedom of religion. It is a matter of seeking truth freely without pressure.

That was how Jesus handled it.

Though constantly mocked and threatened, He patiently answered questions and explained His teachings. Furthermore, He healed the sick and performed miracles to prove what He preached was true.

He had verbally rebuked some people, especially religious hypocrites. And yes, He has once overturned the tables of the money changers, and the benches of those selling doves in the temple (Mathew 21:12), but He never used violence to physically harm those who disagreed with Him or opposed Him, though He could have, given His immense power.

CONCLUDING THOUGHTS

Having pointed out the problems of state-mandated religion, including the tragic history of the Roman Catholic Church, I will not be surprised if many Muslims genuinely and willingly believe in Islam. I respect and appreciate their seriousness and devotion to the God who created the world. I also believe that there is only one creator.

I also think there are moderate, peace-loving Muslims too.

Nevertheless, I sincerely hope that they would consider Jesus' love for them, who was sent by God, as prophesized, to save everyone who is willing, including Muslims.

23 - HINDUISM

The religions known to the world as Hinduism, Buddhism, Jainism, and Sikhism all originated in South Asia, in what are now the countries of India, Pakistan, Bangladesh, Sri Lanka, Bhutan, and Nepal. Hinduism is still the dominant religion of India, encompassing a broad range of beliefs and practices.

The roots of Hinduism can be traced to the second millennium B.C.E. or earlier. It is a minority religion in the other countries of South and Southeast Asia.

Hinduism is a complex religion. There is a variety of different traditions. It has numerous scriptures. Those texts can conflict with each other, and be difficult to interpret and classify. There is no single founder of the faith.

The Sacred

Many Gods and Beyond the Gods: Within Hinduism, we find all types of theism as well as monism, dualism, and more. The complexity is represented by the story of a man who spent his whole life traveling through India, documenting the different deities he encountered. When he finally completed his journey and returned home at age ninety-three, he counted all the gods and goddesses on his list.

There were 330 million.

There is a division in the Hindu understanding of the spiritual. Some speak of an impersonal supreme deity (Brahman), others steadfastly hold to an understanding of the supreme as personal (typically, Vishnu, Shiva, or Devi).

The Basic Human Problem

Trapped by Karma: The atman (eternal soul) is trapped in a cycle of rebirth (*samsara*) because of the law of karma. The law of karma stipulates that we are inevitably determined in our future actions by the effects of our past actions.

Until the inexorable enchainment of karma is broken, the atman's journey through unending rounds of rebirth will continue. For example, a person whose actions are slovenly may cause the atman to experience rebirth as a sloth.

The Cause of the Problem

Desire and Ignorance: The entrapment of the atman by karma is a result of desire, causing us to act with attachment and *avidya* (ignorance) of our true nature. The Hindu understanding of "ignorance" is not a lack of knowledge; it is spiritual confusion about our true human nature and the true nature of all reality. It is delusion, believing that the changing world in which we live day to day is the only reality.

Hinduism teaches that, because of our ignorance, we inevitably assume that the material world is the only reality, and we become attached to that world.

The Goal of Transformation

Liberation (Moksha) from the Cycle of Rebirth: The branches of Hinduism share moksha as the ultimate goal. However, they differ on the nature of the liberated state.

The bhakti movements speak of the communion of the atman with a personal deity in an eternal state of "enjoyment or bliss."

The philosophical schools tend toward a more impersonal view. They typically emphasize that moksha is beyond description. All that we can say is that once the atman experiences liberation, there is no more rebirth, only a state of complete and total release.

The monistic school (Advaita Vedanta) speaks of moksha as a coming to awareness of the identity of the atman with the cosmic oneness (Brahman), a state of absorption often called *Samadhi*.

The Means of Transformation

The Paths of Action, Devotion, and Knowledge: The most common way of designating the different paths to liberation within Hinduism is to speak of *karma yoga* (the way of action), *bhakti yoga* (the way of devotion), and *jnana yoga* (the way of knowledge). Yoga refers to the process of joining or yoking the atman with the spiritual source.

Karma yoga simply means living in accord with dharma (duty, determined principally in Hinduism by gender, caste, and stage of life). Traditionalists believe that by karma yoga, lower-caste individuals can only improve their rank in the next life, while others believe karma yoga opens the door to moksha for any, regardless of caste and gender.

Bhakti yoga is the path of devotion to a personal deity. It is rooted in the Vedic practice of sacrifice to various gods. Hindus are remarkably tolerant of peoples' right to choose different deities as the object of their devotion.

The annual Hindu ritual calendar includes festivals in which the deities are worshiped in special ways. One of the most controversial Hindu customs is the veneration of the cow. At certain times of the year in some locations, cows are venerated as deities, with garlands of flowers placed on their necks.

Jnana yoga is the path of meditation that leads ultimately to an intuitive experience with the ultimate. Through a process of moral, physical, mental, and spiritual discipline, the seeker slowly and patiently reaches a point of final preparation. Meditation often includes focused repetition of a *mantra*, a sacred sound that evokes the spiritual.

My thoughts

About the Sacred

As Professor Young points out, within Hinduism, there are all types of theism, as well as monism, dualism, and more. There are millions of deities, and even for the supreme one, there is division as to whether it is a personal god or an impersonal one.

It contrasts sharply with Judaism and Christianity, which unambiguously hold that there is only one God and that He is a personal God.

A logical question on the sacred for Hinduism is, "Is there only one god, or are there many gods, even millions?"

Furthermore, is it a personal deity, who would converse with human beings, or an impersonal one, like just a force?

As mentioned before, the answer to the question of "no god vs. one god vs. many gods" cannot be "all are true". They are mutually exclusive.

The Relationship between God, Humans, Animals, and Materials

Hinduism's belief in "atman" that humankind has an eternal soul is similar to Christianity's view. However, one unusual scene in India is that cows can roam freely on the road, stopping traffic.

That is because cows are treated even higher than humans and are worshiped as deities, while Christianity does not.

CLEAR DISTINCTION ACCORDING TO JUDAISM AND CHRISTIANITY

Humans should not bow down to animals

As referred to in Part Two, delineating the priorities of Christian life, the Bible teaches clear governing order on earth: God over humans, and humans over animals and materials.

Furthermore, there are definitive differences between them. God created humans "in his own image" (Genesis 1:27). The image here is used figuratively.

It means that "humans share, though imperfectly and finitely, in God's nature, that is, in His communicable attributes (life, personality, truth, wisdom, love, holiness, justice), and so have the capacity for spiritual fellowship with Him."

(Editors: John F. Walvoord and Roy B. Zuck, *The Bible Knowledge Commentary – An Exposition of the Scriptures by Dallas Seminary Faculty, Old Testament* (Wheaton, Illinois: Victor Books, Third printing, 1986), p. 29. Used by permission of David C Cook. May not be further reproduced. All rights reserved.)

In addition, although humans are under God, humans are hugely different from animals and sacred, because they have permanent souls (Genesis 2:7; Ecclesiastes 12:7).

As for animals and plants, they were made "according to their kinds" (Genesis 1:21, 24).

Although some passages state that God's Spirit also creates animals and plants, and thus have the breath of life (Psalm 104:29-30), they do not have a permanent soul like humankind has, let alone the spiritual capacity, as mentioned above, regarding the image of God.

Therefore, human beings should only worship the true God, who created them, and not bow down to the lower animals.

Humans should not worship physical materials either

Isaiah 44:13-19 points out the reason why it is not rational to worship something made by humans:

"¹³ The carpenter measures with a line and makes an outline with a marker;

he roughs it out with chisels and marks it with compasses. He shapes it in human form, human form in all its glory, that it may dwell in a shrine.

"... 16 Half of the wood he burns in the fire; over it he prepares his meal, he roasts his meat and eats his fill. He also warms himself and says, 'Ah! I am warm; I see the fire.'

17 From the rest he makes a god, his idol; he bows down to it and worships. He prays to it and says, 'Save me! You are my god!'

"... 19 No one stops to think, no one has the knowledge or understanding to say, 'Half of it I used for fuel; I even baked bread over its coals, I roasted meat and I ate. Shall I make a detestable thing from what is left? Shall I bow down to a block of wood?'"

The second of the Ten Commandments

The second commandment God gave Moses is about not idolizing anything lower than human beings:

"2 'I am the Lord your God, who brought you out of Egypt, out of the land of slavery. 3 You shall have no other gods before [a]me.

"4 You shall not make for yourself an image in the form of anything in heaven above [sun, moon, stars] or on the earth beneath [animals] or in the waters below [sea lives]" (Exodus 20:2-4).

Footnotes
    a. Or *besides*

In Judaism or Christianity, deifying cows or other creatures is blasphemy. Humans also should not make anything by hand and bow down to it.

Animals like cows should be appreciated; nevertheless, humans should only worship God, who is the one that created both people and animals.

The bottom line is that creatures and objects made by human hands are lower than man. They not only cannot help us, but bowing down to them actually will also offend God, who was the one that created the animals and the physical materials in the first place.

NO SUCH DISTINCTION ACCORDING TO HINDUISM

In short, while Hinduism talks about the preeminence of the spiritual, like atman, it conflates the spiritual world with the world of animals, in that you can worship animals, and even be reborn as an animal.

Aside from cow veneration, I noticed this one popular deity in India, the elephant-headed god *Ganesha*. It looks like a mixture of all four realms: it is a god (revered as a deity), a human (has a human body), an animal (with an elephant head), and it is a physical object made by man.

Reincarnation vs. Resurrection

Some may wonder if there are any differences between Hinduism's reincarnation and Christianity's resurrection.

Hinduism: It can happen many times (cyclical). A Human's soul will be reborn into another life upon death, but not necessarily as a human, and may even as an animal.

Christianity: It will occur only once (linear). At the end of the world, all the dead will return to life as the same individual as before, and still as a human (not animal) with his or her unique permanent soul.

Some claim that Christianity teaches reincarnation, too, saying that John the Baptist is the "reincarnated" Elijah, citing Luke 1:17.

However, the passage says, "And he [John the Baptist] will go on before the Lord [John is to be the forerunner to announce Jesus' coming], in the spirit and power of Elijah, to turn the hearts of the parents to their children and the disobedient to the wisdom of the righteous—to make ready a people prepared for the Lord."

It was in the spirit and power of Elijah, not Elijah himself, which John the Baptist came.

The word "spirit" here should not be interpreted as Elijah's soul, because it is recorded that on a high mountain, Jesus once talked to Moses and Elijah, "Just then there appeared before them Moses and Elijah, talking with Jesus" (Matthew 17:3).

It is evident that Elijah was and still is the same person. He still exists as Elijah. He and John the Baptist are two separate, different beings, each with his own soul, living at the same time.

Except for this particular passage that could be misunderstood, the Bible mentions no incidents of any human "reincarnated".

POSSIBLE CONSEQUENCE OF THE REINCARNATION VIEW

Because of this thinking that relatives who passed away may now be rats, insects, snakes, and other animals, some believers will make sure when they walk, they do not step on insects, for example.

This practice is harmless and understandable, but it may lead to public health issues, when there is a serious community outbreak of diseases brought on by infected animals such as rats. People may be reluctant to act on the threat.

IMPLICATION OF THE RESURRECTION BELIEF

Since it only occurs once, and then all will be subjected to the final judgment, it is imperative that a human being makes the right choice while still alive. There will be no cyclical rebirth to get it right the next time.

The Law of Karma vs. "You Reap What You Sow"

As described before, under the cause of the problem, Hinduism believes that the atman (eternal soul) is trapped in a cycle of rebirth because of the law of karma.

As mentioned earlier, the law of karma stipulates that we are inevitably determined in our future actions by the effects of our past actions.

Most people would agree that it is only fair that we bring on ourselves the results of our own actions. After all, in Christianity, there is this "You reap what you sow" teaching too (Galatians 6:7-8).

In fact, under Christianity, the repercussions are even more severe. Human beings not only will die, but also will be resurrected and subjected to the final judgment and eternal consequence (more specifics later in Part Three and Part Four), while for Hinduism, theoretically, one can try to make it right the next time when reincarnated.

However, there is a critical difference between the two faiths regarding the nature of transgression.

YOU DESERVE IT

I think that under Hinduism, it is like "you deserve it"; "you are suffering because you did something bad in your prior lives, so work out your own salvation. "

The Caste system (priests and sages, warriors, producers [merchants, bankers, and farmers], workers or servants) in Indian society, I feel, epitomizes such precepts.

Although it is less significant in the cities, it is still practiced in the rural areas, according to Professor Young.

Dr. Young writes,

"… In this elaborate system, for a higher caste member to touch a member of a lower caste causes ritual impurity…

"… a fifth social grouping, known as the 'untouchable' or 'scheduled castes,' for example, cremation workers… when members of untouchable jati [birth group] violated the taboos of separation, they were often severely punished, even killed, by members of higher castes… it continues to be a serious problem in modern India" (Young, pp. 63-64).

Under Karma Yoga, "… traditionalist believe that by karma yoga, a lower-caste individual can only improve their rank in the next life, while others believe karma yoga opens the door to moksha [liberation from the cycle of rebirth] for any, regardless of caste and gender" (Young, p. 75).

While some believers may be more accommodating, the overall consequence of the ideology of karma and its related caste system, I think, is not a sympathetic attitude and even allows for cruel actions toward the working people and the poor. The result is a society lacking opportunities and mobility.

WE ALL DESERVE IT

On the contrary, in Christianity, it is like, "we all deserve it," since Scripture says, "All have sinned" (Romans 3:23).

No one can claim that he or she is better than others in the eyes of the Creator. In this sense, there is only one "caste". All will suffer the consequence of sins, which is death, and all need salvation.

However, while God is just, He is also merciful. He loves the world, and all have the chance to be saved (see John 3:16; we will lay out the specific details on how to be saved in Part Four).

Jesus even literally touched a man with leprosy and healed him (Matthew 8:2-3). This starkly contrasts the caste system's treatment of the less fortunate, like the "untouchable."

No wonder there have been so many orphanages, schools, hospitals, etc., established by Christians all over the world. Many have heard about Mother Teresa's untiring, compassionate services to the poor in India. I think it was Christian godly love for fellow human beings that motivated her.

The Yoga Question

Yoga has been quite popular in the West as one of the ways for exercise and relaxation. But is it only a form of physical exercise that some may think it is?

"In Hinduism, yoga (from the Sanskrit term for 'to yoke or join') refers to the variety of methods that seek to join the individual soul to the [Hindu] Ultimate, thus achieve liberation from rebirth.

"... According to a yoga school called "raja yoga," the last stage of its meditative discipline is called "Samadhi," which means "entering into a trance in which oneness with Brahman [Hindu spiritual oneness of all reality], and therefore liberation, is experienced" (Young, p. 70).

If one believes in Hinduism, doing yoga and entering into a trance with a Hindu spiritual source is exactly what one wants. However, some Westerners perhaps are unaware of this Hindu side of yoga.

Is it possible to separate it from its religious aspect and just treat it as a physical therapy?

If it is not, then it is a serious question for people who do not necessarily subscribe to such faith. They might be surprised by the consequence of "yoking" with a spirit they do not even know.

In Summary

It seems that Hinduism is a grand, everything-goes belief system. There is no clear, consistent, non-self-conflicting view of the world.

Is there only one god, or are there many gods? Is it a personal or impersonal deity? It does not seem to matter that there should be objective, coherent truths about the sacred. Each can choose whatever they want to believe in the system.

In addition, God or gods, humans, animals, and objects are all mixed up and receive no distinction. The result is humans worshiping animals and man-made objects, which I believe cannot really help or protect human beings.

I appreciate Hindus' devotion to the spiritual world. They are definitely not atheists. Nevertheless, I sincerely hope that they will ponder the issues raised here.

24 - THERAVADA BUDDHISM

Buddhism began in India in the sixth century B.C.E.; however, it faded as a separate religion in India and survived principally because it spread from India and took root in other cultures of Southeast and East Asia.

As it evolved, Buddhism was divided into three branches, often called "vehicles." They are Theravada (also called Hinayana ("the small vehicle")), Mahayana ("the large vehicle"), and Vajrayana ("the thunderbolt or diamond vehicle").

(Note: The countries where the different branch flourishes are *Theravada* - India, Sri Lanka, Burma, Thailand, and Laos; *Mahayana* – China, Korea, and Japan; *Vajrayana* – Tibet.)

The Founder: Siddhartha Gautama

He was born in about 563 B.C.E. in Nepal, a member of the warrior caste. What follows is one version of the religious biography his followers wrote.

Siddhartha's wealthy father, a chieftain of the Sakya clan, raised him in luxury. He married a lovely princess, and she gave birth to a son. Despite all the affluence, Gautama began to feel an inner longing, an emptiness he could not fill with wine, song, or even the pleasures of family life.

He began to venture out alone. As his chariot journeyed through an "unsanitized" area, Siddhartha experienced what Buddhist tradition calls the "Four Passing Sights." The first was a sorrowful old man. The second was a man racked by illness. The third was a dead man. And he realized that he, too, was destined to grow old, become ill, and die. His despair continued to deepen until one day; he saw the fourth sight: a monk calmly walking alone in a yellow robe.

One night, Siddhartha crept out of his palace, leaving behind his wife and son, and set off to discover the way to escape the inevitable suffering of material existence. He started out with an open mind about the teaching of the Hindu Brahmins. He tried and mastered a meditative approach such as that implied in the Upanishads (a Hindu scripture), but to no avail. Then he tried rigid asceticism, similar to the teaching of the Jains, to the point that his diet consisted of a single grain of rice a day, and fainted beside a stream. When he revived, Siddhartha determined that self-denial would not lead to spiritual fulfillment.

Siddhartha sat down under a fig tree and told himself he would not arise until he reached a state of spiritual enlightenment. As he sat, *Mara*, the god of desire and death, appeared to him and tempted him to turn back to his old life of pleasure.

At that moment, now aware that it was desire that had kept him entrapped, he suddenly "awakened" to a new life beyond its grip. He was now a *Buddha,* one who had "woken up." He was enlightened. The state he now entered, characterized by lack of craving, was *nirvana*.

The Buddha spoke to his former colleagues of a "Middle Way" between the two extremes of his life – self-denial and self-indulgence. This path, he said, had led him to the truth. What he told his fellow seekers has become known as the "Four Noble Truths." They form the core of Buddhist teaching.

The Sacred

Spiritual Atheism: It is an atheistic religion, denying a central role for a personal god or gods. Each person by himself or herself must "work out his or her own liberation."

The Basic Human Problem

The First Noble Truth – Life Is Suffering: The suffering of life is unavoidable. A relationship will end. Friends leave physically or figuratively, or we leave them. Any aspect of life, no matter how seemingly pleasant, already has the seeds of the suffering that is the common denomination of all human experience.

The Cause of the Problem

The Second Nobel Truth – Suffering Is Caused by Craving: We suffer because our craving leads us to become attached to things or people and deluded as to the real nature of our situation in life. For example, we crave the pleasure of friendship, so we become attached to other persons, only to suffer when disputes arise and when friendship ends. We would not suffer if we were not attached, and we will not be attached if we did not crave.

Theravadans believe that even desire for spiritual ends leads to attachment.

The Goal of Transformation

The Third Nobel Truth – The Extinction of Craving: like other religions that originated in India, the "goal" for Theravada Buddhism is the liberation from the cycle of rebirth. When craving is extinguished, suffering ends, as does rebirth.

What follows the cessation of suffering? In a word, nirvana arises when craving ends. Nirvana literally means "blowing out." Existence is ablaze with craving; that is the cause of suffering. When the flame of passion is "blown out," suffering ends.

It is far easier to say what nirvana is *not* in Buddhism than to say what nirvana *is*. Nirvana is not a state of existence after death. Nirvana is a phenomenon experienced whenever a person "wakes up," as did the Buddha. Nirvana is *not* heaven, for that would imply a place where souls dwell.

In the final analysis, the question of the nature of survival beyond death is one most Theravadans stubbornly reject as too speculative, and not helpful in dealing our with basic problem.

The Means of Transformation

The Forth Nobel Truth – The Eightfold Path: the way that leads to the cessation of suffering is the holy "Eightfold Path." The steps in the path are:

Correct belief

Believe in "The Four Noble Truths," no permanent identity, no permanency, etc.

Correct aspiration
Free oneself from sensual desires, greed, and malice; not to "attach" oneself to particular persons with a caring attitude, etc.

Correct speech
Not to lie or gossip; avoid harsh words, etc.

Correct conduct
Not to kill or steal; avoid illicit sexual behavior, intoxicants, gambling, etc.

Correct means of livelihood
Avoid occupations that involve killings, deceptions, astrology, etc.

Correct endeavor
Avoid any unwholesome action and pursue beneficial deeds.

Correct mindfulness
Devote oneself assiduously to focused observation of oneself and others. It is at this level that monks might engage in gazing on decaying bodies and bones, the idea being to let the reality of impermanence completely occupy the mind.

Correct meditation
A state of calmness and peace, a "one-pointedness" in which all attachments have been broken. Once at this stage, nirvana is at hand, and, in a flash of intuition, that state of final bliss dawns.

My Thoughts

On the Belief of Reincarnation

Buddhism also believes in reincarnation, but there is a crucial difference between Hinduism and Buddhism. Hinduism holds that there is a permanent soul. But Buddhism does not believe in anything permanent. There is no eternal self. There is no soul.

Therefore, it is self-conflicting to say nothing is permanent; still, something is going through a cycle of rebirth.

On the Belief of No Eternal Self

REGARDING SELF-IDENTITY

It is extraordinary that no matter how many people have been born and passed, how many people there are now on Earth (more than 7.9 billion as of December 2021), and how many will be born in the future, we have observed and can expect that every human being is uniquely identifiable.

In spite of the fact that there have been billions of us, our DNAs, eyes, fingerprints, etc., are all different! It is like automobiles; each has a unique Vehicle Identification Number.

Granted, this is just the physical evidence we can all witness now. Nevertheless, the Bible describes that this unique human identity is preserved even after one is passed.

As quoted before, on a high mountain, it is recorded that Jesus once talked to Moses and Elijah, "Just then there appeared before them Moses and Elijah, talking with Jesus" (Matthew 17:3).

Moses and Elijah had passed away many years before Jesus. However, their souls continue to exist as two uniquely different individuals.

Christianity believes that each person is created with not just a physical body but also with an eternal soul. And each will be rewarded or held accountable based on what he or she did and said on Earth.

REGARDING THE PERMANENCY

The Bible teaches that although our current body will die when the end of the world comes, all believers will be resurrected with a permanent, imperishable body. And the believer's soul will be with this transformed body.

For unbelievers, their bodies will be resurrected too. But the destination of unbelievers will be different.

In short, contrary to Buddhism, Christianity believes that each of us is unique and has an eternal body and soul.

The fact that all of us are uniquely identifiable, at least at the physical level, such as with our DNAs, and the fact that all of us can witness this, is consistent with that teaching.

On the Concept of Karma

Though Buddhism also holds the view of Karma, it is not like Hinduism because it does not advocate the caste system.

On the contrary, many Buddhists believe in doing good deeds and helping the needy as a means to get out of the suffering of rebirth. Therefore, it does not have the same possible negative social impact of poverty and lack of opportunities as spoken of under Hinduism.

The Question of Nirvana

Buddha means one who has "awoken."
But awaken to what? People may ask. Buddhism believes that it was Siddhartha's desire that had kept him entrapped in the cycle of rebirth; therefore, the goal is to have no more desire – Nirvana.

Siddhartha disapproved of Jainism's self-denial as extreme. Yet, it seems that Siddhartha's belief in seeing all desires as bad was also an extreme reaction to suffering.

NOTHINGNESS VS. JOYFULNESS

Christianity also teaches about spiritual awakening. But the content of awakening is critical. "Awaken to what?" again, is the question. Which is true: Buddhism's "nothingness," or Christianity's "joyfulness"?

Christians believe that humankind is sinful and needs forgiveness from their Creator. Once the sins are forgiven, they will be able to enter a new heaven and new earth in the future, which will be full of joy and people who love God and love each other.

Christianity and Buddhism contrast so much that the two beliefs cannot both be true.

Furthermore, while still on Earth, born-again Christians have strong desires to love people, even though they could be rejected or not appreciated. Because Christian love is "not self-seeking, it keeps no record of wrongs" (1 Corinthians 13:5).

I think one of the reasons that Buddhism holds a negative view of all desires and all relationships, may be due to people not wanting to be disappointed or hurt.

It is understandable, but Christianity sees suffering as temporary, and is the result of sin. Once the sin question is resolved, joy and love replace it. There is hope at the end.

As for Buddhism's nirvana, beyond saying that it is the extinction of craving, one cannot be sure what it really means.

As mentioned earlier regarding the goal of Theravada Buddhism:

"It is far easier to say what nirvana is *not* in Buddhism than to say what nirvana *is*.

"... In the final analysis, the question of the nature of survival beyond death is one most Theravadans stubbornly reject as too speculative, and not helpful in dealing our basic problem "(Young, p. 93).

However, the nature of nirvana is critical in Theravada Buddhism, since it is regarded as its end goal. Without being able to delineate clearly what it really is, its validity is difficult to ascertain and hence becomes questionable.

"The Mindful Revolution"

It is fitting to talk about this subject at this point, since both Hinduism and Buddhism practice some forms of meditation.

Moreover, according to Time magazine's cover story, *"The mindful revolution"* (February 2014, pp. 42-46), like yoga, it has entered the West's mainstream as a relaxation technique.

THE CRITICAL QUESTION IS, "WHAT SHOULD WE BE MINDFUL ABOUT?"

What is the content of this mindfulness? Just imitating its sitting posture is merely superficial.

For Hinduism

As cited before, like Jnana yoga, "it is the path of meditation that leads ultimately to *an intuitive experience with the [Hindu] ultimate. . .* meditation often includes focused repetition of a *mantra*, a sacred sound that evokes the spiritual "(Young, p. 78).

For Theravada Buddhism

It is to "devote oneself to focus observation of oneself and others, such as *the reality of impermanence*... a state of calmness and peace, a 'one-pointedness' in which all attachments have been broken" (Young, p. 95).

The content and the goal of the meditation for Hindus and Theravada Buddhists are actually opposite to each other.

The former seeks to join and be absorbed into the spiritual, while the latter desperately wants to break any "attachments" from any human relationships and anything spiritual (i.e., *spiritual atheism*).

In the West

As for those who practice "mindfulness" in the West, according to Time's article, the basic meditation is "the practice of doing nothing and being tuned in to *your own mind* at the same time... your job is simply to notice that your mind has wandered and to bring your attention back to your breathing."

Although it sounds like a simple physical exercise, the article points out, "Mindfulness is rooted in Eastern philosophy, specifically Buddhism," but "... Kabat-Zinn and other proponents are careful to avoid any talk of spirituality when espousing mindfulness. "

While Kabat-Zinn may avoid talking about spirituality, others also include yoga in their mindfulness retreats, which could involve spirituality.

It brings up the same question I raised regarding yoga, "Is it possible to separate it from its Buddhism origin and just treat it purely as a form of physical therapy?"

Judaism and Christianity

< *Meditation is not new* >

Being mindful and meditation are not new concepts in Judaism and Christianity. It has been practiced for thousands of years.

The critical difference is, again, the content of the meditation.

God reminded Joshua,

"Keep this *Book of the Law* always on your lips; meditate on it day and night, so that you may be careful to do everything written in it. Then you will be prosperous and successful" (Joshua 1:8).

Israelites were encouraged to meditate on God's law:

"[1] Blessed is the one who does not walk in step with the wicked or stand in the way that sinners take or sit in the company of mockers, [2] but whose delight is in the *law of the Lord*, and who meditates on his law day and night" (Psalm 1: 1-2).

Even today, one can notice that devoted followers of Judaism will constantly set aside time to study God's words, which talk about *God's love, justice, and mercy*.

As shared in Part Two, once I was born again, one of the very first things I did was read the Bible eagerly and regularly. And on Saturday mornings, I would spend hours studying the Scriptures and reflecting on their meaning.

It has been a time of peace, encouragement, reminders, and joy away from the daily grind of life.

In fact, when I get up every morning, the first typical thing I do, for almost 40 years now, is spend some time reading the Bible or spiritual books and praying. I know many other Christians do so, too.

GAZING AT THE CORPSE VS. REJOICING IN HAVING CONQUERED DEATH

Theravada Buddhism's "correct mindfulness" is to fix attention, for instance, on the "reality" of "impermanence". For example, "Monks might engage in gazing on decaying bodies and bones, the idea being to let the reality of impermanence completely occupy the mind" (Young, p. 95).

This is in marked contrast to the Christian's belief that a human does have a permanent soul. As for the body, yes, we will all die once; nevertheless, because Jesus has conquered death, all Christians will be resurrected and even transformed to have a new permanent body.

Christians need not keep thinking that our present physical body will die one day, because there is hope for eternal life with a new and glorious body in the future, that will not get sick, old, and then die, as mentioned in Part Two.

SUMMARY ON MINDFULNESS

First

If mindfulness meditation can be separated from the spiritual world, then it is rather limited in its potential benefits. It can only temporarily relieve the stress, but it does not address the source of the anxiety.

What is triggering the anxiety in the first place? It may not be just using too much social media, or too many demands from our work. For example, it can be brought on by our bad lifestyle choices or problematic value judgments and actions.

If those issues are not dealt with, no amount of solely relying on physical therapy, such as just paying attention to breathing, can solve our problems. It will happen again.

Second

If it should include pondering the spiritual aspect of our life, then what should be the correct, thus effective content of it?

As elaborated above, Hinduism, Buddhism, and Christianity offer drastically different understandings of the sacred (we will expound more on Christianity later). Hence, each has a distinct content and focus of meditation.

It all comes down to the fundamental questions regarding the sacred. For instance, is there no god, one God, or are there many gods?

They cannot be all true. Without awareness of this critical spiritual issue, we will be like people trying to drive a car at night without turning on the headlights.

It is also like opening the door to a stranger standing outside our house. To be safe, we do not just open and let anybody come in without asking who the person is and what they are up to.

Similarly, we do not want just to open our mind and let any outside thoughts come into our thinking, especially from those practices that have religious origins, to which we may not subscribe or understand.

A Monk's Quest to Practice Correct Speech

I once read a news article about a person visiting a Buddhist temple in Los Angeles. He noticed a monk who was wearing a sign around his neck. On the sign were two

Chinese words, "禁言" (jìn yán). Literally, it means "forbid speech."

He was told the monk had not uttered a word for three years.

I appreciate the monk's sincerity in wanting to speak correctly. But his method of not speaking for three years is likely futile.

We are given the ability to speak. What we need is the power to speak correctly and not just shut our mouths, hoping this will fix the problem.

THE EIGHT FOLD PATH HAS MORE TO DO WITH GOALS THAN MEANS

I think Theravada Buddhism's means of transformation, the eight fold path, has more to do with goals than means. Because, like correct speech, most religions, including Christianity, also teach proper speech. Even secular schools will teach that one should speak appropriately.

However, what is harder to answer, and indeed is more important, is the question below.

WHAT IS CAUSING PEOPLE NOT TO BE ABLE TO SPEAK CORRECTLY IN THE FIRST PLACE?

Without knowing the root cause of not speaking correctly, one cannot effectively solve the problem.

Theravada Buddhism believes that the source of the problem is craving. But again, why do humans have cravings in the first place? Where does this unwanted craving come from?

For Christianity, the reason people cannot do the right things, like speaking correctly, is the direct result of rebellion against God, who created us.

Romans 5:12 writes,

"Therefore, just as *sin entered the world* through one man [Adam, who disobeyed God], and death through sin, and in this way death came to all people, because all sinned—" (more details on the fall of mankind in Chapter 30).

Consequently, because of our sinful nature, we cannot do what we know is the right thing to do.
Apostle Paul describes such a struggle vividly:

"[18] For I know that good itself does not dwell in me, that is, in my sinful nature.[a] For I have the desire to do what is good, but I cannot carry it out… [24] What a wretched man I am! Who will rescue me from this body that is subject to death?" (Romans 7:18- 24)
Footnotes
    a. Or *my flesh*

THE SOLUTION TO THE ROOT CAUSE

Getting out of such condemnation requires the involvement of God, who placed such judgment on humankind in the first place.
The Bible teaches that God himself offers the solution. And that solution is Jesus.
Apostle Paul triumphantly declares,

"Thanks be to God, who delivers me through Jesus Christ our Lord" (Romans 7:25).
"Therefore, there is now no condemnation for those who are in Christ Jesus, [2] because through Christ Jesus the law of the Spirit who gives life has *set you*[a] *free* from the law of sin and death.

"[3] For what the law was powerless to do because it was weakened by the flesh,[b] God did by sending his own Son in the likeness of sinful flesh to be a sin offering.[c]

"And so *he condemned sin in the flesh*, [4] in order that the righteous requirement of the law might be fully met in us, *who do not live according to the flesh but according to the Spirit* [the Holy Spirit]" (Romans 8:1-4).

Footnotes
- a. The Greek is singular; some manuscripts *me*.
- b. In contexts like this, the Greek word for *flesh* (*sarx*) refers to the sinful state of human beings, often presented as a power in opposition to the Spirit; also in verses 4-13.
- c. Or *flesh, for sin*

When one believes in Jesus, one's sins will be forgiven by God, and on top of that, he or she will be given the Holy Spirit to overcome sinful nature; thus, they *will be able* to speak correctly.

It is a new creation, a transformation from the inside out.

MY OWN EXPERIENCE

I hope this does not come across as boasting. I remember one day at work; I overheard a colleague talking about me in a cubical next to my office. He said, "George is different, he does not curse."

I was surprised to hear that, since it never occurred to me that I did not curse. Indeed, thinking back, since I was born again, it has been not only hard to curse, but also hard to lie either.

A HOLLYWOOD STUNTMAN

There are many testimonies of Christians whose lives changed dramatically.

One of them I read recently was about a Hollywood stuntman.

He had been hesitant when his colleague shared the good news of Jesus with him. However, one day, right before he jumped off a highly dangerous 50- or 60-foot-high catwalk, he said a prayer to give his life to Jesus.

He writes about what happened after the jump:

"I don't know what I was expecting, but there was no immediate change—no obvious physical, emotional, or spiritual sensation. Had God heard me? In any event, I didn't dare tell a soul, just in case what I *thought* had happened hadn't really happened.

"The following weeks confirmed two things: God had indeed heard my prayer, and the stone was gone from my shoe [He was referring to the comments, which his co-worker shared with him, 'were like a small stone lodged in my shoe—a persistent irritant to my comfortable, but godless lifestyle'].

"Before long, I worked up the confidence to evangelize my fellow crew members. And there were sudden changes in my behavior, too.

"Among the first things I noticed was that my go-to indulgences no longer held any appeal, and the dirty humor I once relished no longer struck me as funny.

"Meanwhile, my habit of cursing like a drunken sailor had vanished. After smashing my knee into a steel bolt at work, I started to swear and then stopped myself mid-expletive, surprising everyone within earshot."

(Robert Wilton – *"I Was Filming a Dangerous Action Scene When I Gave My Life to Christ - How a film and television stuntman met the Lord in the air,"* Christianity Today magazine, January/February 2021.)

A POSSIBLE ILLUSTRATION

It is as if now you have put a good break in your car. You can now stop your vehicle effectively when it is going too fast and is about to crash into the car in front of you.

Mr. Wilton was able to stop it "mid-expletive," as soon as he sensed that he was swearing again.

However, it does not mean Christians will be perfect and stop making any mistakes. That said, it is my experience that with our new life, even when we do, we will feel bad.

As remarked in Part One, "now I could see that it was wrong and embarrassing when I cheated in an exam while at the college in Taiwan. It is as if after taking a bath, you can now easily spot dirt on your body. You want to be clean. You are now sensitive to sins."

It is the Holy Spirit indwelling in us that reminds and empowers Christians to do the right thing, including speaking properly.

TO SUM UP REGARDING THE MONK'S QUEST TO PRACTICE CORRECT SPEECH

While trying very hard to speak or do other things correctly can have some effect, because it does not accurately identify the root cause, its prescribed remedies will not fundamentally solve the problem.

I agree with Buddhism that it is sad that people have to get old, sick, and die. But because Siddhartha's teaching does not believe in any God or gods having any role in human liberation, and does not think that mankind did anything wrong in the eyes of any creator being, his way of "working out your own salvation," similar to the monk's own way of just not talking at all, will be challenging to achieve its goal.

The Somber Look

When I was teaching world religions, in one class, after I showed a video clip about a Buddhist temple and the people there practicing rituals, a student asked, "Why do those nuns look so somber and even sad?"

It is a profound observation.

The typical ritual in the temple (and in one's home) is reciting Buddhist scriptures over and over again, all day long. I seldom see any nun or monk look happy or uplifting when they do this.

I think Buddhism points out some valid issues about life, that it is sad that people must suffer aging, sickness, and then death. Having said that, in terms of understanding why it is so, and the solution to fix it, it is a quite pessimistic religion.

The solution is to deny any reality in life, even to reject any form of permanency. Everything is temporary.

And because of that denial, the desire for human relationships is regarded as an "attachment" and should be avoided. "Nirvana" denotes "the extinction of craving," "nothingness," and all desires are harmful; it is all empty and meaningless.

This thinking about life may have contributed to the sad look of Buddhist practitioners.

On the contrary, for Christianity, not all desires are wrong. Hateful wishes or greed is bad; however, wanting to love God and love people is good.

As a matter of fact, to have a peaceful and joyful relationship between human beings and God, and also between fellow humans, is the essence of Christianity.

A Mother's Response to Her Daughter's Visit

I remember a woman in our home evangelistic meeting, who grew up in a Buddhist home, once shared her experience with the religion with us.

She said when she went back to visit her mother after she was married, her mom simply ignored her, and just kept on doing her daily ritual of reciting some Buddhist scriptures in front of a Buddha image in the house.

She sounded sad and disappointed.

It could be due to the belief that all relationships are harmful "attachments" that must be shunned. Her mother might have just wanted to avoid being too close to her daughter, lest she risk getting hurt.

While not all Buddhists would act this way, such behavior seems to be a logical consequence of such teaching.

On the contrary, born-again Christians typically will experience joy and happiness. They would love to meet and care for people, even strangers, not to mention their own daughters.

Yes, we might get our feelings hurt when someone rejects us; however, Christian love is not just about ourselves, but also about loving other people. The focus is on giving, not receiving.

As Apostle Paul encourages Christians,

"In everything I did, I showed you that by this kind of hard work we must help the weak, remembering the words the Lord Jesus himself said: 'It is more blessed to give than to receive'" (Acts 20:35).

While on this subject, I think of Siddhartha's treatment of his family. I understand that he wanted to pursue the answer to human suffering; however, to do that, he just left his wife and children. That might have ironically caused pain and misery to his family.

It is ironic and troubling.

Some of Buddhism's branches evolved later appear to be more positive. One branch holds that one can achieve the goal of going to the "Western Heaven," which is a happy place (not like nirvana, which is difficult to imagine what it really is), if one calls on the name of Amitabha in faith (More on this under Mahayana Buddhism below).

One variant, started by a nun in Taiwan, talks a lot about "the great love," and seeks to reach out and help people. It even sounds a bit like Christianity. However, that was not what the founder of Buddhism, Siddhartha, taught.

25 - MAHAYANA BUDDHISM AND VAJRAYANA BUDDHISM

Of the three major branches of Buddhism, the oldest, Theravada, dominated the nations of Southeast Asia, while Mahayana spread into East Asia and became the principal form of Buddhism in China, Japan, and Korea. The third branch, Vajrayana, took root in Tibet.

At some point in the first century C.E., Buddhist monks crossed the deserts to China. Monasteries sprang up throughout China, and new Buddhist schools, such as *Ch'an* (Zen) and Pure Land, emerged and gained popularity.

Mahayana Buddhism

Different Concept of Buddha

According to Theravada teaching, there is only one Buddha in each age, enlightened beings who have traversed the path to *nirvana* on their own.

THE "THREE BODIES" OF THE BUDDHA

By contrast, according to a Mahayana concept known as the "three body doctrine," also found in the Vajrayana tradition, there are three separate bodies or natures of the Buddha.

One is the earthly body or manifestation of the Buddha – in our age, Siddhartha. Another is the heavenly body of the Buddhas (such as *Amitabha* of Pure Land Buddhism) and bodhisattvas, who inhabit fully spiritual realms. The last is the cosmic body or nature of the Buddha, who is present in all reality. From this perspective, *each* human and every other being has the nature of the Buddha.

Two of the Most Significant Chinese Mahayana Schools

PURE LAND: THE DEVOTIONAL SCHOOL

Faith in "Amitabha" (*infinite light*) – A heavenly Buddha who resides in "Western Paradise" or Pure Land.

Any human can attain Buddhahood through faith in Amitabha.

By the twelfth century, the Pure Land teaching became the basis of a separate Japanese Mahayana School, known as *Jodo-shu* (Pure Land School).

Jodo-shu taught the expression of faith in Amida (the name of Amitabha in Japanese tradition) by chanting his name over and over again. The chant *Namu Amida Butsu* ("I place my faith in Amida Buddha") became the basis for a devotional tradition that is still extremely influential.

CH'AN: THE MEDITATION SCHOOL

"Ch'an" is a Chinese rendering of Sanskrit for meditation (called "Zen" in Japan).

It relies on self, through meditation, as the means to achieve its goal, no outside forces are needed; it mocks attempts to explain truth rationally and sees studying scriptures as worthless.

Vajrayana Buddhism in Tibet

"Vajra" – means both "thunderbolt" and "diamond" and suggests something of immense power, which cannot be broken or split.

It was influenced by Hinduism, Buddhism, and the indigenous Tibetan religion (animism). It seeks the "Vajrayana experience," in which enlightenment comes like a thunderbolt, cutting like a diamond through all that stands in the way of illumination.

Its means of transformation are sacred chants ("mantras"), prayer wheels, fasting, meditation, and others.

My Thoughts

What Is Reality?

I once watched a CBS 60 Minutes TV program. It was about the iconic Steve Jobs, one of the Apple Inc.'s founders. Mr. Jobs reportedly delayed his cancer surgery treatment and died from it at the relatively young age of 56.

The reporter asked Walter Isaacson, Jobs' biographer:

"Why did such a smart guy ignore such a serious illness?" Mr. Isaacson said, "He believed 'if you ignore something, if you don't want something to exist, you can have magical thinking'" (CBS News, *"Steve Jobs, Part 2,"* Oct 23, 2011, YouTube).

Steve Jobs was very interested in Buddhism. In fact, it was a Zen Buddhist monk who married him and Laurene Powell.

(Susan Donaldson James, *"Steve Jobs' Mantra Rooted in Buddhism: Focus and Simplicity - Apple products are beautiful and empowering, but have also enslaved users,"* ABC News, October 6, 2011, 12:12 PM.)

I wonder if he might have been influenced by or had misinterpreted what *"Sunyata"* ("emptiness") means.

WHAT IS SUNYATA?

Professor Young mentioned the concept of "Sunyata" in Mahayana Buddhism. He said that a Buddhist philosopher, Nagarjuna, argued, "Our ideas and language subtly bind us to the constructions of reality that we create, and therefore render us attached to that which is not truly real" (Young, p. 146).

Mr. Young said Sunyata is a difficult concept to grasp. It is not certain what exactly Nagarjuna meant. Nonetheless, I have heard Buddhists say, "If you believe it does not exist, it does not exist." It is perhaps coming from that line of thinking.

It seems to me that Buddhism stresses so much the teaching of non-permanency, saying that it is only because of our craving that creates the "illusion of permanence," that some Buddhists may even think that it is possible to deny the obvious, objective truth like having cancer.

This is a serious matter because we are talking about what constitutes reality. If we think we can just believe the cancer does not exit, and then it will go away, we may miss the critical treatment window that may be beneficial.

We all miss Mr. Jobs' inventive mind. In addition, he lived a modest life even though he was a billionaire. He was not materialistic and appreciated spiritual matters. But it does not seem like he found a definite answer about life.

When the 60 Minutes reporter asked what Jobs thought about the afterlife, Mr. Isaacson said:

"He [Steve Jobs] said, 'Sometimes I believe in God, sometimes I don't, I think 50/50 maybe. But ever since I've had cancer, I have been thinking about it more, and I find myself believing a bit more. I kind of maybe because I wanted to believe in the afterlife. When you die, it does not all disappear. The wisdom you accumulated, somehow, lives on.'

"Then he paused for a second, he said, 'but sometimes I think it's like an on/off switch, click, and you're gone. That's why I don't like putting on on/off switches on Apple devices.'"

Steve Jobs has contributed tremendously to modern technologies. However, it is not certain from this TV interview if he found the answer to the question of the afterlife or believed in God in the end. I sincerely hope he did.

WHAT ABOUT CHRISTIANS' FAITH HEALING?

People may say that the Christians' belief in faith healing also results in not seeking medical treatments.

The Scriptures do not teach that we should not seek medical treatments

Jesus' disciple Luke was a medical doctor (Colossians 4:14). Apostle Paul also advised Timothy to take specific measures to care for his illness (1 Timothy 5:23).

Jesus' miraculous healings were for severe diseases (leprosy, paralytic, blindness, etc.) that did not have effective treatments at the time.

While God can heal any disease, severe or not, those Christians who do not seek available medical treatments, thinking we *only* need to use faith and reject any effective medical therapies, I believe, misapprehend what the Bible teaches.

Medical remedies actually are from God, since it was God who created us and gave us the ability to do scientific research. It does not conflict with having faith in God.

Christians often pray that God will grant wisdom to the doctors treating us. Medical treatments and faith are complementary to each other.

Christians believe the disease is real

Even in the case of not using medical treatments at all, the Buddhist thinking is that if you do not believe it is there, it is not there, while Christians believe the disease is real. Nevertheless, the disease can be healed by God's power by praying to Him. It is different from simply denying that it even exists.

How we view reality, and whether our understanding of it is objectively true or not, can have deadly consequences.

Summary Thoughts on Buddhism as a Whole

I appreciate Buddhists' sincerity in wanting to get out of life's suffering. I find Buddhists are typically truly sincere and non-violent people. However, two issues come to mind:

DRASTIC CHANGES IN THE BUDDHIST BELIEF SYSTEM

There have been drastic changes in the Buddhist belief system, for example:

The question of the sacred

From no deity needed (Theravada Buddhism), to make Siddhartha a divine being (although he did not regard himself as being one), to venerate many gods (Mahayana Buddhism).

The end to achieve

From the abstract concept of nirvana (nothingness, extinguishing any desire in Theravada Buddhism), to a happy land, full of bliss (the "Western Paradise" of Pure Land in Mahayana Buddhism).

The solutions it offers

From "working out your own salvation," to doing enough good deeds, to just chant *"Namu Amida Butsu"* and put faith in a heavenly Buddha.

THE VALIDITY OF THE RELIGION AS A WHOLE

These significant inconsistencies make one question the validity of the religion. Thus, one may legitimately wonder if any of its various versions can effectively address the perceived problems.

Most Buddhists are probably not aware of all these inconsistent and conflicting views, and the various remedies it offers. They just want to be out of this affliction (which is real, and most people would agree), and have a way out of it.

I sincerely hope Buddhists will consider the love of Jesus, because He has pointed out the root cause of human agony, and even offered himself as the effective solution.

The Bible's scriptures and teachings have been consistent, and have not changed for thousands of years. It has withstood the test of times.

I will expound more on Christianity later.

26 - TRADITIONAL CHINESE WORLDVIEW

Daoism and Confucianism are the two major religions that originated in China. Before we dive into the specifics of the beliefs, Professor Young writes an excellent summary of the traditional Chinese worldview as follows.

The Sacred

A fundamental harmony: There is an underlying order in the cosmos as a whole, in nature, and in human societies.

Shang Ti ("Ruler on High")

Early in Chinese history, during the Shang Dynasty (the second dynasty of China, which began around 1750 B.C.E.), a deity who went by the name of *Shang Ti* became the object of worship.

He was thought to determine when and if crops would grow and whether human projects would be successful. For example, the Emperor's diviners consulted him to find out when to go to war or sue for peace.

Shang Ti was the guarantor of the moral order. He ruled over a celestial hierarchy, modeled after the government bureaucracy, with deities in charge of the "ministries" of Thunder, Epidemics, Fire, and so on.

Shang Ti evolved into the Jade Emperor, the central deity in popular Chinese religion to this day.

T'ien ("Heaven")

During the Chou dynasty [or spelled as "Zhou," the dynasty following Shang, 1122 – 222 B.C.], a more impersonal designation of the concept of a heavenly power developed -- T'ien ("Heaven").

Until the last Emperor left the Chinese throne in 1906 C.E., the Emperor was known as the Son of Heaven. He conducted special ceremonies intended to maintain the harmony between Earth and Heaven.

(Note: For an example of these special ceremonies, check out the information on the landmark building in Beijing, China, called *Tiāntán* (The Temple of Heaven).)

According to the traditional Chinese worldview, rulers maintain power only as long as they retain the mandate of heaven. When rulers fail to exercise their responsibility to maintain harmony in society through the promotion of virtue, they lose their right to govern, and a revolution is not only in order, it is inevitable.

The Basic Human Problem

Disharmony: Humans are susceptible to losing the pattern of harmony that is so observable in nature, and therein lies the basic human problem. Confucianism and Daoism (and other religions of East Asia) may describe the situation of disharmony quite differently, but the word applies to the diagnosis of the basic human problem they all affirm.

The Cause of the Problem

Turning from Harmony: According to popular Chinese religions, restless spirits are often the culprits in causing disharmony (although it is the human failure to properly acknowledge and tend to them that causes disharmony to persist).

Humans choose the path that leads to disharmony, and it is up to them to initiate the action (or recognize the "inaction") that will realize harmony.

The Goal of Transformation

Harmony in This Life: Harmony is primarily a this-worldly phenomenon. The ideal of families living in harmony, and a society ruled and inhabited by virtuous persons living harmoniously.

Although life beyond death is a facet of this worldview, the emphasis is placed on the desired transformation occurring within life on Earth.

The specific goals are health, a full life span, prosperity, harmony within the family, continuity of the family lineage, and protection from natural and human disasters.

The Means of Transformation

Discerning and Living in Harmony: The means of realizing harmony are ancestor veneration; the maintenance of worship of gods at temples, shrines, and family altars; and divination. In addition, the important concepts of *de* (virtue) and *xiao* (or *hsiao*, filial piety), are fundamental.

De means inherent power or virtue. In a sense, it is the principle, which allows or creates harmonious human life. Where there is virtue, there is harmony; where it is absent, there is chaos. Although Confucianism and Daoism developed quite different teachings about virtue, they both focus on the question of how to lead virtuous lives, and that concern is deeply imbued in the Chinese way of life.

Although filial piety (*xiao*) rose to prominence later, as one of the principal Confucian virtues, it is a principle deeply rooted in China, as well as in other Eastern Asian cultures. Specifically, filial piety refers to the loyalty shown by a son to his father. More generally, it is the respect and reverence anyone in an inferior social position shows for superiors.

Reverence for elders extends to ancestors. If proper respect is shown to them, they will assist the family.

Many of the popular deities of indigenous Chinese religion are particularly important ancestors who have been accorded the status of gods. For example, the deity *Ma-tsu*, goddess of fishermen, was at first the soul of a young girl who died before her marriage.

Other deities are gods and goddesses associated with natural elements such as the soil.

My Thoughts

On the Understanding of the Sacred

Traditional Chinese religious views, in some respects, are similar to Christianity.

Both believe:

An overriding deity is in control of the world, and He is in heaven.

It is a personal god (for *Shang Ti*, it is a personal god; for *T'ien*, it is more of an impersonal one), to whom we can pray and ask for guidance.

Maintaining a good relationship with him is critical to having peace and a blessed life on Earth.

The government's role is to bear the responsibility given by Him to serve the people and to protect and administer justice.

Romans 13:3-4 states,

"³ For rulers hold *no terror for those who do right*, but for those who do wrong. Do you want to be free from fear of the one in authority? Then do what is right and you will be commended.

"⁴ For the one in authority is *God's servant for your good*. But if you do wrong, be afraid, for rulers do not bear the sword for no reason. They are God's servants, agents of wrath to bring punishment on the wrongdoer."

However, one of the critical differences is that Chinese believe that *Shang Ti*, the Ruler on High, is also in charge of many smaller gods who are ministers of thunder, fire, etc., while Christianity stresses there is only one God, the Creator of the world. There are no other gods.

It is a difference between monotheism (only one god) and henotheism (there are many gods, but one is dominant).

I see the traditional Chinese worldview as a humble, god-fearing culture, seeking to have a good relationship with the supreme power or powers of the universe, so that people can live in peace and prosperity.

That said, by also worshiping many other deities and images made by man, they risk offending the one true God, who warns against bowing down to idols.

On Life beyond Death

Contrasted with the traditional Chinese worldview, which primarily centers on life on Earth, Christianity teaches that life in this world is only temporary.

Christians seek not just to have peace with God and to have stable, harmonious family life here on this planet, but also, more importantly, to look forward to the eternal kingdom of God in the new heaven and the new earth that is to come.

The decisions we make while on Earth, determine if we go to that eternal blessed place in the future when we die.

I sincerely hope that those who adhere to traditional Chinese religions would consider this crucial, eternal aspect of life.

27 - PHILOSOPHICAL DAOISM (DAO JIA)

The name "Daoism" (or Taoism) is ambiguous. It may refer to the philosophical tradition traced to the legendary sage *Laozi* (or *Lao Tzi* or *Lao Tzu*) and first expressed in the collection of poems called the *Daodejing* (or *Tao-Te-Ching*, "The Classic of the Way and Its Power").

Since the Han dynasty, this tradition has been called *Dao jia* ("the philosophy of the Dao"). This is the "Daoism" most widely known in the West today, mostly because of widespread exposure to the translations of the Daodejing.

Philosophical Daoism has faded as a distinct movement in East Asia, but it did have an influence on the Meditation School of Buddhism (Zen), which continues to exercise considerable influence in Japan. It also had a profound influence on the arts and literature in both China and Japan.

However, the Daoism currently practiced in Taiwan and other Chinese communities is more closely associated with a tradition known as *Dao jiao* ("the teaching of the Dao," also called Religious Daoism).

Specifically, Dao jiao involves the worship of deities and the propitiation of spirits through rituals carried out by hereditary Daoist priests. It is one facet of a popular religious movement that evolved from philosophical Daoism, transforming some of its basic teachings.

The Founder - Laozi

The legendary founder of philosophical Daoism is known to tradition as Laozi ("the old Master" or "the old Child"). Some interpreters question if a man called Laozi ever existed as a historical person; others see a real person behind the legends.

According to a second-century B.C.E. biography, Laozi was born in 604 B.C.E. to a virgin. As an adult, he took a government post.

However, he left his position as an archivist because he came to the conclusion that governments, with their laws and bureaucracies, distort the simplicity by which humans should live.

He withdrew from society and resolved to live a solitary life. He was besieged by visitors (including Confucius, according to the legend) and decided to leave society all together.

As he traveled on his ox, the gatekeeper at the pass into the western regions recognized Laozi as a renowned scholar, and would not allow him to pass, until he wrote down his philosophy of life. In the form of short, enigmatic poems, he wrote a treatise on how to live, calling it the *Daodejing*.

The Daodejing

It is timeless in its basic meaning. After the Christian Bible, it is the most translated book in the world. The Daodejing is a short work, with eighty-one chapters, including only about five thousand Chinese characters. It has become the most widely known Chinese classic.

It may have been written originally as a political work, a manual to instruct those who would aspire to rule in the art of governing, but like all great literary works, it has various levels of meaning.

Politically, the Daodejing must be considered a failure. No Chinese government, or probably any other in history, has made a serious attempt to implement on a large scale its philosophy of passive government.

Its lasting impact has been at other levels. The Daodejing's teaching of natural, simple living has inspired millions of readers to examine their own lifestyles and to let go of that which has been forcing them into uncomfortable, even destructive patterns. It has also served to spiritually inspire many with its teaching of a mystical, harmonious process that is true reality.

The Sacred

The Nameless and Eternal *Dao*: We should first clarify what the Dao ("way") is not. The Dao is not God, at least in any personal sense (4, 60) **(the numbers here are chapter references of Daodejing: Chapter 4 and Chapter 60)**. The Dao is not a being of any sort, yet all beings are manifestations of the Dao.

Feminine images point us toward the Dao. The Dao is the Mother, the source of life (1, 25). The Dao is the womb of all reality. Stated more philosophically, the Dao is the "nonbeing" from which all "being "comes (40, 25), yet the Dao is also everything that is!

The Basic Human Problem

Resisting the Flow of the Dao: In a sense, the basic problem humans face, according to the Daodejing, is that we do not know who we truly are. Our fundamental choice is either to acknowledge that reality and let ourselves go with the flow of the Dao (23), or to resist who we are and try to establish our own, separate identities (13).

The Cause of the Problem

Striving for Permanence and Virtue: As Buddhism teaches, the Daodejing suggests that when we allow ourselves to succumb to the illusion of a unique, permanent self we fall victim to desire and craving (1, 9). We strive to "become," to "make something of ourselves." For philosophical Daoism, this human striving for permanence is the cause of the dilemma to be overcome.

The Daodejing also makes the intriguing claim that if we strive to be virtuous, the result will not be harmony but chaos (38).

The Goal of Transformation

The goal of human life is the same as the goal of all life: harmony with the Dao (15, 55). For humans, this means a natural and simple life (8), seeing both life and death as part of the eternal Dao (16, 33).

The ideal life is that of the Sage (22, 33, 47). The goal of Daoism is at both an individual and communal level, for if those who are leaders practice the life of natural goodness, then the society will be in harmony with the Dao.

The notion of a "goal" is ironic in Daoism, for the "goal" is to realize the natural, cosmic process that is already present. "Goal" implies striving, and that is the problem we must overcome. Therefore, in a sense the real goal in Daoist philosophy is to stop having a goal!

The Means of Transformation

Action without Assertion (*wu wei*): What is the simple life through which one experiences harmony with the Dao? The term *wu wei* ("inaction" or "nonpurposiveness") expresses it most clearly.

To practice wu wei is to act without asserting oneself (2, 47). On the one hand, wu wei means to have no ambitions, no desire for fame or power, no need to influence or dominate others. It is to be not what others think you should be, but to simply "be yourself" in the most basic and natural sense.

Such a person may seem weak willed, passive, and even stupid to those who live by desire and striving. However, such a person "achieves without achieving." How can that be? By living spontaneously, the person is allowing the Dao to come to its true expression, and "virtue" (de) will be natural rather than contrived (18, 38).

Others will be positively influenced not by an effort to influence them, but by the power of the Dao being actualized. As we will see, the attitude toward the "virtuous life" is much different than that taught by Confucian ethicists.

My Thoughts

Philosophical Daoism vs. Christianity

NOT A RANDOM ACT, BUT WHAT CAUSED IT?

Philosophical Daoism believes that an impersonal originator dictates how all things come to exist.

I read the Daodejing and thought perhaps when Laozi looked at the natural world, he was so awed by its beauty and orderly fashion, that he was convinced there must be something out there that made all this happen.

He did not know what it was, so he called it "Dao" ("the way"). That is why he wrote, "不知其名，強名曰道" (bù zhī qí míng, qiáng míng yuē dào), meaning "I do not know what it is, and therefore, do not know how to name it, but if I have to, I call it 'the way'."

He further believed that humans should respect "the way," not resist it, and go with the flow.

Regardless of how Laozi came up with the idea of "the way," it is apparent that He did not believe that the universe was the result of some random acts of nature. Something was definitely controlling the orderly fashion that he did not know what to name.

Daoism is close to Christianity in the sense that it teaches the universe is not the result of some accidents in nature, but was caused by something beyond the natural world.

However, while Laozi did not know what it was and just gave it an abstract and impersonal name, for Christianity, Scripture clearly and forthrightly says, in the very first verse of the very first book of the Bible:

"In the beginning God created the heavens and the earth" (Genesis 1:1).

Furthermore, throughout the Bible, it reveals that God is a personal God, who enjoys engaging and interacting with the human beings he created.

In short, both do not believe that the universe is the result of some chance occurrence, but one calls it a mysterious, impersonal "Dao," while the other unambiguously proclaims the existence of a personal Creator.

SEEKING HARMONY WITH THE SACRED, BUT HOW?

Daoism's seeking harmony with the sacred is similar to Christianity's teaching that humans must maintain a good relationship with the sacred in order to have a blessed life.

Nonetheless, they are quite different regarding how to achieve that peaceful relationship.

For Daoism, one does not need to do anything. There is no need for any purpose in life or to do any good deeds; just be yourself and avoid getting in the way of "the Dao."

For Christianity, as mentioned before, the salvation is free. However, once one is born again with a new life, God expects us to do good deeds to serve and love people (Ephesians 2:10).

A life of joyful actions and purpose begins.

WANTING TO LIVE A SIMPLE LIFE, BUT IS LIFE THAT SIMPLE?

Philosophical Daoism desires a simple life. Many people would agree that it is an attractive and ideal lifestyle to have.

Nevertheless, as pointed out before, Daoism does not believe what Christianity does, that it was a personal God that created the world (not a mysterious "Dao" that is difficult to describe), and that the Creator enjoys engaging and interacting with humans.

In addition, Christianity teaches that God is a God of morals, and that men and women do have a role to play in those dynamics.

And most importantly, Christianity teaches that how a person responds to God's moral standards and fulfills their own part will determine if one can lead a blessed life.

In reality, life, I believe, is not as simple as Daoism maintains. Therefore, any religion that discounts any human's role in that dynamics is too passive to be able to deal with human issues effectively.

Philosophical Daoism vs. Buddhism

Professor Young writes, describing Daoism's view on the cause of the problem, "as Buddhism teaches, the Daodejing suggests that when we allow ourselves to succumb to the illusion of a unique, permanent self we fall victim to desire and craving (1, 9)" (Young, p. 124).

WAS IT POSSIBLE THAT BUDDHISM INFLUENCED DAOISM?

Mr. Young seems to suggest that Daoism might be influenced by Buddhism. Nevertheless, Laozi was born in 604 B.C., much earlier than Siddhartha Gautama (who was born in 563 B.C.). In addition, Buddhism did not begin to spread to China until the first century A.D.

Daoism originated in China hundreds of years before Buddhism reached the country. They are two independently developed belief systems in the two countries, in two different periods, and with dissimilar world views.

ON THE CONCEPT OF "A UNIQUE AND PERMANENT SELF"

Chapters 1 and 9 of Daodejing talk about the vanity of striving to possess wealth. In that sense, it is not permanent. However, it does not say that there is no unique, permanent self as Buddhism holds.

On the contrary, Professor Young mentioned, "In speaking of the eternal Dao, sections of both the Daodejing and Zhuangzi seem to suggest that whoever is in harmony with the Dao *lives forever*" (Young, p. 122).

Therefore, if this is a correct interpretation of Daodejing, Daoism does believe in a unique and permanent self, while Buddhism does not.

THE MEANING OF "NO PERMANENCY" IS DIFFERENT

I think Daoism's view of "no permanency" results from observing the powerful nature and teaches the vanity of striving to possess wealth, while Buddhism is the reaction to the pains and afflictions of humans and teaches avoidance of any relationships. It is looked at in a different context.

Therefore, Daoism's sense of "no permanency" is vastly different from that of Buddhism's "no permanency," both in term of its meaning and how to deal with it.

I feel that using "vanity" instead of "no permanency" will be more definitive in describing Daoism's concept, lest it be confused with the term used for Buddhism.

THE GOAL IS DIFFERENT

Theravada Buddhism seeks to achieve the state of nirvana in which there are no more desires and there is nothingness. It is a highly negative view of the world.

On the contrary, Daoism is to have harmony with the Dao. It is a positive and appreciative attitude toward nature.

THE MEANS ARE DIFFERENT

Theravada Buddhism's method to solve the perceived problem is the eight-fold path, which is about virtuous acts (correct speech, correct conduct, etc.), while Daoism is the opposite, claiming that if we strive to be virtuous, the result will not be harmony but chaos. It is to respect nature and seek to follow the Dao.

In short, Philosophical Daoism was a much earlier independently developed philosophy. The world and its perceived problems were seen from a critically different perspective. They might sound similar in some respects, yet are, indeed, two distinct worldviews.

28 - RELIGIOUS DAOISM (DAO JIAO)

As described before, Dr. Young writes that Daodejing and Zhuangzi seem to suggest that whoever is in harmony with the Dao lives forever. He went on to write:

This intimation of immorality in the classic texts, combined with popular concern for health, happiness, and long life, became the basis for a new branch of Daoism, often called in the West "Devotional," "Religious," "Ritual, " "Applied," or sometimes "Magical" Daoism.

By the second century C.E., there was an organized Daoist "religious" movement, focusing on the pursuit of immortality and well-being, which continues today. The facet of this movement dealing with rituals of cosmic renewal, carried out to renew the community's relationship with deities and spirits, is called Dao jiao.

A variety of paths to "immortality" developed. One was alchemy, the search for some elixir that could be taken to preserve the vital force. Another was a hygienic and dietary regime, in which foods with energies thought to correspond to the five basic elements were eaten, and foods that caused the vital essence to dissipate were avoided. Breath control techniques and physical exercises also developed as a means to preserve the *qi* (breath). Finally, living a life of virtue was thought to be essential to becoming an "immortal".

Associated with this branch of Daoism is an elaborate array of hierarchically arranged spiritual beings, organized on the bureaucratic model of the Han dynasty. Highest is the unmanifest Dao, next the primordial chaos of breath (qi), followed by The Three Officials (or Three Heavenly Worthies), and many others.

My Thoughts

Religious Daoism is drastically different from Philosophical Daoism in that, instead of just believing in one singular sacred (the Dao) and living a passive life, it now embraces polytheism, revering a pantheon of deities, and actively practicing many rituals.

It also departs from the "action without assertion" and "no purpose" way about life to actively seek a specific objective: immortality.

While whether or not the various ways to attain immortality, as prescribed by religious Daoism, are effective is questionable, it is more assertive in the sense that it believes humans can do something to improve life.

That attitude is also quite distinct from Theravada Buddhism, which looks at life so negatively that it even denies any permanent thing exists, let alone feel the need to pursue it.

29 - CONFUCIANISM

In China, the tradition called Confucianism in the West was known as the *ru* tradition (rujia), a literati (intellectual) movement rooted in the self-cultivation of moral virtue.

For two thousand years, until the early twentieth century, Confucianism dominated the philosophy of education and the approach to government, first in China, then in Korea and Japan. It is undergoing a contemporary resurgence.

Indeed, the influence of Confucianism on East Asian culture is difficult to overemphasize. Many attribute the miraculous postwar recovery of Japan, Korea, and Taiwan (not to mention the resurgence of China) to an innate commitment to Confucian ideals.

The Founder – Master Kong (Confucius)

Confucius was born in the ancient feudal state of Lu, now the area known as Shantung, in about 551 B.C.E. Shortly after his birth, his father died, and his mother had to sacrifice to provide him with an education, helping to instill in him the value of learning.

At about the age of fifty, he was appointed to a high office in the administration of the Duke of Lu. However, his policies were not adopted, and he resigned or was forced out of office.

Confucius was about fifty-five when he began a thirteen-year period of wandering from state to state, teaching a program of political and social reform. At age sixty-seven, he returned to Lu and spent the rest of his life teaching and (according to tradition) editing the Confucian classics.

When he died in about 479 B.C.E., he was discouraged by his failure to have more influence on government. However, he left a band of followers committed to his teaching.

The Analects and Other Texts

The Four Books

1. The *Analects* (*Lunyu*) are one of the *Four Books*. They are the reputed sayings and conversations of Confucius. They were compiled after his death, over a long period of time, in various layers. However, the major Confucian teachings are present in the Analects, making them an important source for the ideas of Confucius himself and his early disciples. The Analects became the principal cornerstone of both the Chinese educational system and the examination system for government officials. It has also continued to serve as an inspiration for personal reflection. An example of a saying from the Analects reflects the timeless quality of the teaching (4:16): "The Master said, 'a gentleman takes as much trouble to discover what is right as lesser men take to discover what will pay.'"

2. The *Great Learning* (*Daxue*) is a short discussion of the character and influence of the noble person.

3. The *Doctrine of the Mean* (*Zhongyong*) deals with the relationship between humanity and the moral order, emphasizing the avoidance of extremes and maintaining harmony in all things.

4. The *Book of Mencius* (*Mengzi*) is the third-century B.C.E. collection of the sayings of Mengzi, one of the principal disciples of Confucius. It is the first attempt at a systemic philosophical statement of the teachings of Confucius.

The Five Classics

1. The *Shujing* (Book of History) focuses on the *Zhou* (Chou) dynasty (ca. 1100 – 256 B.C.E.);

2. The *Shijing* (Book of Poetry), a collection of 300 poems, also from the *Zhou* dynasty;

3. The *Liji* (Book of Rites), a description of ancient ceremonies and their meaning;

4. The *Yijing* (Book of Changes), basic pattern of the universe, was used to guide the nobility in how to face future events;

5. The *Chunqiu* (Annals of Spring and Autumn), historical records of the State of Lu.

The Sacred

Making the Dao Great: Confucius sidestepped questions such as, "What is the nature of the spirit?" He is reputed to have said that you cannot treat spirits and divinities properly before you learn to treat your fellow human beings properly (Analects 11:12). He advised his followers to treat the spirits "as though they were real" (3:12).

Some have called his teaching a "spiritual agnosticism". He professed no knowledge of the spiritual, but still felt that maintaining religious rituals as critical to his central concern: social harmony.

Confucius spoke of the Dao, but not like a philosophical Daoist. According to the Analects, it is humans that make the Dao great, not the Dao that makes humans great (15:29). In other words, if there to be a "way" for things to go, an underlying harmony, it will be because humans manifest it in their commitment to virtue.

For philosophical Daoists, the way to virtue is to let the Dao happen. Striving to be virtuous results in a lack of virtue, they argued. For Confucians, the way to the Dao is to seek virtue actively. From this perspective, perhaps Confucianism is the *yang*, and philosophical Daoism is the *yin* of East Asian culture!

The Basic Human Problem

Social Chaos: The social chaos of the Warring States period, brought on by the collapse of the feudal system.

The Cause of the Problem

A Breakdown of Virtue: When rulers and educated elite did not live virtuous lives, a social breakdown occurred. In particular, this breakdown occurred because people failed to follow their social roles.

For example, princes failed to behave as princes should, and fathers no longer performed the roles they should play. At the same time, as Mengzi observed, people were not corrupt by nature, and virtue seemed to depend on how people were educated. Confucian teaching pointed to an earlier age, when rulers naturally displayed virtue (*de*) and sought to recover that kind of society.

The Goal of Transformation

Leaders of Characters (*jun-zi*) and the Harmonious Society: The goal was the restoration of the harmony of the feudal order, and the right pattern of human relationships. The harmonious society would be created by sages, "ideal persons" who lived virtuous lives, and they would do so by the force of their moral character.

The "gentleman" (*jun-zi* or *chun-tzu*) that Confucius envisioned would remain committed to virtue through all of life's hardships. Jun-zi had meant an aristocrat or a person of noble birth; Confucius taught that anyone could become an "ideal person" through a process of moral formation leading to harmony (*ho*).

For Confucius, the ideal was not to withdraw from the world but to realize one's inherent human potential for goodness, immersing oneself in human life – in the family but also in society through public service. *This* is the Confucian way to achieve identification with the cosmic order.

According to the Master, the gentleman was the son always filial, the father ever just and kind, the official unfailingly loyal and faithful, the husband completely righteous and judicious, and the friend always sincere and tactful.

The Means of Transformation

The Virtuous Life: The path to the harmonious society – and the "ideal person" who would create it by the force of their moral character – lay in education in specific virtue.

The gentleman would maintain a balance between what we might call "inner" (*nei*) virtues (relating to one's basic attitude and orientation) and "outer" (*wai*) virtues (having to do with how one behaves toward others.

The primary inner virtue is *ren* (humaneness, thoughtfulness, empathy, and kindness; also written as *jen*). Related to *ren* is *shu* (reciprocity). Shu means not doing to others what you would not have them do to you. It is sometimes called the "silver rule," for it is gentler than "the golden rule," to which it has been compared.

The most basic external virtue is *li* ("propriety, good form," or "doing what is proper for the situation"). *Li* has a variety of meanings in different contexts. It can refer to the rites and rituals of a society; it can mean courtesy in human interaction or treating others with reverence and respect. In general, *li* is a right and proper order to be followed in any circumstance.

Another outer virtue deserving mention is *xiao* (or *hsiao*, "filial piety"). Confucianism is the principal carrier of this virtue. "Filial piety" means respect for one's elders, especially within the context of family. You will not find many nursing homes in societies rooted in Confucian values, because keeping one's elders within the context of the family is seen as a basic social obligation. Not only are they kept physically, but they are valued and honored.

Confucius emphasized respect for elders and others in authority, but it is important to emphasize that "filial piety" also includes parents treating their children (and those in authority treating people in their charge) with respect and courtesy.

My Thoughts

Similarities between Confucianism and Christianity

There are similarities between the two worldviews regarding virtues, for example:

THE "SILVER RULE" OF CONFUCIANISM

It teaches, "*Not* doing to others what you would *not* have them do to you," while Christianity urges, "So in everything, do to others what you would have them do to you, for this sums up the Law and the Prophets" (Matthew 7:12), which is regarded as the "golden rule".

Although Christianity's rule is stated positively, both principles are similar in that they all respect other's rights.

THE VIRTUE "REN"

It teaches "ren:" be kind and thoughtful. The Chinese character of "ren" suggests one must consider the other person also, not just him or herself. The Bible encourages us to "Love your neighbor as yourself" (Matthew 22:39).

THE FILIAL PIETY

It teaches respect for one's elders, especially within the family context. One of the Ten Commandments taught in the Bible is "Honor your father and your mother, so that you may live long in the land the Lord your God is giving you" (Exodus 20:12).

Differences between Confucianism and Christianity

While some similarities between the two worldviews are present regarding what constitutes a virtuous life, there are critical differences in how to achieve that goal.

IS EDUCATION AN EFFECTIVE MEANS TO LIVE A VIRTUOUS LIFE?

Although Confucianism includes religious rituals as part of its prescribed means, it believes that the education of virtues is the most important solution.

I think that while education can help alleviate human relationship problems to some extent, it does not address the root cause of human conflicts.

This is the same case with many religions, in that the teachings they offer are more about goals than solutions.

As discussed before regarding Theravada Buddhism, which offers the eight-fold path as the remedy, like correct speech, what is causing people to be unable to speak correctly in the first place? We all want to communicate appropriately, but why is it difficult for us to do that?

Confucianism believes that if we are all educated to live a virtuous life, we can all get along harmoniously.

But the question is, again, we all want to live a virtuous life, yet why can we not live that way in the first place? Is it just for lack of education?

What is the origin of humankind's misbehavior?

ARE PEOPLE GOOD OR CORRUPT BY NATURE?

Professor Young mentioned that Confucius's follower Mengzi believed that people were not naturally corrupt, and virtue seemed to depend on how people were educated. In other words, it believes our nature is not flawed; it is the lack of education that causes problems.

I remember a long-time neighbor came to me one day and said, "My two-year old just said to me 'Bad Daddy, go away!'"

He was somewhat sad, because he and his wife had tried very hard to have children, and finally, they had two. He had been an excellent dad and spent much time caring for them.

Apparently, my neighbor did not teach their kids to act like that. That two-year-old must have gotten that attitude somewhere else.

I think, fundamentally, it is not about training, it is about something that is inherent in our nature.

As shared in the chapter regarding Theravada Buddhism, Christianity points out that the reason for human suffering is humankind's rebellion against God, the Creator. As a result, people are born with a sinful nature (Romans 5:12).

It does not mean that our nature is all bad. However, it is tarnished.

By fixing that rebellion issue, Christians not only will be free from the condemnation of sins, but also will be given the power (the Holy Spirit) to overcome that sinful inclination and, therefore, to be able to speak correctly and to treat each other politely.

It is that transformation from the inside that will genuinely and effectively change a person's outward behavior.

DO WE NEED ONLY GOD, ONLY HUMANS, OR BOTH?

Scholars view Philosophical Daoism as representing the passive "Yin" (no action needed), while Confucianism is the active "Yang" (man must actively pursue it).

As commented before, Daoism does not believe any effort is required for humans; just do not get in the way of the "Dao," and everything will go smoothly.

On the other hand, Confucianism only deals with human relationships by advocating living a virtuous life through education.

It avoids facing the question of divinity. No answer is provided to such inquiry as where we came from or where we are going after death, claiming it is unknowable (spiritual agnosticism).

It stresses that humans can actively do something to fix their own problems and ignore any possible role from God or gods in human affairs.

Thus, Daoism believes that only Dao is needed, while Confucianism holds that only human effort is called for.

However, Christianity holds that *both* God and humans are vital to achieving a harmonious world.

We need God's power to help us overcome our shortcomings. And to access that assistance, human beings must be willing to acknowledge God's existence and actively seek his help, while carrying out our own responsibilities.

Christians believe it is a world where God and humans engage in a dynamic, loving relationship.

30 - QUESTIONS ABOUT CHRISTIANITY

I will start with the basic questions according to Dr. Young's analytical framework, and then provide additional answers to some questions people might have.

The Sacred: What Is Trinity?

Christians believe in the triune God: God the Father, God the Son, and God the Holy Spirit, the Trinity. This triune God created the world, including human beings on Earth.

He is not an impersonal deity, such as a controlling force. The triune God is a personal god; He communicates with humans and cares about them. In fact, He is love (John 3:16).

As explained before, the Trinity is not about multiple gods (polytheism); it is one God in three persons. In other words, it is one essence revealed in three distinct persons. It is not like 1+1+1 = 3; it is like $1 \times 1 \times 1 = 1^3$.

I understand it isn't easy to comprehend. However, although the word Trinity does not occur in the Bible, it clearly points to this conclusion. Some of those passages are listed below.

One God

DEUTERONOMY 6:4

"Hear, O Israel: The Lord our God, the Lord is one. [a]"
Footnotes
> a. Or The Lord our God is one Lord; or The Lord is our God, the Lord is one; or The Lord is our God, the Lord alone

ISAIAH 46:9

"Remember the former things, those of long ago; I am God, and there is no other; I am God, and there is none like me."

MARK 12:29

"The most important one," answered Jesus, "is this: 'Hear, O Israel: The Lord our God, the Lord is one. [a] '"
Footnotes
> a. Or The Lord our God is one Lord

Note that Jesus was quoting Deuteronomy 6:4 in the Hebrew Bible.

In Three Persons

ISAIAH 48:16

"Come near me and listen to this: 'From the first announcement I have not spoken in secret; at the time it happens, I am there.' And now the Sovereign Lord [the Father] has sent me [the Son], endowed with his Spirit [the Holy Spirit]."

ISAIAH 61:1

"The Spirit [the Holy Spirit] of the Sovereign Lord [the Father] is on me [the Son], because the Lord has anointed me to proclaim good news to the poor. He has sent me to

bind up the brokenhearted, to proclaim freedom for the captives, and release from darkness for the prisoners, [a]"
   Footnotes
   a. Hebrew; Septuagint *the blind*

MATTHEW 28:18-20

"[18] Then Jesus came to them and said, "All authority in heaven and on earth has been given to me. [19] Therefore go and make disciples of all nations,

"baptizing them in *the name* [singular in Greek] of *the* [a definite article, indicating distinctness] Father and of *the* Son and of *the* Holy Spirit, [20] and teaching them to obey everything I have commanded you. And surely I am with you always, to the very end of the age.""

All Three Are Equally God

THE FATHER IS CALLED GOD

1 Corinthians 8:6

"yet for us there is but *one God, the Father*, from whom all things came and for whom we live; and there is but one Lord, Jesus Christ, through whom all things came and through whom we live."

THE SON IS CALLED GOD

Isaiah 7:14

"Therefore the Lord himself will give you[a] a sign: The virgin[b] will conceive and give birth to a *son*, and[c] will call him *Immanuel*.[d] [*God with us*]"
   Footnotes
   a. The Hebrew is plural.

b. Or *young woman*
c. Masoretic Text; Dead Sea Scrolls *son, and he* or *son, and they*
d. *Immanuel* means *God with us.*

Isaiah 9:6

"For to us a child is born, to us a *son* is given, and the government will be on his shoulders. And he will be called Wonderful Counselor, *Mighty God,* Everlasting Father, Prince of Peace.

John 1: 1

"¹ In the beginning was the Word, and the Word [Jesus] was with God, and *the Word was God.*

THE HOLY SPIRIT IS CALLED GOD

Acts 5:3-4

"³ Then Peter said, 'Ananias, how is it that Satan has so filled your heart that you have *lied to the Holy Spirit* and have kept for yourself some of the money you received for the land? ⁴ Didn't it belong to you before it was sold? And after it was sold, wasn't the money at your disposal? What made you think of doing such a thing? *You have not lied just to human beings but to God.*"

Yet They Act in Unity as One

JESUS' TESTIMONIES

John 17:11

"I will remain in the world no longer, but they [the believers] are still in the world, and I am coming to you. Holy Father, protect them by the power of[a] your name, the name you gave me, so that they may be one *as we are one.*"

Footnotes
   a. Or *Father, keep them faithful to*

John 10:25-30

"[25] Jesus answers, "I did tell you, but you do not believe. The works I do in my Father's name testify about me, [26] but you do not believe because you are not my sheep.

"[27] My sheep listen to my voice; I know them, and they follow me. [28] I give them eternal life, and they shall never perish; no one will snatch them out of my hand.

"[29] My Father, who has given them to me, is greater than all[a]; no one can snatch them out of my Father's hand. [30] *I and the Father are one.*"

Footnotes
   a. John 10:29 Many early manuscripts *What my Father has given me is greater than all.*

John 10:37-38

"[37] Do not believe me [Jesus] unless *I do the works of my Father.* [38] But if I do them, even though you do not believe me, believe the works that you may know and understand that *the Father is in me, and I in the Father.*"

JESUS' BAPTISM

Matthew 3:16-17

"[16] As soon as Jesus was baptized, he went up out of the water. At that moment heaven was opened, and he saw the *Spirit* of God descending like a dove and alighting on him. ¹⁷ And a voice from heaven said, "This is my Son, whom *I* [*God the Father*] love; with him I am well pleased."

It is remarkable to see that in this single event, all three Persons of the Trinity were present and participated.

BAPTISM FOR ALL WHO BELIEVE

As mentioned earlier, all believers are to be baptized in the "name" (singular in Greek) of all three persons of the one true God: of the Father, of the Son, and of the Holy Spirit (Matthew 28:19).

APOSTLE PAUL'S FINAL GREETING TO THE CHURCH AT CORINTHIAN

Apostle Paul says the blessing from the Triune God well:

"May the grace of the Lord Jesus Christ, and the love of God [God the Father], and the fellowship of the Holy Spirit be with you all" (2 Corinthians 13:14).

We see time and time again, throughout the Old and the New Testament periods (For the Old Testament times, refer to Isaiah 48:16, and Isaiah 61:1 as cited earlier), that all three Persons work in unison, and *function as one*, in their ministries to humankind.

What Is the Basic Human Problem?

The relationship between God, the Creator, and man, the created, is broken.

All human problems, as spoken of before, like sickness, aging, death, wars, and even natural disasters, directly resulted from this broken relationship. Humans and the Earth are under the curse of man's rebellion against God.

What Is the Cause of the Problem?

The Fall of Humankind

When God created the Earth and humans, He did not make them as robots but as living beings with free will, to choose whether to obey His commands or not.

"^{15} The Lord God took the man [Adam] and put him in the Garden of Eden to work it and take care of it. ^{16} And the Lord God commanded the man, 'You are free to eat from any tree in the garden; ^{17} but you *must not* eat from the tree of the knowledge of good and evil, for when you eat from it *you will certainly die*'" (Genesis 2:15-17).

Despite such a specific warning, Adam and Eve were tempted and did not follow God's order:

"^{1} Now the serpent [the devil, in the form of a snake (Revelation 20:2)] was more crafty than any of the wild animals the Lord God had made. He said to the woman, 'Did God *really* say, 'You must not eat from any tree in the garden?'

"^{2} The woman said to the serpent, 'We may eat fruit from the trees in the garden, ^{3} but God did say, 'You must not eat fruit from the tree that is in the middle of the garden, and you must not touch it, or you will die.'

"^{4} 'You will not certainly die,' the serpent said to the woman. ^{5} 'For God knows that when you eat from it your eyes will be opened, and *you will be like God*, knowing good and evil.'

"⁶ When the woman saw that the fruit of the tree was good for food and pleasing to the eye, and also desirable for gaining wisdom, she took some and ate it. She also gave some to her husband, who was with her, and he ate it. ⁷ Then the eyes of both of them were opened, and they realized they were naked; so they sewed fig leaves together and made coverings for themselves" (Genesis 3:1-7).

Consequences of the Fall

DEATH

As God forewarned Adam and Eve, "when you eat from it you will certainly die." When God created Adam and Eve, He did not prohibit them from eating from the Tree of Life, which would have enabled them to live forever.

Physical death

Since they willfully chose to eat from the forbidden tree of the knowledge of good and evil, humans are no longer allowed to live forever (Genesis 3:22).

This is why the human body now dies from old age or sickness.

Spiritual death

Though the human soul is eternal, it is now dead in the sense that it is separated from God. The spiritual relationship with God is broken.

SIN ENTERED THE WORLD

As previously stated in Part Three, Scripture tells us,

"Therefore, just as sin entered the world through one man [Adam], and death through sin, and in this way death came to all people, because all sinned—" (Romans 5:12).

Sin (*Hamartia* in Greek) means "A *missing of the mark*... It is the most comprehensive term for moral obliquity. It is used of sin as (a) a principle or source of action, or an inward element producing acts, e.g., Rom. 3:9; 5:12..."
(W. E. Vine, *Vine's Expository Dictionary of Old and New Testament Words* (Grand Rapids, Michigan: Fleming H. Revell, a division of Baker Book House Company, 1981), Volume 4, p. 32)

From the Book of Genesis, which describes how humankind fell, it is evident that sin means humans have missed the mark set by God.

It is the acts that deviate from God's moral principles, but it also denotes a perverted spiritual condition.

Since the fall of Adam and Eve, we have all been born with that sinful inclination, being rebellious, for instance. King David admits in Psalm 51:5, "Surely I was sinful at birth, sinful from the time my mother conceived me."

As stated before, Prophet Isaiah mourns, "We all, like sheep, have gone astray, each of us has turned to our own way; and the Lord has laid on him the iniquity of us all" (Isaiah 53:6).

Hatred, conflicts, murders, and wars between human beings ensued. In fact, right after the fall of Adam and Eve, as recorded in Chapter 3 of Genesis, the following chapter documents the first murder of mankind. The first son of Adam and Eve, Cane, killed his younger brother, Abel, because of jealousy (Genesis 4:1-8).

THE EARTH IS CURSED

Not only will humans not live peacefully with each other, but the environment is also tarnished. Adam and Eve were driven out of the Garden of Eden. People must work hard to make a living, "... Cursed is the ground because of you; through painful toil you will eat food from it all the days of your life" (Genesis 3:17).

STRUGGLE BETWEEN SATANIC FORCES AND HUMANITY FOLLOWED

"^{14} So the Lord God said to the serpent, 'Because you have done this, 'Cursed are you above all livestock and all wild animals! You will crawl on your belly and you will eat dust all the days of your life.

"^{15} And I will put enmity between you and the woman [Eve], and between your offspring[a] and hers; he [Christ] will crush[b] your head, and you will strike his heel" (Genesis 3:14-15).

Footnotes
    a. Or *seed*
    b. Or *strike*

According to Dr. Allen P. Ross,
"The 'offspring' of the woman was Cain, then all humanity at large, and then Christ and those collectively in Him. The 'offspring' of the serpent includes demons and anyone serving his kingdom of darkness, those whose 'father' is the devil (John 8:44).

"Satan would cripple mankind (you will strike at his heel), but *the* Seed, Christ, would deliver the fatal blow (He will crush your head)."

(Editors: John F. Walvoord and Roy B. Zuck, *The Bible Knowledge Commentary – An Exposition of the Scriptures by Dallas Seminary Faculty*, *Old Testament* (Wheaton, Illinois: Victor Books, Third printing, 1986), p. 33. Used by permission of David C Cook. May not be further reproduced. All rights reserved.)

FINAL JUDGMENT

Hebrews 9:27 warns, "Just as people are destined to die once, and after that to face judgment."

At the end of the world, all humankind's bodies will be resurrected to face the final judgment. Then, their souls and the resurrected bodies will be eternally separated from God in the torment of hell. (More information about the end-time judgment and the supporting Scriptures in Part Four.)

I am aware that it sounds horrible. Some Bible interpreters even scoff at this, saying we should take the passages symbolically, not literally.

Incidentally, these Christians typically do not believe that Jesus actually bodily resurrected either. Despite the fact that it is explicitly stated in the Bible that Jesus showed the unbelieving Thomas the nail marks on his hands, and even ate a broiled fish in front of them (John 20:24-28; Luke 24:36-43).

I remember that in one of our home evangelistic meetings, a woman laughed when I mentioned the dire consequences of sin, saying it sounded like a horror movie.

On the other hand, a pastor once said that one day, the father of one of his church members came to the church and loudly complained to him, questioning, "If the judgment and hell is true, why have I not been told about it? It is a serious matter!"

I believe that while some descriptions in the Bible may be symbolic, many others are meant to be literally true, especially regarding the prophecies on the things to come, since they have been fulfilled literally.

I will expound more on the interpretation of the Bible, later in the section on the differences between the three branches of Christianity.

Why Would God Not Allow Adam and Eve to Eat from the Tree of the Knowledge of Good and Evil?

Some may be puzzled by such a command. It seems that the Devil had a point. Does God not want humans to have the knowledge of good and evil? Is it not a good thing for us to have?

First of all, I do not think it is about knowing good and evil. From the Bible's first book to the last one, it is full of the standard of good and evil. God wants us to know that.

WHO SHOULD BE BEST TO SET MORAL STANDARDS?

The critical question is, "Who should be best to say what is evil, and what is good; God, or humans?"

1 Kings 15:5 says,

"For David [King David] had done what was right *in the eyes of the Lord* and had not failed to keep any of the Lord's commands all the days of his life—except in the case of Uriah the Hittite."

1 Kings 15:25-26 records,

"[25] Nadab son of Jeroboam became king of Israel in the second year of Asa king of Judah, and he reigned over Israel two years. [26] He did evil in the eyes of the Lord, following the ways of his father and committing the same sin his father had caused Israel to commit."

It is apparent that according to the Scriptures, God should be the one that sets the moral standards. Although no specific reason is given in the Bible about this, it is not difficult to understand and accept.

A POSSIBLE EXPLANATION

I thought of what humans typically do when buying a brand-new car, especially those who care about safety. We would open the manual, read it carefully, make sure we know how to operate the vehicle, particularly on the new features, and check out if there are any safety warnings.

Nobody will say, "Why do I have to follow what the manual says? I can make my own decisions."

Because we know, it is the designers and the manufacturer of the car that built the car and wrote the manual. Only they know for sure how the new features work, what the procedures are to operate them, and if there are any safety precautions.

To illustrate the point, if the instruction manual cautions the driver not to exceed a speed of 55 miles an hour on a rainy day, due to the possibility of the new tires losing traction and causing your vehicle to spin out of control (*hydroplaning*), it would be best for us to heed this advice.

Those who respect and heed the warning will enjoy driving the car without having a preventable accident.

Likewise, if we believe that God created us, of course, it will be best that He tells us what is right and wrong, so we can enjoy living our lives safely and happily.

For example, Bible warns,

"Do not get drunk on wine, which leads to debauchery. Instead, be filled with the Spirit," (Ephesians 5:18).

If we drink too much, our bodies will not function well, to put it mildly. That is how we are made. We must be aware of our limitations.

It is sad to note that we hear this quite frequently, even from some celebrities, declaring, "There is no right or wrong, I do whatever I want."

Having said that, as stated before, God did not make us like robots; we are given free will to choose to either heed or ignore his forewarnings.

What Is the Goal of Transformation?

The Kingdom of God

Jesus' very first message, "'The time has come,' he said. 'The kingdom of God has come near. Repent and believe the good news!'" (Mark 1:15).

The end goal is to be able to enter The Kingdom of God, where there is eternal justice, peace, and joy.

But first, the broken relationship between mankind and God must be restored. We are under the condemnation of sins and are destined to die and face judgment. Thus, we must repent and believe the good news, so as to be reconciled with our Creator.

I will describe more specifics regarding the Kingdom of God in Part Four.

What Are the Means of Transformation?

Repent and Believe the Good News

Jesus said the way to go to the Kingdom of God is to repent and believe the good news. So, what was Jesus talking about regarding "the good news"?

THE GOOD NEWS

John 3:16 proclaims,

"For God so loved the world that he gave his one and only Son, that *whoever believes in him* [Jesus Christ] shall not perish but have eternal life."

By the way, we hear "Jesus Christ" all the time, even when somebody is cursing. Does his name have any particular meaning?

THE MEANING OF "JESUS"

Matthew 1:21 records about Jesus' birth,

"She [Mary] will give birth to a son, and you are to give him the name Jesus, [a] because he will save his people from their sins."

Footnotes
- a. *Jesus* is the Greek form of *Joshua,* which means *the Lord saves.*

The footnote points out that *Jesus* means *the Lord saves.*

THE MEANING OF "CHRIST"

It is the Greek word for *the anointed*, which is the word *Messiah* in Hebrew.

To summarize, *Jesus Christ* means the one *anointed* by God the Father, to *save* the world from their sins. In short, it means *the Anointed Savior.*

WHAT DOES "BELIEVE IN JESUS CHRIST" MEAN?

You may wonder what "believe in Jesus Christ" means. Chapter 32, "How you can truly be saved," will lay it out clearly for you.

Why Would God Not Stop the Sufferings Now?

When I was helping the Indo-Chinese refugees back in the early 1980s, I recall one young woman asking me, "Why would God not stop the sufferings now? Why is the end of the world still to come?"

She and her two younger sisters (both in their teens) had struggled through the chaos and brutalities of war in Cambodia. I am not sure exactly what happened to their parents and other family members, except they were the only ones who escaped from the Communist regime. It was tragic and must have been particularly painful for them.

I shared with them this passage:

"[8] But do not forget this one thing, dear friends: With the Lord a day is like a thousand years, and a thousand years are like a day. [9] The Lord is not slow in keeping his promise, as some understand slowness. Instead, he is patient with you, not wanting anyone to perish, but everyone to come to repentance "(2 Peter 3:8-9).

I said, "If Jesus comes right now, it would be to judge the world, and you will not have the opportunity to be saved." At the time, they were not Christians yet.

I also said, "On the Day of Judgment, all who shed innocent blood and did not repent of their crimes, will be held accountable. Justice will come to those who thought they had gotten away with murder."

It is common to hear some people say, "If there is God, He should stop the pains and injustices in the world right now." I understand the feeling; nevertheless, God wants us to have a chance to repent before that dreadful judgment day comes.

Why Did Jesus Have to Die in Order to Save Us?

God Is both Just and Merciful

He is just; therefore, the consequence of man's sin cannot be ignored. And that consequence is death. However, He is also merciful, sending Jesus to die for our sins.

It is called "substitutionary atonement".

That was what John the Baptist declared in John 1:29,

"The next day John saw Jesus coming toward him and said, 'Look, the Lamb of God, who takes away the sin of the world!." (For further explanation of such sacrificial love, refer to Philippians 2:5-8).

I thought of a possible illustration: On a freezing night, a father warned his son that he would be kicked out of the house and freeze in the cold if he violated a particular rule. But the son did it anyway. However, his mother chose to leave the house instead, so the son could be spared.

It Is a Relationship of Life and Love

This is not to say that the relationship between the three persons of the Triune God is the same as that of the human parents. Nevertheless, it is similar in the sense that, between God and humans, the relationship is one of life and love, like the relationship between parents and their children.

There are many occurrences in the Scriptures, where God the Father and God the Son use the relationship between parents and children to explain God's love for the humans He created.

For example, in Psalm 103:13, it says,

"As a father has compassion on his children, so the Lord [God the Father] has compassion on those who fear him."

As cited in Part One, Jesus says:

"[11] 'Which of you fathers, if your son asks for[a] a fish, will give him a snake instead? [12] Or if he asks for an egg, will give him a scorpion?

"[13] If you then, though you are evil, know how to give good gifts to your children, how much more will your Father in heaven give the Holy Spirit to those who ask him!" (Luke 11:11-13).

Footnotes
    a. Some manuscripts *for bread, will give him a stone? Or if he asks for*

What Is the Significance of the Virgin Birth of Christ?

Only the Sinless Can Die for the Sinful

Since all have sinned (Romans 3:23), no human being on Earth can die for us. Jesus was born by the Virgin Mary through the Holy Spirit, not from her husband Joseph (Matthew 1:18-20).

In addition, He committed no sins in his life on Earth either. Hebrews 4:15 states, "For we do not have a high priest who [Jesus] is unable to empathize with our weaknesses, but we have one who has been tempted in every way, just as we are—yet he did not sin."

Jesus Is the Eternal God the Son Who Exists before Mary

Colossians 1:16-17 tells us, "¹⁶ For in him [Jesus] all things were created: things in heaven and on earth, visible and invisible, whether thrones or powers or rulers or authorities; all things have been created through him and for him. ¹⁷ *He is before all things*, and in him all things hold together."

Jesus himself says,

"'Very truly I tell you', Jesus answered, 'before Abraham was born, I am!'" (John 8:58).

Mary did not give birth to a new life. Jesus always existed. He is God who came in the flesh (1 John 4:2).

Why Is Jesus the Only Way?

He Is Not Like Other Religions' Founders

It is remarkable that Jesus is unlike other religions' founders in many aspects. I will list three examples here.

SIDDHARTHA GAUTAMA VS. JESUS

Buddhism's founder, Siddhartha Gautama, was raised in luxury, yet he was unhappy and felt emptiness. He was further troubled by seeing people destined to get old, sick, and die.

He then left his family and wandered the country, trying to figure out the reason and the solution. He tried Hinduism and Jainism, but none worked for him. Finally, after enduring many difficult trial-and-errors, he claimed he had discovered the answer.

On the contrary, Jesus came and immediately proclaimed,

"*I am the way* and the truth and the life. No one comes to the Father except through me" (John 14:6).

He did not wander around in search of an answer to humans' afflictions. He says He is the answer, the truth, and He knows why there are sufferings in the world. He did not go out into the world and try to find a solution in other religions; He says He *is* the solution and *the only way* to fix the problem.

LAOZI VS. JESUS

Philosophical Daoism's founder Laozi, working as a government archivist, became troubled by the government's laws and bureaucracies, believing that it distorted the simplicity by which humans should live. He withdrew from society and resolved to live a solitary life.

Obviously, living alone would not solve his perceived problems for humankind, since only some have the space and resources to do the same as Laozi.

Jesus says that the root cause is our broken relationship with our Creator. It is our heart that needs to be changed. Solitary life will not solve the real issue.

Jesus tells us that everyone can restore that relationship, if one is willing to repent and believe that God sent him to save us, regardless of whether you live alone in the countryside or with many people in a crowded city.

ALL OTHERS VS. JESUS

Looking at the world's major religions, I have not found any of them say their founder died for them so that they can achieve their goal of transformation.

Even for someone like the Bodhisattvas (literally "a being [intended] for enlightenment") in Mahayana and Vajrayana Buddhism, they merely just "postponed final enlightenment and nirvana for himself or herself, in order to help other beings in their spiritual quests" (Young, p. 145).

Most importantly, Jesus says He is *God the Son* of the Trinity, who came in flesh to save us.

Is Jesus Not "Open" and "Tolerant"?

I understand some may strongly object to Jesus' assertion, given the prevailing sentiment of needing to be "open" and "tolerant".

But as I asked that sincere Buddhist on a flight to L.A., if there was only one medicine that could cure his wife's cancer, would he like his doctor to tell him the truth? His answer was a definite yes.

Yes, we need to be tolerant and open in the sense that we must respect the right of others to their own opinions, choices of lifestyle, or preferences of what faith to believe in, etc.

Nevertheless, this is about the truth and what it is. Jesus declares He is the only way to the truth, and "the truth will set you free" (John 8:30-32).

That said, He did not then, and does not now, use force to compel us to believe Him. It is up to us to decide.

Why Is Belief in Jesus Not a Blind Faith?

Jesus Proved His Divinity and Truthfulness with His Miraculous Works

Jesus did not just claim that He was the Son of God who came in the flesh to save the world, but also performed many miracles to prove it. He healed the blind, cast out demons, and even raised Lazarus from the dead (John 11:43-44).

John 20:30-31 writes,

"[30] Jesus performed many other [miraculous] signs in the presence of his disciples, which are not recorded in this book. [31] But these are written *that you may believe* [a] that Jesus is the Messiah [The anointed one], the Son of God, and that by believing you may have life in his name."
Footnotes
    a. Or *may continue to believe.*

However, some Jews still did not believe him and asked him,

"[24] ... 'How long will you keep us in suspense? If you are the Messiah, tell us plainly.'
"[25] Jesus answered, 'I did tell you, but you do not believe. The works [miracles] I do in my Father's name testify about me,
"'... [36] what about the one whom the Father set apart as his very own and sent into the world? Why then do you accuse me of blasphemy because I said, 'I am God's Son'?

"'37 Do not believe me unless I do the works of my Father. 38 But if I do them, *even though you do not believe me, believe the works* [*the miracles*], that you may know and understand that the Father is in me, and I in the Father'" (John 10:24-38).

In fact, one of the most critical miracles that Jesus did and continues to do even today, is that He frees those who trust Him from sins and gives them a new, joyful life - a new creation.

My forty years of changed life, which is still changing and growing, is one of those hundreds of millions of solid proofs.

How the FDA Approves a Medicine

It is interesting to note how we, in the 21st Century, will trust a particular medicine to be as effective as claimed and take it, risking our health and even possibly our lives, because it has received the FDA (the Federal Food and Drug Administration of USA)'s approval.

What the FDA does for the approval process is to examine the submitted results of clinical trials of a drug that the pharmaceutical company conducted.

According to the FDA's requirement, the size of the trial, at a later stage, is only 300 to 3,000 volunteers who have the disease or condition, for a length of study of 1 to 4 years (https://www.fda.gov/patients/drug-development-process/step-3-clinical-research, as of 2019).

I then think of the amazing transformations in the lives of hundreds of millions of born-again Christians throughout the past two thousand years, including myself, that have testified to the effectiveness of Jesus' regenerating power.

That is a "clinical trial" on the scale of tremendous "size" of so many millions of people, over a "length of study" of a vast period of thousands of years.

And it is still happening today.

I have no doubt that the Christian faith is a solid, time-tested truth. It has far more concrete proof than even our current 21st century requirements for the efficacy of medicinal treatment.

Is the Solution "Too Easy"?

I once heard a physicist commenting on YouTube:

"... It is too easy to have the meaning of life to come down from heaven to our lap. We have to work for it; we have to create our own meaning.

"... I'd say there is no equation out there that can give you meaning to your life, you have to find yourself. Search inside yourself, because that's where true meaning is going to be found, because if I tell you the meaning is the equation, you are not going to believe me..."

He made two arguments: first, it is too easy; second, we should be able to come up with our own solution.

Is Easiness a Problem?

I think in the search for truth, the question is not about whether it is easy or hard to find it but if it is true. As cited before, we now know that the force of gravity between any two masses follows a remarkably simple, straightforward rule: $F = (G \ast m1 \ast m2)/r^2$.

No scientists question its validity because that formula seems too easy or simple.

As a matter of fact, Einstein believes that there must be a formula that could even further unify all the known forces in the universe with just one simple formula, i.e., the forces of gravity, electromagnetism, strong force that binds together atomic nuclei, and a weak force that governs radioactive decay.

Is It Necessary that We Have to Find Our Own Solution?

It really does not matter whether it is from heaven, me, or others, as long as it is true.

To say, "we have to create our own meaning" and not accept something as accurate, simply because it is not from my own self, seems to be more like a personal attitude issue than the objective nature of finding what the truth is.

As referred to before, after the fall of Adam and Eve,

"We all, like sheep, have gone astray, each of us has turned to our *own way*; and the Lord has laid on him the iniquity of us all" (Isaiah 53:6).

Sadly, our self-centeredness and arrogance created such a dire situation. We do not want anybody to tell us what is true or what is right.

Consequently, there are no common principles among us. It is no wonder we cannot get along with each other. We want to have our own rules.

How Do I Know That the Bible Is Telling the Truth?

I have been quoting the Bible to answer many questions. Understandably, people want to know if the Bible is telling the truth. Can I trust what it says?

There are two aspects of this question:

Have the Manuscripts We Read Today Been Correctly Copied from the Original Writings, Since They Were Written Thousands of Years Ago?

THE OLD TESTAMENT (THE HEBREW BIBLE)

Dead Sea Scrolls (DSS)

In 1947, a young Bedouin stumbled upon several jars, containing leather scrolls in a cave near the northwest shores of the Dead Sea.

The first cave the young shepherd discovered contained seven scrolls. Between 1952 and 1956, ten more caves were found. Over eight hundred ancient Jewish manuscripts were eventually recovered.

According to Dr. Geisler,

"The DSS manuscripts date from the third century B.C. to the first century A.D. They include one complete Old Testament book, Isaiah, and thousands of fragments, which together represent every Old Testament book, except Ester. William F. Albright called this 'the greatest manuscript discovery of modern times.'"

(Norman L. Geisler, *Baker Encyclopedia of Christian Apologetics* (Grand Rapids, Michigan: Baker Books, 1999), p. 187. Used by permission of Baker Academic, a division of Baker Publishing Group.)

Through Carbon 14 dating, paleography (ancient writing forms), orthography (spelling), and archaeological dating, Dr. Geisler said,

"There was no reasonable doubt that the Qumran manuscripts came from the century before Christ and the first century A.D. Thus, they are *1000 years older than the Masoretic manuscripts* of the tenth century. Before 1947, the Hebrew text was based on three partial and one complete manuscript dating from about A.D. 1000.

"The scrolls give an overwhelming confirmation of *the faithfulness with which the Hebrew text was copied through the centuries.* By the tenth-century Masoretic copies, few errors had crept in.

"... Gleason Archer observes that the two copies of Isaiah discovered in Qumran Cave 1 'proved to be word for word *identical with our standard Hebrew Bible* [based on the Masoretic manuscripts of the tenth century] in more than 95 percent of the text. The 5 percent of variation consisted chiefly of obvious slips of the pen and variation in spelling'" (Ibid., p. 187).

It is breathtaking that two copies of the same book, though copied one thousand years apart, only have very few differences.

The utmost respect for the Scriptures

We can also see the utmost respect for the Word of God by the Jews since ancient times from this passage, which records what God told Moses to tell the person who would become the new king what to do with the Scriptures:

"[18] When he takes the throne of his kingdom, he is to write for himself on a scroll a copy of this law, taken from that of the Levitical priests.

"[19] It is to be with him, and he is to read it all the days of his life so that he may learn to revere the Lord his God and follow carefully all the words of this law and these decrees,

"[20] and not consider himself better than his fellow Israelites and turn from the law to the right or to the left.

Then he and his descendants will reign a long time over his kingdom in Israel" (Deuteronomy 17:18-20).

THE NEW TESTAMENT

The New Testament manuscripts were written in Greek. So far, scholars have counted more than 5,000 copies.

As stated by Dr. Geisler,

"It is not uncommon for classics from antiquity to survive in only a handful of manuscript copies. According to F. F. Bruce [*The New Testament Documents: Are They Reliable?*], nine or ten good copies of Julius Caesar's *Gallic War* survive, twenty copies of Livy's *Roman History* ... (Bruce, 16).

"The most documented ancient secular work is Homer's *Iliad*, surviving in 643 manuscript copies. Counting Greek copies alone, the New Testament text is preserved in some 5686 partial and complete manuscript portions that were copied by hand from the second (possibly even the first) through the fifteenth centuries ...

"... Most other ancient books are not nearly so well authenticated. New Testament scholar Bruce Metzger [*Chapters in the History of New Testament Textual Criticism*] estimated that the *Mahabharata* of Hinduism is copied with only about 90 percent accuracy and Homer's *Iliad* with about 95 percent. By comparison, he estimated the New Testament is about 99.5 percent accurate" (Norman L. Geisler, ibid., pp. 532-533).

Judging from the above data, one can be confident that the New Testament we read today is fundamentally the same as what was originally written by Jesus' apostles and his followers.

Is the Content True?

It is true in all senses of reality: scientifically, historically, and spiritually.

SCIENTIFICALLY

For instance, Isaiah 40:22 records,

"He [God] sits enthroned above the *circle* of the earth, and its people are like grasshoppers. He stretches out the heavens like a canopy, and spreads them out like a tent to live in."

Job 26:7-8 states,

"⁷ He spreads out the northern skies over empty space; *he suspends the earth over nothing.* ⁸ He wraps up the waters in his clouds, yet the clouds do not burst under their weight."

It was an observation that could only be seen from above the Earth.
It is stunning that even though the passage was written at least two thousand years ago, it correctly describes that the Earth is not flat and is suspended over nothing.
Scientists did not know or agree on these facts until only a few hundred years ago.
Even if one argues that ancient Greek astronomers might have found out about this also, Scripture's description has proven to be scientifically correct, whether the book of Job was written before or after the time of the ancient Greek period or not.
Furthermore, the Scriptures were written correctly, even in minute detail.
Luke 10:30 writes,

"In reply Jesus said: 'A man was going *down from Jerusalem to Jericho*, when he was attacked by robbers. They stripped him of his clothes, beat him and went away, leaving him half dead.'"

Since Jerusalem is on the mountain ridge area (about 2400 feet above sea level), and Jericho is down on the plain region (about 800 feet in elevation), Scripture correctly describes it geographically.

However, the Bible is not intended to be a comprehensive textbook on science. Nonetheless, when it is related to science, it is accurate.

In addition, keep in mind that science, as we know it, is limited compared to the vast universe out there. Moreover, we have to revise our understanding of the world all the time, because we are constantly learning new information.

For example, scientists are still unsure how the universe was started. That is why the current thinking is called the "Big Bang Theory." As for the question of what preceded the "Big Bang," different models have been proposed. We are still trying very hard to figure out how this tremendous universe began.

On the contrary, as mentioned before, according to Revelation 22:13,

"I [Christ] am the Alpha and the Omega, the First and the Last, the Beginning and the End."

As pointed out before, humans may know A, B, and is seeking to discover C, but God is A and Z. He is the ultimate. That is why the Scriptures have never had to be changed. But our science, as we know it, is changing constantly.

HISTORICALLY

Christians believe that archeology does confirm the historicity of the Bible. The following examples are some of the many discoveries.

On the Creation accounts

Dr. Geisler and Mr. Brooks write: "The recent discoveries of Creation accounts at Ebla confirm this [that the creation account in the Bible is historically true and is not a myth]. This library of more than 17,000 clay tablets predates the Babylonian account by about 600 years. The creation tablet is strikingly close to Genesis, speaking of one being who created the heavens, moon, stars, and earth. People at Ebla even believed in Creation from nothing."

    (Norman L. Geisler, Ron Brook, *When Skeptics Ask* (Grand Rapids, Michigan: Baker Books, 1996), p. 182)

On account of the invasion of Israel's Northern Kingdom by the Assyrians

"We have learned a great deal about the Assyrians, mostly because of 26,000 tablets found in the palace of Ashurbanipal, the son of Esarhaddon who had taken the Northern Kingdom in 722 B.C. … Several of these records confirm the Bible's accuracy.

    "*Every reference in the Old Testament to an Assyrian king has proven correct*. Even though *Sargon* [an Assyrian king] was unknown for some time, when his palace was found and excavated, there was a wall painting of the battle mentioned in Isaiah 20" (Ibid., pp. 198-199).

    Dr. Geisler is correct; we see the name of the king of Assyria, *Sargon*, clearly mentioned in verse 1 of Isaiah 20, which says, 'In the year that the supreme commander, sent by Sargon king of Assyria, came to Ashdod and attacked and captured it."

About the question regarding "Gallio, the proconsul of Achaia"

Acts 18:12 records, "While Gallio was proconsul of Achaia [a province of the Roman Empire, a part of today's Greece], the Jews of Corinth made a united attack on Paul and brought him to the place of judgment."

The designation of Gallio, the proconsul, was thought to be impossible. Yet Dr. Geisler writes, "... an inscription at Delphi [an ancient religious sanctuary dedicated to the Greek god Apollo] *notes this exact title* for the man, and it dates him to the time Paul was in Corinth (A.D. 51)" (Ibid., p. 201).

By the way, it is remarkable that the Scriptures would record events down to the specifics of the exact year and the month of the occurrences.

As an illustration, in 1 Kings 6:1, it states,

"In the four hundred and eightieth year after the Israelites came out of Egypt, in the fourth year of Solomon's reign over Israel, in the month of Ziv, the second month, he began to build the temple of the Lord."

It is evident that the Bible was written as a historical witness to what has, in fact, happened.

Biblical prophecies

On top of documenting what has happened in the past, the Scriptures also declare what will occur in the future throughout the Old and New Testaments.

In fact, there are hundreds of prophecies in the Bible.

Dr. Walvoord points out:

"... for about *one fourth of the Bible was prophecy when it was written*... the revelation of prophecy in Scripture serves as an important evidence that the Scriptures are accurate in their interpretation of the future. Because approximately half of the prophecies of the Bible have already been fulfilled in a literal way ...

"It justifies the conclusion that the Bible is inspired of the Holy Spirit and that prophecy which goes far beyond any scheme of man is instead a revelation by God of that which is certain to come to pass."

(John F. Walvoord, *The Prophecy Knowledge Handbook* (Colorado Springs, Colorado: Victor Books, 1990), p. 10. Used by permission of David C Cook. May not be further reproduced. All rights reserved.)

< *Why are there prophecies in the Bible?* >

The Bible answers this question directly,

"[9] Remember the former things, those of long ago; I am God, and there is no other; I am God, and there is none like me. [10] *I make known the end from the beginning*, from ancient times, what is still to come. I say, 'My purpose will stand, and I will do all that I please'" (Isaiah 46:9-10).

"[3] I foretold the former things long ago, my mouth announced them and I made them known; then suddenly I acted, and they came to pass. [4] For I knew how stubborn you were; your neck muscles were iron, your forehead was bronze.

"[5] Therefore I told you these things long ago; before they happened I announced them to you *so that you could not say,* 'My images brought them about; my wooden image and metal god ordained them'" (Isaiah 48:3-5).

God uses prophecies to prove to humankind that only He is the real God who can make things happen, not those idols humans made with their own hands.

Most importantly, it is to demonstrate that God is in control of history. And He has a plan for humankind's future. Whoever believes and heeds the advice and warnings of the prophecies will be blessed:

"Blessed is the one who reads aloud the words of this prophecy, and blessed are those who hear it and take to heart what is written in it, because the time is near" (Revelation 1:3).

"Look, I [Jesus] am coming soon [at the time of the end]! Blessed is the one who keeps the words of the prophecy written in this scroll [the Book of Revelation]" (Revelation 22:7).

In Part Four, we will cover the specifics regarding the end-time judgment on believers and non-believers, and how one can genuinely be saved.

< An example of fulfilled prophecies – Prediction about King Cyrus >

Prophet Isaiah predicted in Isaiah 44:24-28, that a king called Cyrus would allow the city of Jerusalem to be rebuilt after it was ruined:

"²⁴ This is what the Lord says— your Redeemer, who formed you in the womb: I am the Lord, the Maker of all things, who stretches out the heavens, who spreads out the earth by myself,

"²⁵ who foils the signs of false prophets and makes fools of diviners, who overthrows the learning of the wise and turns it into nonsense,

"²⁶ who carries out the words of his servants and fulfills the predictions of his messengers, who says of Jerusalem, 'It shall be inhabited,' of the towns of Judah, 'They shall be rebuilt,' and of their ruins, 'I will restore them,'

"... ²⁸ *who says of Cyrus*, 'He is my shepherd and will accomplish all that I please; he will say of Jerusalem, *'Let it be rebuilt,*' and of the temple, 'Let its foundations be laid.'"

This was an unusual prophecy, since the city and the temple (built by King Solomon) were still standing at the time of his writing. It was not destroyed, and reconstruction was not needed.

Furthermore, Dr. Walvoord writes, "The name of the person [Cyrus] is given *before he was born*..."

"... This prophecy of Isaiah was given *150 years before its fulfillment*. Cyrus, king of Medo-Persia, who conquered Jerusalem in 539 B.C., in the following year gave the Jews permission to return to their land and build a temple" (Walvoord, ibid., p. 111).

In addition, as referred to before, the reestablishment of the nation of Israel in 1948, after more than two thousand years of the dispersion of Jews, is one of the most astonishing examples of a fulfilled prophesy that the people of our recent generations can all witness.

Based on the fact that those prophecies predicted to occur in the past have materialized, I am convinced that those that are yet to come, as prophesied in the Bible, such as the day of judgment and the new heaven and the new earth, will undoubtedly come to pass too.

SPIRITUALLY

As commented under the previous question, "Why is belief in Jesus not a blind faith?" the transformations of the lives of tens of millions of born-again Christians testify to the truthfulness and the effectiveness of the Scriptures.

How About Those Miracles Recorded in the Bible, Are They Believable?

I worked in the computer industry for about 15 years. It is common knowledge that we can write codes to provide an override to a standard routine application.

That is why the cashier at a store can ask the manager to come and enter a code, so that the cashier can make an exception to the transaction at hand.

From that perspective, one will find that it is quite logical that God, who designed and created the world, can, of course, override the general physical laws, which God himself set in the first place.

Christianity Is a Foreign Religion to Me; Why Should I Accept It?

Some may reject Jesus because it is a foreign religion to them. However, if we are searching for the truth, then it should be universal and transcend any boundaries, like ethnic, cultural, or other barriers.

Many of us have no problem buying a particular brand of foreign-made car, because it is more dependable and safer. Many will purchase a smartphone if it is of superior quality and at a good price (or even at a higher price), regardless of where it is designed and made.

In search of the answers to the big questions, such as where we came from, where we are going, and what the meaning of life is, which are of the utmost seriousness for our life, should we let such thinking deprive us of the real answers?

What Are the Differences between the Three Major Branches of Christianity?

The History of the Three Branches

EARLY CHURCH ERA

As discussed before on the church and the state issue, for close to three hundred years since Jesus was crucified in 33 A.D., despite the Roman Empire's constant persecution, the early Christians persevered and continued to preach the gospel fearlessly but peacefully, and the faith continued to grow throughout the empire.

ROMAN CATHOLICISM

The persecution of Christians did not end until 313 A.D., when Emperor Constantine issued the Edict of Milan, making Christianity legal.

Furthermore, under the reign of Emperor Theodosius (379-395), Christianity was declared the empire's *official* religion. The state religion of Roman Catholicism and the Papacy began.

As spoken of before, it might sound good for Christianity. However, the opposite happened. Christianity, I believe, under the authoritarian rule of the Bishop of Rome, who was now both a political and religious power, became a tool of political dominance, exploitation, and oppression.

The clergies had the sole authority and wealth without any accountability.

For more than a thousand years, the Catholic Church brutally put down any opposition against its rule. Those who criticized the Church's corruptions or questioned its interpretations of the Scriptures were often condemned as a heretic and burned at the stake.

EASTERN ORTHODOXY

As the religious and political power of the Pope in Rome grew, with the Pope even claiming to be the head of all Christians, the patriarchs of the East refused to recognize it. This came to a head in 1054, when Pope Leo IX excommunicated the Patriarch of Constantinople, and Patriarch Michael Cerularius responded in kind, resulting in the "Great Schism" between the two Churches.

PROTESTANTISM

As noted before, in the early sixteenth century, under the German Martin Luther, the Protestant Reformation movement seriously challenged the absolute power and the abuse of the Roman Catholic Church.

Martin Luther was a Catholic priest and a professor, teaching Bible courses at the University of Wittenberg, Germany. Through studying the Scriptures, Luther became convinced that salvation was not for the Church to dispense through the sacraments; instead, it was God's free gift of grace, received by each individual through faith.

Furthermore, he was deeply troubled by the Pope's practice of selling the so-called indulgences, which the Roman Church claimed gave remission before God of temporal punishment due to sins.

In 1517, Luther posted his demands for change and reformation on the door of the castle church of

Wittenberg in the form of *Ninety-Five Theses*. Pope Leo X subsequently excommunicated Luther.

Fighting for religious freedom from the dictates of the Papacy ensued. Millions died.

With continued struggles between Protestant Christians and the Catholic Church, many Protestants in Germany and other parts of Europe finally gained their liberation, and restored the biblical teachings to what they should have been in the first place, as in the early church era: To freely worship God truly from our hearts without coercion.

Common Beliefs

Before we lay out the differences, it is essential to note that some aspects of the fundamental tenets of the three branches are the same, although each may have a different emphasis.

All believe in the Trinity, the incarnation of Christ, his crucifixion, and resurrection. All accept the problem, the cause, and the end goal of life as described in the Scriptures (but check below under "A word of caution").

Common Scriptures except for Minor Variations

All recognize the 66 books of the New and Old Testaments.

However, Catholicism has seven more books for the Old Testament, while Eastern Orthodoxy accepts an extra 12 books.

This is because Catholicism and Eastern Orthodoxy's Old Testaments are based not on the original Masoretic Hebrew Bible, but on the Greek translation, the *Septuagint*, which has these additional texts.

As for the New Testament, all three have exactly the same 27 books.

All the citations of the Scriptures in my book are from the 66 books recognized by the three branches.

A WORD OF CAUTION

It must be pointed out that while all three branches essentially hold common scriptures, their interpretations of them can be very different. It could happen even within the same branch.

Metaphorical or Literal?

For example, some regard the creation account of Adam and Eve as just a metaphor. In other words, it is like a fairy tale. It did not actually happen. Therefore, it does not contradict the evolution theory.

In fact, Pope John Paul declared:

"... The first account of man's creation, which, as we observed, is of a theological nature, conceals within itself a powerful *metaphysical content*... He [Adam] is defined in a way that is *more metaphysical than physical...*"

("*Analysis of the Biblical Account of Creation*," (General Audience, Wednesday 12 September 1979), as part of the series of Original Unity of Man and Woman, "*Catechesis on the Book of Genesis*," by Pope John Paul II, (General Audiences, 1979-1980).)

In his short analysis of the account of Creation, he invoked the word "metaphysical" five times. There is not a single instance in which he used the word "literal." And when he mentioned the word "physical," it was used to say, "It was more metaphysical than physical."

Apparently, Pope John Paul II holds the view that the account of Adam and Eve is not literally applicable. And he made sure that the Roman Church officially published it for all to know that.

Many Bible scholars and Christians strongly disagree with this interpretation.

The Scriptures do indeed use metaphorical language. Jesus sometimes employs parables to illustrate spiritual principles, like *The Parable of the Lost Son* in Luke 15:11-3.

Even for the record of Adam and Eve, some figures of speech are used. In describing the perpetual struggle between satanic forces and humankind, it says,

"And I will put enmity between you and the woman, and between your offspring[a] and hers; he will *crush*[b] *your head* [a fatal blow], and you will *strike his heel* [crippled mankind]" (Genesis 3:15).
Footnotes
  a. Or *seed*
  b. Or *strike*

However, keep in mind that though symbolic words are employed here, the prophetic message is still meant to be literally true: that Christ will defeat Satan in the end.

A dangerous slipping slope

Furthermore, it is a dangerous slipping slope, when one begins to treat even non-symbolic words as just figurative speech.

For instance, on the account of Adam and Eve, regarding the location of the Garden of Eden, Scripture painstakingly describes with actual geographic names:

"[10] A river watering the garden flowed from Eden; from there it was separated into four headwaters. [11] The name of the first is the *Pishon*; it winds through the entire land of Havilah, where there is gold. [12] (The gold of that land is good; aromatic resin[a] and onyx are also there.)

"¹³ The name of the second river is the *Gihon*; it winds through the entire land of Cush.[b] ¹⁴ The name of the third river is the *Tigris*; it runs along the east side of Ashur. And the fourth river is the *Euphrates*" (Genesis 2:10-14).
Footnotes
a. Or *good; pearls*
b. Possibly southeast Mesopotamia

From these detailed names of the lands and the rivers, scholars believe the Garden of Eden could likely be located in the Persian Gulf.

As for their descendants, from Adam to Noah, the genealogy is meticulously listed with specific names and the number of years each generation lived, starting with this verse,

"This is the written account of Adam's family line,"

And ending with this passage,

"After Noah was 500 years old, he became the father of Shem, Ham and Japheth" (Genesis 5:1-32).

It is abundantly clear that the intent of the author for the story of Adam and Eve is that it is a historical account.

Adam and Eve were real, literal, living human beings created by God, and had descendants. It is not metaphorical at all.

Therefore, the central point of the record, that humans were created by God (not evolved from some random acts of nature), that humans chose to rebel against God, that humankind is thus under the curse of sins, and that there will be a Savior to defeat Satan, should be best taken as the author intended: literally true.

The Present vs. the Ultimate

Some may feel pressured to try to make certain texts just figurative, so as to conform to whatever the current science claims.

Yes, with our telescopes, we have discovered that the Earth is circling the sun, and not the other way around. We have also been able to observe and calculate the laws of planetary motion.

Nevertheless, questions such as how humankind came to exist, is still a huge debatable issue.

As mentioned before, while we have learned a lot about our environment on Earth, and as much as we can regarding outer space, by looking as far as we could into the cosmos, we still know very little compared to what is out there.

Furthermore, our understanding will keep changing and revising as we continue to observe the universe.

The current notion that humans are just the result of some chance encounters of atoms, as the evolutionists claim, is highly hypothetical and premature.

As spoken of earlier, according to the Scriptures, God is the alpha and the omega (Revelation 22:13). He is the source of all knowledge. He is the ultimate science.

God's revealed words tell us the truth and have withstood the test of time for thousands of years. We can be confident in what it says literally, when it is meant to be literally true.

Major Differences

THE AUTHORITY

Roman Catholicism

The Pope: The doctrine of "papal infallibility" dictates that when a Pope is speaking in the capacity of his office on matters of faith and morals, his utterances are without error.

Eastern Orthodoxy

The patriarchs and bishops collectively: This branch consists of a number of independent national churches, for instance, the Greek Orthodox Church and the Russian Orthodox Church.

"The Orthodox Churches do not recognize the central authority of any one leader, believing that decisions should be made collectively, through the consensus of all patriarchs and bishops "(Young, p. 209).

Protestantism

The Scriptures: Protestants hold that Scripture *alone* is the standard by which church teachings should follow.

THE MEANS OF SALVATION

Roman Catholicism

Grace, faith, and the sacraments dispensed through the Church.

Eastern Orthodoxy

Orthodox teaching is similar to the Catholic Church in that God's grace is accessed through the Church, and the Church's sacraments are the instrument of divine grace.

Protestantism

Grace and faith: Humans are saved by each individual's personal response in faith to the grace of what God has done in Christ alone, not through merits or sacraments administered by the Church.

Additional Thoughts

CATHOLICISM

On the question of authority

The Roman Catholic Church claims that Peter and his successors (the Popes installed by the Catholic Church) hold the authority of all Christian churches, based on the passage of Matthew 16:16-19,

> "¹⁶ Simon Peter answered, 'You are the Messiah, the Son of the living God.' ¹⁷ Jesus replied, 'Blessed are you, Simon son of Jonah, for this was not revealed to you by flesh and blood, but by my Father in heaven. ¹⁸ And I tell you that you are Peter,[a] and *on this rock I will build my church*, and the gates of Hades[b] will not overcome it.
>
> "¹⁹ *I will give you the keys of the kingdom of heaven*; whatever you bind on earth will be[c] bound in heaven, and whatever you loose on earth will be[d] loosed in heaven.'"
> Footnotes
> a. The Greek word for *Peter* means *rock*.
> b. That is, the realm of the dead.
> c. Or *will have been*.
> d. Or *will have been*.

< *On what foundation is Christ's church built?* >

Catholic Church claims that *"this rock"* was Peter and his successors.

However, by examining the relevant Scriptures, it is evident that the church is built upon Jesus himself, not Peter:

Isaiah 28:16

Isaiah writes about the coming Messiah, "So this is what the Sovereign Lord says: 'See, I lay a stone in Zion, a tested stone, *a precious cornerstone for a sure foundation*; the one who relies on it will never be stricken with panic."

Matthew 21:42

Jesus says about himself, "Have you never read in the Scriptures [the Hebrew Bible]: 'The stone the builders rejected has become the *cornerstone* [Jesus]; the Lord has done this, and it is marvelous in our eyes'[a]?"
Footnotes
    a.   Psalm 118:22,23

1 Corinthians 3:3-11

Apostle Paul explicitly warns not to elevate any particular church leader:
"³ You are still worldly. For since there is jealousy and quarreling among you, are you not worldly? Are you not acting like mere humans? *⁴ For when one says, "I follow Paul," and another, "I follow Apollos," are you not mere human beings?*

"... *⁹ For we are co-workers* [no one is superior to any other] in God's service; you are God's field, God's building.

"¹⁰ By the grace God has given me, I laid a foundation as a wise builder, and someone else is building on it. But each one should build with care. ¹¹ *For no one can lay any foundation other than the one already laid, which is Jesus Christ."*

Galatians 2:11-13

Ironically, Peter was rebuked openly by Apostle Paul for hypocrisy:

"[11] When Cephas [Peter] came to Antioch, I opposed him to his face, because he stood condemned.

"[12] For before certain men came from James, he used to eat with the Gentiles. But when they arrived, he began to draw back and separate himself from the Gentiles because he was afraid of those who belonged to the circumcision group. [13] The other Jews joined him in his hypocrisy, so that by their hypocrisy even Barnabas was led astray."

As Peter's hypocrisy demonstrates, God built His church on the solid, perfect foundation of Christ, not on fallible humans.

Acts 4:8-11

Even Peter himself acknowledges it by referring to the exact passage of Psalm 118:22, which Jesus has told them before, "[8] Then Peter, filled with the Holy Spirit, said to them: 'Rulers and elders of the people! ... [11] Jesus is 'the stone you builders rejected, which has become the *cornerstone.*'[a]"

Footnotes
   a. Psalm 118:22

What did Peter think of himself?

Peter claims to be nothing more than just one of the twelve apostles, and one of many elders in many churches: "Peter, an apostle of Jesus Christ" (1 Peter 1:1); "To the elders among you, I appeal as a fellow elder" (1 Peter 5:1).

In fact, Peter prohibited anyone to bow down to him, saying,

"...'Stand up,'... 'I am only a man myself.'" (Acts 10:25-26).

Despite Peter's clear objection, seeing the Pope let people kneel before him even today is particularly disturbing. It is a serious offense to the one true God. Because only to God should people bow.

How did the church in Jerusalem regard Peter's role?

From the council meeting at Jerusalem, on the issue of the circumcision of the Gentiles, we can observe that Peter spoke, but others, like James, also did. In the end, the decision was made with collective consensus:

"*[22] Then the apostles and elders, with the whole church, decided* to choose some of their own men and send them to Antioch with Paul and Barnabas. They chose Judas (called Barsabbas) and Silas, men who were leaders among the believers" (Acts 15:6-22).

Obviously, neither Peter acted as if he was in charge of the church, nor did the church in Jerusalem regard him as such.

Above all, what did Jesus say about Peter?

It is interesting that at one time, the apostles actually got into an argument about which one of them was the greatest; Jesus cautioned:

"[25] Jesus said to them, "The kings of the Gentiles lord it over them; and those who exercise authority over them call themselves Benefactors.
"[26] But you are not to be like that. Instead, the greatest among you should be like the youngest, and *the one who rules like the one who serves*. [27] For who is greater, the one who is at the table or the one who serves? Is it not the one who is at the table? *But I am among you as one who serves*" (Luke 22:25-27).

Jesus clearly did not say any one of them was the greatest among them. Instead, He advised them not to think like pagans wanting to use power to lord it over people, but to serve, just as Jesus was serving them.

He then told the twelve apostles (not just Peter), that they *all* would sit on thrones to judge Israel's 12 tribes in the final judgment (Luke 22:30).

Peter was only one of many among the apostles and prophets

Peter did have a role in the building of the Church, but he was only one of many prophets and apostles who participated.

Ephesians 2:19-22 describes how it is built:

"[19] Consequently, you [the non-Jewish believers] are no longer foreigners and strangers, but fellow citizens with God's people and also members of his household, [20] built on the foundation of *the apostles and prophets*, with <u>Christ Jesus himself as the chief cornerstone</u>.

"²¹ In him [Christ] the whole building is joined together and rises to become a holy temple in the Lord. ²² And in him [Christ] you too are being built together to become a dwelling in which God lives by his Spirit."

But what was Jesus saying about Peter in Matthew 16:16-18?

Dr. Louis Barbieri, Jr. comments:
  "Peter (*Petros*, masc.) was strong like a rock, but Jesus added that on this rock (*Petra*, fem.), He would build His church.
  "Because of this change in Greek words, many conservative scholars believe that Jesus is now building His church on Himself… It seems best to understand that Jesus was praising Peter *for his accurate statement about Him [Jesus Himself]*, and was introducing His work of building the church on Himself (1 Cor. 3:11)."
  (Editors: John F. Walvoord and Roy B. Zuck, *The Bible Knowledge Commentary – An Exposition of the Scriptures by Dallas Seminary Faculty, New Testament* (Wheaton, Illinois: Victor Books, Eighth printing, 1988), p. 57. Used by permission of David C Cook. May not be further reproduced. All rights reserved.)
  It is also the position of the Eastern Orthodox Church:
  "… the Orthodox became ever clearer in their exegesis of the keys: the church was built upon Peter's confession of faith (which the Orthodox had preserved intact), *not upon Peter himself or his sometime wayward successors*. More recently, the Orthodox found the declaration of infallibility [of the Pope] almost as offensive as did Protestants."

(Editor: Walter A. Elwell, *Evangelical Dictionary of Theology* (Grand Rapids, Michigan: Baker Book House, Eighth printing, 1991), p. 823.)

< Who has the keys to the kingdom of heaven? >

Not just Peter, but all the disciples

Not long after Jesus told Peter about the keys to the kingdom of heaven, Jesus said,

"Truly I tell you [all the disciples], whatever you bind on earth will be[a] bound in heaven, and whatever you loose on earth will be[b] loosed in heaven" (Matthew 18:18).
   Footnotes
   a. Or *will have been.*
   b. Or *will have been.*

Dr. Wiersbe writes:
"Peter was given the privilege of opening 'the door of faith' to the Jews at Pentecost (Acts 2), to the Samaritans (Acts 8:14 ff), and to the Gentiles (Acts 10). But the other apostles shared this authority (Matt. 18:18), and Paul had the privilege of 'opening the door of faith' to the Gentiles outside of Palestine (Acts 14:27).

"Nowhere in this passage, or in the rest of the New Testament, are we told that Peter or his successors had any special position of privilege in the church."

(Warren W. Wiersbe, *Be Loyal (Matthew) – Discovering the excitement of knowing and serving the King of Glory* (Wheaton, Illinois: Victor Books, 1980), p. 113. Used by permission of David C Cook. May not be further reproduced. All rights reserved.)

As a matter of fact, all believers are "Ambassadors of Christ."

Apostle Paul tells the people at the church of Corinthian:

"[17] Therefore, if anyone is in Christ, the new creation has come:[a] The old has gone, the new is here! [18] All this is from God, who reconciled us to himself through Christ and gave us the ministry of reconciliation:

"[19] that God was reconciling the world to himself in Christ, not counting people's sins against them. And he has committed to us the message of reconciliation. [20] *We are therefore Christ's ambassadors*, as though God were making his appeal through us. We implore you on Christ's behalf: Be reconciled to God" (2 Corinthians 5:17-20).
   Footnotes
      a. Or Christ, that person is a new creation.

The Great Commission for all believers of all time

Furthermore, as cited before, in Matt. 28:18-20, Jesus gave the great commission to His followers, not just the apostles, but also to all believers (Luke 24:33), before He ascended to heaven.

< *To sum up regarding the question of authority* >

Regarding the foundation of the Church, Jesus himself is the chief cornerstone upon which the Church is built. Peter was only a small part of God's plan, among many prophets and other apostles.

It is especially noteworthy that even for the future city of New Jerusalem, it says explicitly that on the twelve foundations of the city's wall, there are the names of the twelve apostles.

Peter is just one of the twelve equally named (Revelation 21:14).

As for the keys to the kingdom of heaven, one can undeniably conclude from the Scriptures that sharing the good news of the kingdom of heaven is not just Peter's responsibility and privilege, but also that of all the disciples.

In fact, the great commission is for all believers to be the ambassadors of Christ to the people of the world until the end comes.

The assertion that only Peter and his supposed successors have the power of the keys of the kingdom of heaven, fundamentally misconstrues what Jesus is saying in Matthew 18:18, and ignores all other relevant passages of the Bible.

In short, the Scriptures do not support the Catholic Church's claim that Peter and his successor hold supreme authority over the entire Christian Church.

This claim is frankly a blatant violation of the clear and critical biblical teachings.

On the means of salvation

As said earlier in Part Two, it is a free gift from God. Ephesians 2:8-9 declares,

"^{8} For it is by grace you have been saved, through faith— and this is not from yourselves, it is the *gift* of God— ^{9} *not by works, so that no one can boast.*"

It is free, not because it is cheap, but because so that no one can brag about it. No good deeds or money can buy it. We are saved by God's grace and through our faith in Jesus alone. Nothing else is required.

The Catholic Church claims that merits such as various sacraments and charitable deeds are required for salvation.

Some may cite the passage in the Book of James (2:14-19) for support. But James is not saying works is a part of the condition of salvation, but is pointing out that genuine faith will be evidenced by good deeds. A truly born-again Christian will naturally *want* to help and love people, because he or she has been transformed from the inside out and will show genuine faith through actions.

In other words, good deeds are the result of being born again and saved. They are not the condition of salvation.

Martin Luther rightly called the Catholic Church's selling indulgences, violating this fundamental scriptural principle.

In fact, Apostle Peter personally condemns such behavior:

"[20] Peter answered: "May your money perish with you, because you thought you could buy the gift of God with money! ..." (Acts 8:20-23).

On the veneration of Mary (Mariolatry)

< Do we need any intercessors other than Christ? >

As stated in Part Two, Jesus is our high priest. Christians can pray to God through Jesus (Hebrews 4:14-16) for assistance in our time of need.

Jesus says,

"And I will do whatever you ask *in my name*, so that the Father may be glorified in the Son" (John 14:13).

Apostle Paul writes,

"For there is one God and *one mediator* between God and mankind, the man Christ Jesus" (1 Timothy 2:5).

No other intermediary, not the Pope, Mary, or any saints, is needed. There is no scriptural support for such additional intercessors, once Jesus' redemption work was completed on the cross (Hebrews 8:6; 9:15).

< Is Mary sinless? >

Mary was a devoted, blessed servant of God, but she was only a human.
Mary herself says,

"My soul glorifies the Lord and my spirit rejoices in God *my Savior*" (Luke 1:46-47).

Only sinners need a savior. Mary personally admits her own guilt and her need for salvation.
As mentioned before, all have sinned (Romans 3:23); there is no exception, not Abraham, Moses, the Apostles, Mary, or anyone.
Venerating any human beings or praying to any of them, including Mary, is a distraction from, and an offense to, the one true Savior and mediator. (More is elaborated on this subject under "Jesus is your high priest" in Part Four.)

On making statues/images

As indicated before, the second one of the Ten Commandments in the Bible strongly warns against making and worshiping any man-made objects.
But in countries like Spain, it is concerning that one can find statues of Mary prominently erected in many churches. In one church, as part of the annual religious

event, a throne of Mary weighing several tons carried by several hundred bearers is paraded around the city.

< Israelites who bore and paraded idols >

God has specifically warned the Israelites, who also bore and paraded idols:

> "[1] Bel bows down, Nebo stoops low; their idols are borne by beasts of burden.[a] The images that *are carried about* are burdensome, a burden for the weary. [2] They stoop and bow down together; unable to rescue the burden, they themselves go off into captivity.
>
> "[3] Listen to me, you descendants of Jacob, all the remnant of the people of Israel,
>
> you whom I have upheld since your birth, and have carried since you were born. [4] Even to your old age and gray hairs I am he, I am he who will sustain you. I have made you and *I will carry you*; I will sustain you and I will rescue you" (Isaiah 46:1-4).
>
> Footnotes
> a. Or *are but beasts and cattle*

"Bel" and "Nebo" were Babylonian's gods. On Babylon's New Year's Day festival, large images of those gods were carried about in the city.

It is ironic that the heavy idols they made, not only had to be lifted by themselves and were burdensome to them, but the idols also could not prevent the Israelites from being conquered either. At the same time, the true God, Jehovah, needs no men to carry Him and can actually "carry" (support and rescue) them.

< The foolishness of worshiping idol >

God further admonished Israelites for the foolishness of worshiping objects made by man:

"⁵ With whom will you compare me or count me equal? To whom will you liken me that we may be compared?
⁶ Some pour out gold from their bags and weigh out silver on the scales; they hire a goldsmith to make it into a god, and they bow down and worship it.
"⁷ They lift it to their shoulders and carry it; they set it up in its place, and here it stands. *From that spot it cannot move.* Even though someone cries out to it, it cannot answer; it cannot save them from their troubles" (Isaiah 46:5-7).

In Taiwan, one of the annual major religious festivities is for the statue of "Ma-Tsu," a Chinese sea goddess, to be carried out of the temple and paraded all over the island.

I appreciate Catholics' sincerity about their belief and their desire to please Mary. Carrying her statue weighing tons is not an easy task.

Nevertheless, watching the parade, I wondered what the difference between it and pagan idol worship was. It ironically offends the only true living God, the Trinity, who finds veneration of any man-made objects distasteful.

On the issue of separation of church and state

Today, although the Pope no longer possesses both religious and political power, and hence cannot force people to accept its doctrines, the Catholic Church still has serious issues, I believe, in the following two areas:

< *Structural corruptions still exist* >

Because it retains its rigid, hierarchical, and secretive church polity, there is still a lack of accountability of the clergies' behavior to the outside world, and this creates opportunities for abuse.

For instance, as the case reported below in Boston revealed, priests who sexually abused children in their parishes, were often simply moved from one place to another, and were allowed to continue their despicable acts for years. Incidents in U.S. cities and countries around the world, have been ignored or even covered up.

The Scandal in Boston

Newsweek prints in its cover story, *"Sex, Shame and the Catholic Church – 80 Priests Accused of Child Abuse in Boston – And New Soul-Searching Across America"*:

"For years, Boston's cardinal kept on priests who had been accused of molesting children. Now Catholics across America are confronting similar scandals and questioning the secretive culture of the church" (Newsweek, March 4, 2002, pp. 43-45).

The Abuse in the Vatican

Even after the explosive exposure of this magnitude in Boston, this kind of problem appears to continue. It even allegedly happened in the city of the Vatican itself.

The National Public Radio (NPR) of the United States reports:

"Two priests are going on trial in the Vatican court — one accused of sexually abusing an altar boy and the other charged with aiding and abetting the alleged abuse, which allegedly took place at the St. Pius X youth seminary. The seminary's residents are known as the 'pope's altar boys' and serve Mass in St. Peter's Basilica."

(Sylvia Poggioli, *Vatican Court Hears Unprecedented Sexual Abuse Criminal Trial*," NPR, October 26, 2020, 4:52 PM ET.)

The Instructions that do not go far enough

As of 2020, while the Church has made some measures to deal with this systemic problem, it does not seem to be serious enough to address it.

Check the report written by Elisabetta Povoledo for details, *"Vatican Tells Bishops to Report Sex Abuse to Police (but Doesn't Require It)"* (New York Times, Published July 16, 2020, Updated October 21, 2020).

< Troubling agenda >

The Assisi Prayer Service

I can still recall vividly reading a news report in 1986 that Pope Johan Paul II invited the leaders of all major religions (African and American Indian Animism, Hinduism, Buddhism, Japanese Shintoism, Judaism, Islam, etc.) to Assisi, Italy, and held a prayer service in which each *pray to their own god or gods* for world peace.

It was quite troubling that such a thing could happen.

Although he said, "The fact that we have come here does not imply any intention of seeking a religious consensus among ourselves or of negotiating our faith convictions" (Roberto Suro, New York Times, October 28, 1986, Section A, Page 3 of the National edition with the headline: "*12 Faiths Join Pope to Pray for Peace*"), he allowed this to happen:

"... The Buddhists, led by the Dalai Lama, quickly *converted the altar* of the Church of San Pietro by *placing a small statue of the Buddha atop the tabernacle* and setting prayer scrolls and incense burners around it" (Ibid., New York Times).

In fact, he also willingly accepted idols from Buddhists as gifts to him later in the 1990s.

It is good that all religions should seek to advance world peace. However, many of these beliefs are mutually exclusive and could not be all true. Therefore, it raised the question of whether these prayers to different perceived deities could be effective.

Furthermore, the Bible explicitly warns: "[3] 'You shall have no other gods before (Or *besides*) me. [4] You shall not make for yourself an image [idol] in the form of anything in heaven above or on the earth beneath or in the waters below'" (Exodus 20:3-4).

It is the very first of the Ten Commandments, which the Pope is supposed to uphold. It is detestable in the eyes of the one true God to accept idols.

For example, Buddhism does not believe or seek to have anything to do with one true God. They are either spiritual atheists (Theravada Buddhism), or polytheists (Mahayana and Vajrayana Buddhism).

Though the Pope did not "worship" other gods per se, inviting and willingly allowing a Buddhist to convert a Christian sanctuary to a Buddhist temple to worship a different deity, and also accepting a Buddhist idol as a gift, is concerning.

What is the cause of wars?

According to the Scriptures, the reason that there have been wars (and many different religions) is the result of humanity's rejection of the one true God, and hence, as mentioned before, "We all, like sheep, have gone astray, each of us has turned to our own way" (Isaiah 53:6).

Pope John Paul II's invitation to all religious leaders to pray to their own god or gods for world peace ignored this specific warning.

It is appalling and offensive to the one true God.

John Paul II said at the event, "... If there are many and important differences among us, is it not true to say that at the deeper level of humanity, there is a common ground whence to operate together in a solution of this dramatic challenge of our age: true peace or catastrophic war?" (Ibid., New York Times)

His remark is apparently saying we may be praying to different gods; still, it is not as important as our shared desire for peace.

He was proposing that we humans can solve our own problems, as long as we all desire to have peace, and that, by the way, it does not matter much that we are praying to different god or gods.

Nonetheless, according to the Scriptures, it is our bowing down to our own perceived masters, while rejecting the one true God, that has resulted in our being under the curse of sin, and thus not being able to live peacefully with each other in the first place.

It is deeply dismaying that he ignored this clear and crucial Biblical truth.

It seems that the Catholic Church, having lost its political and military power to force people to accept its doctrines, is now doing a 180-degree turn, and downplaying the differences between religions, saying all religions are now welcome to practice whatever they want, and the differences do not matter anymore.

Perhaps he was still hoping to play a leadership role, at least in the religious world, but sadly, at the expense of Christian spiritual principles.

Some may be troubled and wonder why this could even happen.

The Woman on the Beast

Revelation 17:3-6 describes a woman regarding things to come:

"³ Then the angel carried me [Apostle John] away in the Spirit into a wilderness. There I saw a woman sitting on a scarlet beast that was covered with blasphemous names and had seven heads and ten horns.

"⁴ The woman was dressed in purple and scarlet, and was glittering with gold, precious stones and pearls. She held a golden cup in her hand, filled with abominable things and the filth of her adulteries. ⁵ The name written on her forehead was a mystery:

> BABYLON THE GREAT
> THE MOTHER OF PROSTITUTES
> AND OF THE ABOMINATIONS OF THE EARTH.

"⁶ I saw that the woman was drunk with the blood of God's holy people, the blood of those who bore testimony to Jesus. When I saw her, I was greatly astonished."

Dr. Walvoord explains:

"The woman was dressed in purple and scarlet, and was glittering with gold, precious stones, and pearls. Her adornment is similar to that of religious trappings of ritualistic churches today... here they reveal a false religion that prostitutes the truth...

"... The Bible is full of information about Babylon as the source of false religion... Crowns in the shape of a fish head were worn by the chief priests of the Babylonian cult to honor the fish god.

"The crowns bore the words 'Keeper of the Bridge,' symbolic of the 'bridge' between man and Satan. This handle was adopted by the Roman emperors, who used the Latin title *Pontifex maximus*, which means 'Major Keeper of the Bridge.'

"And the same title was later used by the bishop of Rome. The Pope today is often called the *pontiff,* which comes from *pontifex.*

"When the teachers of the Babylonian mystery religions later moved from Pergamum to Rome, they were influential in paganizing Christianity and were the source of many so-called religious rites which have crept into ritualistic churches.

"Babylon then is the symbol of apostasy and blasphemous substitution of idol-worship for the worship of God in Christ."

(Editors: John F. Walvoord and Roy B. Zuck, *The Bible Knowledge Commentary – An Exposition of the Scriptures by Dallas Seminary Faculty, New Testament* (Wheaton, Illinois: Victor Books, Eighth printing, 1988), p. 970-971. Used by permission of David C Cook. May not be further reproduced. All rights reserved.)

The Roman Church's historical violent persecution of anyone who opposed it in the past, Pope John Paul II's problematic behavior, and the subsequent Popes' permissive approach toward other religions today, appear to be consistent with the related aspects of the description regarding the woman.

It would be alarming if the Papacy is what Scripture predicts the coming of the spiritually adulterous and physically violent entity symbolized by the woman on the beast.

How to achieve real peace

If there is only one true God, then there is only one effective authority, and the best way to live is according to the way prescribed by that authority.

Praying to other perceived deities will offend the real one and, in fact, will be an obstacle to real peace.

I am not saying we should engage in violent religious warfare.

As mentioned, countless Protestant Christians lost their lives fighting for their religious freedom from the Roman Catholic Church's oppression. It should not happen again.

We should always respect the people's right to worship according to their own conscience.

However, it is critical that we recognize that not all faiths are the same, and that they are actually mutually exclusive.

What should be the focus for every one of us human beings?

We should urgently seek and find out what the spiritual realities are before the end of time comes. Only when we find the truth and respond correctly can real peace come.

For example:

- Is there God?
- Is there only one God, or are there many gods?
- Is Christ the only way, as he claims he is?
- What are the spiritual truths?

I am talking about civil, non-violent pursuit of the answer, while respecting the freedom of worship for the believers of other faiths.

That is why I wrote this book.

Ignoring these conflicting views and continuing praying to our own favored master or masters, or just relying on our own desire to have peace, is the opposite of what we should be doing.

It is like we are burying our heads in the sand.

According to the Bible, the real eternal world peace can only be realized when Jesus comes again at the time of the end, and the world is united under His reign.

Those who believed in Him will be part of that kingdom of eternal peace.

To sum up my additional thoughts regarding Catholicism

Although the Catholic Church tried to modify somewhat some of its most controversial teachings, such as the so-called papal infallibility and Marian veneration (as in the Vatican Council II, convened in 1962), overall, it remains a very problematic branch of Christianity, in terms of its doctrinal, structural, and agenda issues.

Having said that, many Catholic Christians probably are not aware of these concerns.

I do not doubt that many of them, especially the lay believers, are indeed born again and are sincere followers of Christ, if they believe and confess that Jesus is their Lord and Savior.

EASTERN ORTHODOXY

Its historic collective leadership has made it less susceptible to abuse and corruption.

However, since it is often the dominant religion in the countries of Eastern Europe, I feel that people might easily become just cultural Christians.

This would be a similar concern in Catholic states like Italy and Spain, or predominantly Protestant countries like England and Scotland as well, although church attendance in the last two nations is declining.

Nonetheless, like Catholic parishioners, I will not be surprised that many Eastern Orthodox adherents are devoted followers of Christ, and are truly born again, if they believe and confess that Jesus is their Lord and Savior.

PROTESTANTISM

"Sola Scriptura"

As noted before, the authority of the church, according to the Scriptures, is not the Pope. Neither is any person, such as a particular popular Protestant pastor.

The authority for Christian faith and practice rests solely upon Scripture itself, as the Latin phrase *Sola Scriptura ("by Scripture alone")* means.

Apostle Paul earnestly warns the church at Corinth, not to follow any person or anything but the inspired Scriptures:

"[6] Now, brothers and sisters, I have applied these things to myself and Apollos for your benefit, so that you may learn from us the meaning of the saying, *"Do not go beyond what is written."*

"Then you will not be puffed up in being a follower of one of us over against the other. [7] For who makes you different from anyone else? What do you have that you did not receive? And if you did receive it, why do you boast as though you did not?" (1 Corinthians 4:6-7).

From early church believers, we can also see that it is the Scriptures that one should depend on to discern whether what is said is true or not:

"Now the Berean Jews were of more noble character than those in Thessalonica, for they received the message with great eagerness and *examined the Scriptures every day to see if what Paul said was true*" (Acts 17:11).

This principle is reflected in the Protestant Church's services that center on the teachings of the Bible, especially on how to apply it to our everyday lives.

Catholic mass may also include some homily time, but it is relatively short. The mass seems to focus on performing a variety of rituals.

< *Catholic Church's traditions* >

The Council of Trent in 1546 (the Roman Catholic Church's conference) decreed that the traditions of the Catholic Church (as declared by the papal pronouncements) had equal authority with Scripture.

As shown before, the numerous papal claims and practices, such as purporting that the Roman Catholic Church has the authority over all Christion churches; requiring sacraments and good deeds, in addition to faith for salvation; venerating Mary; and erecting images and statutes, etc., are in direct contradiction to the clear teachings of the Scriptures.

By its actions, in effect, it asserts that the Pope has higher authority than Scripture, not just equal to it.

As referred to before regarding Islam about prophecy, Jesus warns:

"¹⁸ I warn everyone who hears the words of the prophecy of this scroll: If anyone *adds anything* to them, God will add to that person the plagues described in this scroll.
"¹⁹ And if anyone *takes words away from* this scroll of prophecy, God will take away from that person any share in the tree of life and in the Holy City, which are described in this scroll" (Revelation 22:18-19).

While the above passage regards the things to come, it can be inferred that God's revelation to humankind was completed after Jesus revealed it to the Apostle John, who wrote down the Book of Revelation in the first century A.D.

Nothing is allowed to be added to, or taken away from, what has been revealed after the last book of the Bible, the Revelation, was completed. It is final.

The Roman Catholic Church's edicts that countermand and or add to the completed teachings of the Scriptures are dangerous and ignore the forewarning given by Christ himself.

Saved by grace through faith

As explained under "My thoughts" regarding Catholicism, contrary to the Catholic Church's position, Protestantism holds that people are saved by God's grace, through his or her faith in Christ alone, not by works.

In Part Four, we will detail the specific actions one can take regarding how to be born again.

No statues/images in the church

To avoid venerating idols, one will typically not find statues or images in Protestant sanctuaries except a simple cross symbol. Protestant Christians respect but do not venerate Mary or any saints.

Anabaptist movement

The Protestant Reformation has two major wings. One is Lutheran (by Martin Luther) and Reformed (by Calvin), and the other is the Anabaptist movement.

In addition to the beliefs in the authority of the Bible and justification by faith alone, the Anabaptist movement further advocates the believer's baptism and the separation of church and state, among other teachings.

< Believer's Baptism >

Denominations like the Baptists and the Mennonites stress the importance of only baptizing those who are old enough to be able to make a personal confession of faith in Jesus, as contrasted to infant baptism.

< Separation of church and state >

As noted before, Protestant Christians restored what Christianity should be in the first place, and how it looked in the early church era: To freely worship God genuinely from our hearts without compulsion.

As Jesus says,

"Yet a time is coming and has now come when the true worshipers will worship the Father *in the Spirit and in truth*, for they are the kind of worshipers the Father seeks" (John 4:23).

These Protestants strongly believe in the separation of church and state, freedom of religion, and, accordingly, also the freedom of speech, so that all can freely search for truth and practice their faith according to their conscience.

Congregational church polity

In marked contrast to the Catholic Church's strict top-down hierarchical structure ruled by the Pope, many Protestant churches, for example, the United Church of Christ and the Baptists in the U.S., are governed by local congregations, based on the principle of the "*priesthood of all believers*" (1 Peter 2:9). Each local church is subject to its own members' collective check and balance.

"Congregationalism maintains that local congregations, consisting of men and women who acknowledge the Lordship of Jesus Christ and seek his will, can minister and govern themselves through congregational vote, covenant, and participation.

"Congregationalists view this polity as a more complete fulfilment of the Reformation principle of the priesthood of all believers.

"... Historical Congregationalism came to America with the Separatist Pilgrims of Plymouth and the Puritans of the Massachusetts Bay Colony."

(Coordinating editor: Daniel G. Reid, *Dictionary of Christianity in America*, (Downers Grove, Illinois: InterVarsity Press, 1990), p. 309)

Congregational polity does not guarantee a corruption-free church, but it can act as a deterrent against possible wrongdoings.

Above all, I believe it is structured according to the early church's organization, the Scriptures' teaching regarding the "priesthood of all believers," and the fact that there is no scriptural support for the sole papal primacy as discussed before.

As for church leaders, Scripture cautions:

"² Be shepherds of God's flock that is under your care, watching over them—not because you must, but because you are willing, as God wants you to be;

"not pursuing dishonest gain, but eager to serve; ³ *not lording it over* those entrusted to you, *but being examples to the flock*. ⁴ And when the Chief Shepherd [Christ] appears, you will receive the crown of glory that will never fade away" (1 Peter 5:2-4).

We are not to use our position in the church to amass power and wealth for ourselves, but to serve and live an exemplary life.

It is an excellent reminder for all who wish to minister in the church.

SUMMARY OF MY ADDITIONAL THOUGHTS REGARDING THE THREE BRANCHES

I conclude that Protestantism overall is most consistent with the biblical teachings of the Scriptures. However, again, I do not doubt that there are believers in other branches of Christianity who are indeed born again, if they trust and accept Jesus as their Lord and Savior from their hearts.

Why Would Some Christians Vote for an Apparently Amoral Political Candidate?

People may be puzzled, or even disgusted, by seeing some Christians vote for an apparently amoral candidate. I completely get that.

As a matter of fact, I was also quite upset and sad when this happened. I am particularly concerned that some might misconstrue what Christianity is really about, and thus miss the opportunity to be saved.

Possible Reasons

FALSE RELIGIOUS ELITES

Jesus reserved the most scathing rebuke for the religious elites at the time when He was ministering to the people in Galilee and Judea:

"^{27} Woe to you, teachers of the law and Pharisees, you hypocrites! You are like whitewashed tombs, which look beautiful on the outside but on the inside are full of the bones of the dead and everything unclean.

"^{28} In the same way, on the outside you appear to people as righteous but on the inside you are full of hypocrisy and wickedness" (Matthew 23:27-28).

Unfortunately, this hypocrisy has continued throughout the church's history, and will get even worse in the future. Jesus forewarns that there will be false teachers, false prophets, and even false Christs, when the end of time approaches:

"^{22} For false messiahs and false prophets will appear and perform signs and wonders to deceive, if possible, even the elect. ^{23} So be on your guard; I have told you everything ahead of time" (Mark 13:22-23).

SECULAR CHURCH ATTENDANTS

Such people are in the church for social connections, personal business opportunities, or reasons other than religious ones.

I still can recall meeting a person from mainland China in a church a while ago, who said to me, "I am a 'Christian' because it is the mainstream religion in America; if I were in Iran, I would be a 'Muslim'."

I must say I was surprised and dismayed by his seemingly candid, unapologetic admission.

NOMINAL CHRISTIANS

Some people may think they are Christians, but might not be born again. I was such a person before I was truly saved. Without the Holy Spirit inside them for guidance, they are not acting much differently than nonbelievers.

POLITICAL PARTISAN BELIEVERS

I remember right before a recent presidential election, a leader in a Bible study of a church said, "I guess we have to hold our noses and vote for him. "

Unfortunately, some may be genuinely saved, but are tempted and give in to partisan politics or tribalism.

These people would say, "He may be a bad guy (or even worse expression), but he is *our* bad guy."

However, I believe partisan politics should not be in Jesus' church. At the end of the world, it is in front of Christ's judgment seat, not before a particular earthly political party's boss, that Christians will be held accountable for what they did and spoke.

MISINFORMED CHRISTIANS

The last probable reason is that there might be misinformed Christians. Some may be genuine believers and sincerely think they are advocating for God, thinking they must accept a candidate, no matter what, because of a particular moral issue.

First, will God use a very immoral person who continues sinning to accomplish a good cause?

The prophets God raised in the Old Testament era, and the apostles Jesus called in the New Testament times, were all of good character. Although they were imperfect and made mistakes at times, they were God-fearing and upright people overall.

Even in the case of Apostle Paul, though he was persecuting Christians before Jesus revealed to him on the road to Damascus, he was a *changed person* and was filled with the Holy Spirit, when he started to serve Jesus and preached the gospel (Acts 9:17).

Paul served God honorably and behaved righteously after being called and transformed on that road to Damascus.

Some may think of Judas, who betrayed Jesus later on. But as soon as he did that, he committed suicide. Jesus did not let him continue to serve as his disciple, even though he was filled with sorrow and regretted what he did (Matthew 27:3-5).

As for the kings that God chose to rule Israel, when King Saul started to disobey God's commands and became arrogant, God raised David to replace him (1 Samuel 15: 23-25; 16: 1-13). Throughout Israel's history, God would punish bad kings without mercy.

While there may be exceptions, it would be highly unusual that God will use an immoral person who *continues to sin* to serve Him, especially in the context of choosing a leader of our country.

We must be careful when making decisions; be sure to base them on sound biblical ground and not on a misunderstanding of what the Bible teaches.

Second, regarding advocating for a particular moral issue

There is a good reason why there are Ten Commandments, not just one, in the Bible. Christianity is not about a specific sin. On the contrary, it is about "*All* have sinned" (Romans 3:23).

When the religious leaders brought in a woman caught in adultery and said to Jesus,

"Teacher, this woman was caught in the act of adultery. ⁵ In the Law Moses commanded us to stone such women. Now what do you say?" ⁶ They were using this question as a trap, in order to have a basis for accusing him."

Jesus said:

"⁷ ... Let any one of you who is without sin be the first to throw a stone at her.

"⁹ At this, those who heard began to go away one at a time, the older ones first, until only Jesus was left, with the woman still standing there. ¹⁰ Jesus straightened up and asked her, "Woman, where are they? Has no one condemned you?" (John 8:4-6, 7, 9-10).

It is clear that one must be careful not to single out a specific sin. Generally speaking, we must consider all the issues, such as abortion, greed, corruption, etc.

While that is the general principle, I agree that there are situations when one pressing concern of the time is paramount, for instance, the abolition movement regarding slavery in 1860s, and the civil rights issues in the 1960s.

Those Christians who fought bravely, and even sacrificed their lives, to free the enslaved people, or to give the African Americans and other minorities the fundamental human civil rights of equality, were fighting for noble principles, despite the fact that many of them were not slaves or persons of color.

God hates injustice. Those Christians did the right things and will be remembered and rewarded by God.

However, I believe that one must be diligent and sure of three conditions, before deciding to pay attention to only one single matter:

- That it *is* indeed the overriding problem of the time;

- That it is *applied consistently*, and not just being used for partisan, political wedge issues;

- That it is *a public matter*, and should be mandated by the government and not a private concern, which should be best handled and decided privately by the citizens themselves.

< Abortion issue as an example >

On the first point

Is abortion indeed the overriding problem of the time?

How about greed and corruption? As mentioned above, God gave us ten commandments, not just one. The sin of murder is not even at the top of the list. It is about the worshiping idol that is at the top.

Scripture warns,

"The love of money is a *root of all kinds of evil*. Some people, eager for money, have wandered from the faith and pierced themselves with many griefs" (1 Timothy 6:10).

    Many believe that part of the reason the United States political system is in a lot of trouble today, is the out-of-control campaign money pouring into the pockets of congressional politicians and our state officials.

    The most severe blow occurred in 2010 when a huge floodgate was opened by the Supreme Court's ruling in *Citizens United v. Federal Election Commission*, which reversed century-old campaign finance restrictions and allowed billionaires, corporations, and other outside groups to spend *unlimited* funds on elections.

    Rampant greed and corruption ensued in the government institutions and private sector companies, which are supposed to be under our elected officials' watch on behalf of the people.

    Furthermore, it is apparent, in my opinion, while greed is not limited to just a particular political party, the party in the U.S. that is anti-abortion, is also the party that has been known to be pro-big businesses, but is against workers and the protection of the consumers and the environment.

    One will seldom see this party advocate any meaningful campaign reform. It is this mantra, "the more money the better."

    Under such situations in our society today, to fix attention on just one single, narrowly defined issue, such as abortion, in every election cycle, and use it to claim the moral high ground, amounts to practicing selective morality.

That is why people are troubled and disgusted by this hypocrisy, and it makes Christianity look bad.

On the second point

Let us assume that abortion is the most important moral issue in our time. But is it applied consistently and not just used as a partisan, political wedge issue?

Personally, I believe that Scripture teaches that life starts from conception and that we must value life (Psalm 51:5; Luke 1:40-44; Exodus 20:13).

That said, I find it perplexing that many pro-life supporters use the "sanctity of life" argument to only talk about the unborn, yet seemingly not interested in those lives that have already been born.

Does Scripture teach that it is only about the unborn? God's command, "thou shall not murder," includes all lives, the unborn and the born.

How about those lives that were lost because of the lack of access to affordable health care, caused by a corrupt, broken, and outrageously expensive system? The irony is that although the United States is the highest spending country worldwide per person regarding health care, it has the worst health outcomes among high-income countries, and does not guarantee affordable health care for all its citizens.

How about those lives that were lost due to an unnecessary war, initiated and perpetuated by lies told by profiteering politicians and companies?

How about those lives that were lost, as a result of the toxic dumps created by greedy, irresponsible corporations?

How about those lives that were lost, because of drug companies knowingly pushing unsafe or addictive medicines?

How about our parents, grandparents, and spouses in nursing homes who lost their lives, because heartless corporations failed to protect our most vulnerable populations and lobbied against any protective regulations?

How about those kids shot dead in schools, because of the lack of common-sense gun safety laws that were blocked by the lobbying of companies and the corrupt elected officials who took their money?

So many innocent lives have been lost due to various sinful behaviors in our society, not just abortion. Yet I seldom hear any of these advocates mentioning these tragic losses of lives as described above.

In fact, many of these anti-abortion activists belong to the same political party, which is against any reasonable regulations to seek to hold corrupt corporations accountable for causing harm and the loss of human lives.

Yes, abortion is problematic, especially when the mothers' lives are not in danger. But are those lives the only ones the Bible teaches us to care about and protect?

In short, we should care for and protect all lives. It should be applied consistently. If not, then it is suspected of being just used for a partisan wedge issue.

On the third point

Is abortion a public matter, that should be mandated by the government, or is it a private concern, which should be best decided privately by the citizens themselves?

As remarked above, personally, I believe Scripture teaches that life starts from conception and that we must value life.

When my mother was pregnant with me, I was to be the sixth child of the family. She told me that, at that time, she was asked if she wanted the child, since they already had five kids, and she was thirty-nine years old, a risky age to have more children.

She said, "Yes, I want to keep it. Because life is given by God and should be cherished."

I am deeply grateful that she made the right choice. However, the question we need to ask ourselves is:

"Should this be the kind of decision dictated by the government, or made by the citizens themselves, according to their conscience and belief, like what my mother did?"

It is puzzling that often, those anti-abortionists are also fervent anti-government activists who preach small government when it is about supporting business interests, at the expense of consumer and environmental protection; nevertheless, when it comes to the abortion issue, they have no problem with the big government dictating our personal lives.

A reminder

Do we really care about the abortion issue because of Christian love?

It is troublesome to note that some anti-abortion activists seem only to condemn those women/girls for their behavior, and seek to block abortion in any way they can, but do not actually want to help them constructively.

I believe some of them, like teenagers in low-income families, probably do not have health insurance for prenatal and after-birth care. They probably are also scared of caring for the baby since they are still minors.

How about supporting public policies to render medical care and provide financial aid for those who need it? How about offering adoption alternatives?

I seldom hear those pro-life advocates talk about helping teenagers this way; instead, they often only condemn them.

If we do care about "the sanctity of life," we should care about the life of the would-be mother and the wellbeing of the baby once it is born, too, and help as much as possible, not just attack them.

Summary on the issue of abortion

To pick one out of the Ten Commandments and many other sins, apply that to only the narrow aspect, i.e., the unborn, and then use it to claim the moral high ground, as mentioned before, is, in effect, practicing selective morality.

It smells hypocritical and partisan. That is contrary to what Christianity is about. That is why I am concerned that it may drive away potential believers of Christ, thinking that it is a hypocritical and political religion.

How Should Christians Handle Politics?

Having discussed the unfortunate situations above, it is not to say Christians should avoid public affairs. On the contrary, Christians should care about them. They should participate and vote, especially because it tremendously affects people's daily lives, including ours.

My wife and I have never missed any presidential elections since we became citizens many years ago. We vote on local issues as well.

Here are my suggestions for how we can best handle politics.

KEEP THE OVERALL BIBLICAL PRINCIPLES IN MIND

It is precisely because it affects our lives that we must be cautious about how we manage it. We must not consider a candidate based on a politically motivated, selected moral single issue or party affiliation; instead, we should consider him or her based on the overall biblical principles first.

Does the person generally have integrity compared with other candidates? We are not looking for a perfect person. People make mistakes. Nevertheless, among others, does the person have the humility to admit wrongdoing and correct it, or just blame everyone except themselves?

Does the person have honesty and not lie so easily? Does the person have a genuine servant attitude for the people, or just claim to be for the people? Is the person just in it for the power, money, and fame?

Children of the devil

As mentioned in Part Two, Jesus issued one of the sternest warnings against lying, saying that liars, in fact, are children of the devil:

"[43] Why is my language not clear to you? Because you are unable to hear what I say [the truth]. [44] *You belong to your father, the devil*, and you want to carry out your father's desires. He was a murderer from the beginning, not holding to the truth, for there is no truth in him. When he lies, he speaks his native language, for *he is a liar and the father of lies*" (John 8:43-44).

While lying is not the only immoral behavior, it is particularly critical in this context, because trustworthiness is vital when we elect a person to represent us. Some may promise whatever we want, but do not intend to keep it.

On the other hand, if they are honest and have that overall biblical character, then it is worthy of our consideration whether the person is a Democrat, Republican, or Independent; or whether he or she is white, black, brown, or of other races.

EVALUATE THE CANDIDATE'S POLICIES

Then, we can evaluate if the candidate's policies are the best for addressing our public issues. Is there only one crucial concern, or are there multiple pressing problems to which we must also pay attention?

Avoid candidates who are evasive and refuse to be transparent on issues. There is no way to evaluate what they will do, if all you get are empty slogans or catchy 15-second TV sound bites.

We must spend time to educate ourselves so that we can make an informed decision. Do not just watch one particular TV channel, or visit only one website, especially those media that are known to be one-sided.

Consider arguments from both sides. Verify the truthfulness of the reports or claims. Above all, pray to God for guidance.

CHOOSE APPROPRIATE TIMES AND PLACES TO ENGAGE IN POLITICS

While we must actively participate in politics, there are proper times and places to do so. We can volunteer for a particular campaign in the campaign's offices or join a rally at the campaign-designated site.

But I believe it is best to avoid using churches for political purposes if possible.

I understand that sometimes it is the only place in town that is large enough and available for public meetings. In such circumstances, using the facility for non-partisan discussion of public issues might be fine.

However, at least when sharing the gospel with people, studying the Bible together in a class, or worshiping God in a Sunday morning service inside the church, we must avoid injecting politics, especially if we cannot present it fairly and non-biasedly.

Jesus loves all the people, regardless of our political affiliations or views. It is a distraction and is divisive to insert partisan politics in such a gathering.

My Experience on This Regard

When I held evangelistic meetings in my house a while ago, there were Chinese unbelievers from various parts of the world with vastly different political backgrounds.

Several couples are from mainland China, which is ruled by the authoritarian Chinese Communist Party. That government has been trying to take Taiwan and threatening to invade the island if Taiwan officially declares independence.

Some attendees are from Taiwan, where democracy is flourishing, and many people there are against the rigid regime of communist China.

Others are from Hong Kong and Singapore, which have varying degrees of different political systems and views.

I gave a six-part lesson, one every other Saturday. At the beginning of the first meeting, I said, "We will not be talking about politics here. What I will be sharing with you is about Jesus' good news of the coming kingdom of God. And Jesus loves all people, regardless of where you are from, or what your political view is."

We kept that principle and focused on what the Bible says for all humankind. At the end of the sixth meeting, I gave an invitation to accept Jesus' saving grace. Although I am from Taiwan, I was delighted to see some of those who raised their hands are from communist China!

I practiced that same principle when I pastored Chinese churches. I am very thankful that those I had the honor to baptize are from mainland China, Taiwan, and even Vietnam.

It is reassuring to witness that the love of Christ is for all the people, and that all human beings, regardless of diverse political backgrounds, indeed have the same longing to want to be liberated from the bondage of sins and to be free!

In Conclusion

Please do not let those people, such as hypocritical false religious elites, political partisans, or misguided believers, stop you from seeking to know the saving grace of Jesus Christ. It is a matter between you and God.

Please do not let anybody or anything stand in your way of receiving the love of Jesus.

Apostle Paul encourages believers in Romans 8:38-39,

"[38] For I am convinced that neither death nor life, neither angels nor demons, [a] neither the present nor the future, nor any powers, [39] neither height nor depth, nor

anything else in all creation, will be able to separate us from the love of God that is in Christ Jesus our Lord."
Footnotes
    a. Or *nor heavenly rulers*

    While Apostle Paul is talking to Christians who are under persecution, if the love of God is so great that no oppression, not even death, can separate us from it, it is undoubtedly worth having it in the first place.

    Fundamentally, it is the eternal, everlasting Kingdom of Heaven, which is to come, not the temporary, earthly political parties or governments, which are going away, that is at stake for you.

PART FOUR - You Can Truly Be Saved Too

31 - EVERYONE IS CHERISHED IN GOD'S EYES

You do not have to continue to be held captive by sins, and to face the final judgment, when the end of the world comes.

2 Peter 3:8-10 urges us:

"⁸ But do not forget this one thing, dear friends: With the Lord a day is like a thousand years, and a thousand years are like a day. ⁹ The Lord is not slow in keeping his promise, as some understand slowness. Instead he is patient with you, not wanting *anyone* to perish, but *everyone* to come to repentance.
"¹⁰ But the day of the Lord will come like a thief. The heavens will disappear with a roar; the elements will be destroyed by fire, and the earth and everything done in it will be laid bare[a]."
Footnotes
   a. Some manuscripts *be burned up.*

Hebrews 9:27 warns us:

"Just as people are destined to die once, and after that to face judgment."

Regardless of who you are, what your ethnicity, gender, religion (atheist, agnostic, Judaist, Muslim, Hindu,

Buddhist, Confucian, Daoist, New Ager, etc.), and political party is, whether you are rich or poor, Jesus' salvation is available to all.

It is astounding to note that almost two thousand years ago, the book of Galatians declares:

"There is neither Jew nor Gentile, neither slave nor free, nor is there male and female, for you are all one in Christ Jesus" (Galatians 3:28).

Racism, gender bias, economic classes, or any form of discrimination has no place in God's eyes because, as remarked before, all have sinned. Nobody is better or superior to anybody else before God.

All need salvation. All are precious in God's eyes.

Signs of the End Times

One might wonder, "What are the signs of the end times, and of the coming of the final judgment?"

Jesus answered this question specifically in Mathew 24: 4 – 8,

"^{4} Jesus answered: 'Watch out that no one deceives you. ^{5} For many will come in my name, claiming, 'I am the Messiah' and will deceive many.

'^{6} You will hear of wars and rumors of wars, but see to it that you are not alarmed. Such things must happen, but the end is still to come. ^{7} Nation will rise against nation, and kingdom against kingdom. There will be famines and earthquakes in various places. ^{8} All these are the beginning of birth pains.'"

In short, as the end of the world approaches, there will be <u>rampant deceptions</u> by false Christs (Mathew 24:5), and false prophets (Mathew 24:11), and there will be <u>widespread wars and massive natural disasters</u>, including pestilences (Luke 21:11; Revelation Chapter 6 through 19).

However, this chaotic, violent, corrupt, and deceptive world of ours will end, when Christ comes to judge the world, and all of us will be held accountable for what we have said and done.

The Final Judgment

The Judgment Seat of Christ

Those who have believed and accepted Jesus' forgiveness of their sins, will be resurrected (or raptured, if alive when Jesus comes again) and be judged in front of the judgment seat of Christ (2 Corinthians 5:10).

It is an assessment for rewards (as discussed in Part Two under "Believers will be rewarded for a job well done").

It is not about life or death. All believers will have eternal life and will enter the eternal kingdom of God; first, in the millennium on Earth (Revelation 20:4-6), then in the Holy City of the New Jerusalem under a new heaven and a new earth (Revelation 21:1-2).

In that city of the New Jerusalem, the perfect God will dwell with mankind. There will be no more injustice, and

"4 'He [God] will wipe every tear from their eyes. There will be *no more death*' [a] *or mourning or crying or pain*, for the old order of things has passed away" (Revelation 21:4).
Footnotes
    a. Isaiah 25:8

Yes, there is hope. Yes, there is a way out of this madness of ours. Although it will get worse before it gets better, a new, peaceful, and joyful eternal kingdom of heaven will come.

The Great White Throne of God

On the other hand, those who have rejected Christ will also be resurrected, but will be condemned to the eternal lake of fire (Revelation 20:11-15).

Incidentally, some may have been particularly upset and troubled that there are so many injustices and corruptions in the world today, and criminals and liars are getting away with it. Rest assured that all these wrongdoers will be dealt with at the final judgment.

Revelation 20:12-15 warns:

"12 And I saw the dead, great and small, standing before the throne, and books were opened. Another book was opened, which is the book of life. The dead were judged *according to what they had done* as recorded in the books.

"13 The sea gave up the dead that were in it, and death and Hades gave up the dead that were in them, and each person was judged according to what they had done.

"14 Then death and Hades were thrown into the lake of fire. The lake of fire is the second death. [All, including Christians, will die once (the first death). But unbelievers will die a second time.]

"15 Anyone whose name was not found written in the book of life was thrown into the lake of fire."

Revelation 22:14-15 reiterates:

14 "Blessed are those who wash their robes, that they may have the right to the tree of life and may go through

the gates into the city [the Holy city of the New Jerusalem]. ¹⁵ Outside are the dogs, *those who practice magic arts, the sexually immoral, the murderers, the idolaters and everyone who loves and practices falsehood."*

Please note that this is a simplified summation of what will happen in the coming days. For particulars of *the Seven Year Tribulation*, *the Armageddon* (the biggest war in history), *the Millennium* (the one thousand years of Christ's reign on Earth), *the Final Judgment*, and *the New Heaven and the New Earth*, please consult the book of Revelation, the book of Daniel (Chapter 7; 9), and other relevant passages.

32 - HOW YOU CAN TRULY BE SAVED

Our spiritual journeys may differ; some may be dramatic, some may not, but all can be saved. One of the most essential promises from God is in John 3:16, "For God so loved the world that he gave his one and only Son [Jesus Christ], that *whoever believes in him* shall not perish but have eternal life."

If You Will Tell God that You:

1. *Admit* that you have sinned, "for all have sinned and fall short of the glory of God"(Romans 3:23).

    (We all have violated God's moral standards in one way or another, like lying, stealing, etc. See Romans 1:28-32 for more examples; also refer to Mark 1:15 and Acts 2:36-38 regarding repentance.)

2. *Believe* in your heart, that Jesus Christ, God the Son, sent by God the Father, died for your sins, and that God the Father raised him from the dead (Romans 10:9b; John 3:16; Romans 5:8; 1 Corinthians 15:3-6); and

3. *Confess* with your mouth, that Christ is your Lord and Savior (Romans 10:9a);

Your sins will be forgiven, and you will be saved *right away*. Your life will begin to change, starting at this very moment! It is a brand-new beginning!

Jesus Is Your High Priest

You do not need to do this through any person, like a pastor or a priest. It is between you and God. Jesus has paid the price for your redemption. He has opened the door for you. Nobody else needs to be your intermediary.

Jesus himself is our high priest (Hebrews 2:17). When Jesus died on the cross, the curtain of the temple was torn in two, from top to bottom. It signified that access to God was open to everyone from then on, and there was no need to go through any human priest anymore (Matthew 27:51; Hebrews 6:19-20).

It Is a Free Gift from God

As previously stated in Parts Two and Three, it is a gift for all willing to believe and accept. It is *free*. Ephesians 2:8-9 declares:

"[8] For it is by grace you have been saved, through faith—and this is not from yourselves, it is the *gift* of God— [9] *not by works, so that no one can boast.*"

I thought of a possible illustration of accepting a free gift by faith.

It is like a significant sum of money is deposited for everyone, including you. All you have to do is trust that it is real, go to the bank, claim it, and you will have it.

It might sound too simple and not serious, but if the gospel is for everyone, rich and poor, highly educated or not, it should not be too complicated for people to understand and respond to.

On the other hand, those who think it is too easy to be true, snub it, and do not even bother checking it out, will miss that precious opportunity.

That actually is the wisdom of God.

More on this point under the subtitle, "However, He will oppose the proud and the arrogant," later in Chapter 33.

About Baptism

After you put your trust in Jesus and are born again, you can ask a church to baptize you. In fact, it does not even have to be done inside an institution.

Acts 8:26-39 records a beautiful story about how a eunuch from Ethiopia was baptized as soon as he trusted in Jesus, after disciple Philip shared the gospel with him:

"... 36 As they traveled along the road, they came to some water and the eunuch said, 'Look, here is water. What can stand in the way of my being baptized?' [37] [c]

"38 And he gave orders to stop the chariot. Then both Philip and the eunuch went down into the water and Philip baptized him. 39 When they came up out of the water, the Spirit of the Lord suddenly took Philip away, and the eunuch did not see him again, but went on his way rejoicing."

Footnotes
   c. Some manuscripts include here *Philip said, "If you believe with all your heart, you may." The eunuch answered, "I believe that Jesus Christ is the Son of God."*

Why Baptism?

When Jesus gave the great commission to his followers before He ascended to heaven, as part of the commission, they were to baptize those who believed (Matt. 28:18-20).

Later on, Apostle Peter, following Jesus' directive, at Pentecost, told those who were willing to listen and asked him what they should do:

"Peter replied, *'Repent and be baptized*, every one of you, in the name of Jesus Christ for the forgiveness of your sins. And you will receive the gift of the Holy Spirit" (Acts 2:38).

Christians are to be baptized because that is what Jesus specifically commands us to do.

What Is the Meaning of Baptism?

At baptism, when one is immersed in water, it symbolizes he (or she) is dead to his sinful life in the past. When he emerges from the water, it signifies that he is raised to a brand-new life.

Apostle Paul reminds believers about the meaning of their baptism:

"³ Or don't you know that all of us who were baptized into Christ Jesus were baptized into his death? ⁴ We were therefore buried with him through baptism into death in order that, just as Christ was raised from the dead through the glory of the Father, we too may live *a new life*.

"⁵ For if we have been united with him in a death like his, we will certainly also be united with him in a resurrection like his. ⁶ For we know that *our old self was crucified with him so that the body ruled by sin might be done away with*,[a] that we should no longer be slaves to

sin— [7] because anyone who has died has been *set free from sin*" (Romans 6:3-7).
> Footnotes
> a. Or *be rendered powerless.*

Apostle Peter says,

"and this water symbolizes baptism that now saves you also—not the removal of dirt from the body but the pledge of a clear conscience toward God.[a] It saves you by the resurrection of Jesus Christ" (1 Peter 3:21).
> Footnotes
> a. Or *but an appeal to God for a clear conscience*

I find that the chapter title of the passage in Romans 6, on the meaning of baptism by the New International Version of the Bible, sums it up well: "Dead to Sin, Alive in Christ"!

Is Baptism a Condition of Salvation?

As mentioned, Roman Catholicism and Eastern Orthodoxy hold that the sacraments through the Church, including baptism, are instruments of divine grace. In other words, they are part of the conditions for salvation, administered by the Church.

However, Protestant reformers believe that, according to the Scriptures, God's grace is received by man's faith alone.

Some claim that Peter's reply in Acts 2:38, "Repent and be baptized," denotes that baptism is also required for salvation in addition to repentance.

However, an overwhelming number of other passages firmly establish that forgiveness of sin is solely based on faith.

Jesus' own saying in John 3:16 and Luke 24:47, Peter's remarks in Acts 10:43 and 5:31, Paul's statements in Ephesians 2:8-9, 4:1-17, and Romans 3 and 4, etc., all testify to that conclusion.

Protestant Christians do accept baptism (together with the Lord's Supper) as an ordinance (not as a condition for salvation) that Jesus commands us to do, *after* we are saved. It is to show our love and obedience to Christ, now that we are his children.

It is the believer's public declaration that they have accepted Jesus as their personal Savior.

Believer's baptism

As discussed in Part Three, Protestant denominations, like the Baptists and the Mennonites, stress the importance of only baptizing those who are old enough to be able to make a personal confession of faith in Jesus, in contrast to infant baptism.

MY EXPERIENCE

I was baptized twice.

As shared in Part One, when I was baptized in Taiwan, although I was already in college, and thus was old enough to make conscientious decisions, I was perhaps only halfway on the right track to understanding the faith.

I was convinced of the existence of a creator, but I did not know who Jesus was. I was not aware of my sinfulness. My life was not changed.

Thankfully, while working in Dallas, God showed me my iniquities, and I was truly born again. After that, I started to eagerly serve in my church in various ministries.

Then, one day, I strongly felt I should be baptized again, since now I had indeed understood and felt my sinful condition, and the reason why Jesus died for me.

I asked the church's senior pastor if it was okay to do that. He was very kind and said, "Yes. As a matter of fact, my mother was baptized twice too."

However, some at the church were skeptical of my request.

One mockingly said to me, raising her voice, "George, you are running already, why are you trying to learn to crawl again?" (This is my English literal translation of her remark in Chinese.)

At the meeting before the church leadership, tasked to consider requests for baptism, one asked, "What are you trying to prove?" (He actually said it in English.)

I was surprised by such a question because I was not trying to prove anything. I said, "I just want to follow what the Bible says: repent, and then be baptized."

Fortunately, my application was granted. At the baptism, I shared with the church how I was not really saved until I was 32 years old.

Interestingly, that same woman who ridiculed me, apparently now seeing my reason, called the pastor and asked him to invite me to write about my testimony in our church's publication.

The bottom line is that baptism without repentance, and the understanding and acceptance of Jesus' salvation *first*, is not much different from just getting oneself wet, to put it plainly.

I am grateful to live in America today, where religious freedom is protected. I thought of the many Anabaptists who were persecuted in the 16th century.

Many of them were tortured, burned, or drowned at the hands of the Catholic Church, and even some Protestant groups, because of their belief in the believer's baptism, and perhaps for their advocacy of pacifism, and the separation of church and state as well.

Although I do not agree with some of their tenets, certainly, the principles of the believer's baptism and the separation of church and state are grounded in Scripture.

All who died for being faithful to sound biblical teachings will be blessed, for Jesus says, "Blessed are those who are persecuted because of righteousness, for theirs is the kingdom of heaven" (Matthew 5:10).

On the other hand, those who persecuted and shed innocent blood of the righteous will be held accountable (2 Kings 24:3-4; Revelation 22:15).

About Growing Spiritually and Doing Good Deeds with Other Fellow Believers

All Believers Are Now God's Children in a Spiritual Family

Hebrews 10:24-25 says to fellow Christians,

"*24 And let us consider how we may spur one another on toward love and good deeds, 25 not giving up meeting together, as some are in the habit of doing, but encouraging one another*—and all the more as you see the Day [Christ's second coming at the end of the world] approaching."

It is crucial and a privilege for Christians to help build each other up, meeting either in person (at church, at home, and other places) or online. The format or method is not important.

In fact, it is not just for spiritual growth, but also for supporting each other in times of need. Ephesians 4:28 writes,

"Anyone who has been stealing must steal no longer, but must work, doing something useful with their own hands, that they may have something to share with those in need." (Also check 1 John 3:17.)

It is also about spurring one another on and working together to serve others in the community, as Ephesians 2:10 reminds us,

"For we are God's handiwork, created in Christ Jesus to do good works, which God prepared in advance for us to do."

We can all witness the many non-profit hospitals, schools, orphanages, food pantries, and other charity organizations in America and around the world, especially in poor, less developed countries, as the result of Christians' good works.

Encouraging "One Another" Passages

There are many other great "one another" passages in the Scriptures; the following examples are some of them:

1 John 4:7,

"Dear friends, let us love one another, for love comes from God. Everyone who loves has been born of God and knows God."

Colossians 3:16,

"Let the message of Christ dwell among you richly as you teach and admonish one another with all wisdom through psalms, hymns, and songs from the Spirit, singing to God with gratitude in your hearts."

Galatians 5:13,

"You, my brothers and sisters, were called to be free. But do not use your freedom to indulge the flesh[a]; rather, serve one another humbly in love."
   Footnotes
   a. In contexts like this, the Greek word for *flesh* (*sarx*) refers to the sinful state of human beings, often presented as a power in opposition to the Spirit; also in verses 16, 17, 19 and 24; and in 6:8.

James 5:13-16, Ephesians 4:32, Romans 12:16, and 2 Thessalonians 1:3 are also especially helpful and affirming.

Good Churches to Join

As for considering joining a church, while there is no perfect one, a good church, I believe, is one that has less partisan politics, and more Bible and Christ-centered teachings and ministries.

The focus of such a congregation is on building up believers and sharing the gospel's message with unreached people, while serving the community and reaching out to the poor.

A good place to find information about a congregation is on the church's website. Pay attention, particularly to its beliefs, look under "about us," "our church," "our beliefs," or "our statement of faith".

Also, note the teachings of the church. Sometimes, the official statement of faith may be solid, but what they preach can be quite different.

However, Be Mindful

Always remember that a particular organization or church may change after joining.

Make sure to check if its statement of faith is changed. In addition, regarding the group's leadership, pay attention if it has also been replaced and different people are now in charge.

As mentioned in Part Two, the current status of the Billy Graham Evangelistic Association under his son, Franklin Graham, and his other family members' administration, is concerning.

Even if the leadership of a congregation stays the same, a person could succumb to temptations, unfortunately.

1 Peter 5:8 warns,

"Be alert and of sober mind. Your enemy the devil prowls around like a roaring lion looking for someone to devour."

On top of the possibility of a leader giving in to temptation, 2 Peter 2:1-3 alerts us that there will be false teachers among Christian churches:

"[1] But there were also false prophets among the people, just as there will be false teachers among you. They will secretly introduce destructive heresies, even denying the sovereign Lord [Jesus] who bought them—bringing swift destruction on themselves... "

Furthermore, for a particular organization, even if the leadership continues to be upright and faithful, and there is no false teacher in it, as pointed out before in Part Three, Apostle Paul cautions believers not to elevate a particular person, not Peter, not Paul himself, but only to exalt Christ, and not to any human (1 Corinthians 3:1-23; 4:6-7).

In short, study and follow God's inspired, time-tested word in the Bible, fellowship with sincerely devoted Christians, and work together to reach out and help people.

Above all, worshiping only Jesus and ensuring that you do not idolize any particular human being, organization, or church, is vital to personal healthy spiritual growth.

Some May Think, "I Have Sinned So Much, I Am Not Worthy of Anything."

When Jesus says in Mark 1:15, "The kingdom of God has come near. Repent and believe the good news!" it does not mean you have to be perfect to be saved.

On the contrary, it means you just need to admit that you are imperfect, have sinned, and are willing to accept Jesus' offer to forgive your sins.

When Christ was hung on the cross with the other two condemned criminals beside him,

"[39] One of the criminals who hung there hurled insults at him: 'Aren't you the Messiah? Save yourself and us!'

"[40] But the other criminal rebuked him. 'Don't you fear God,' he said, 'since you are under the same sentence?

41 We are punished justly, for we are getting what our deeds deserve. But this man has done nothing wrong.'

"42 Then he said, 'Jesus, remember me when you come into your kingdom.[a]'

"43 Jesus answered him, *'Truly I tell you, today you will be with me in paradise'*" (Luke 23:39-43).

Footnotes
   a. Some manuscripts *come with your kingly power*

I am sure I will see him in Heaven!

Others Might Say, "I Have Never Done Anything Illegal, What Sins Have I Committed?"

I remember reading a true story about a Chinese student, who came to the U.S. to study around 1930, and returned to mainland China upon receiving his Ph.D..

One day, he was invited to a Dr. John Sung's evangelistic gathering. (Dr. Sung was a renowned Chinese evangelist in the 1930s, who became a born-again Christian while studying in the United States. After he earned a doctorate in chemistry from Ohio State University, he went back to China and started preaching the gospel all over the country.)

When he heard Dr. Sung say, "You must repent of your sins so that you will be saved," he felt very offended, because he did not think he had done anything wrong at all.

He wanted to leave, but he was sitting in the middle of a bench and could not get out easily in the packed place. Then, Dr. Sung urged the audience to pray to God to reveal to them their sins. He decided to give it a try.

After he prayed, he saw this scene in his mind: One day, when he was four or five years old, he was playing in the living room and accidentally knocked down a ceramic vase and broke it. His mom heard the noise, came in, and asked, "Who did this?" He immediately pointed his finger at the maid in the room and said, "She did it!"

God revealed to him that, even as a little child, he blamed an innocent person for his own misbehavior. He repented and accepted Jesus as His Lord and Savior. His life changed, and he even became a minister later on.

People May Ask, "I Have Been Going to Church Since I Was a Child, Am I Saved?"

As I have shared in Part One, although I grew up in a Protestant Christian home, it was not until I was 32 that I was truly saved.

The Conversation between Jesus and Nicodemus

John 3:1-8 records,

"[1] Now there was a Pharisee, a man named Nicodemus who was a member of the Jewish ruling council. [2] He came to Jesus at night and said, 'Rabbi, we know that you are a teacher who has come from God. For no one could perform the signs you are doing if God were not with him.'

"[3] Jesus replied, 'Very truly I tell you, no one can see the kingdom of God *unless they are born again.*[a]'..."

Footnotes
    a. The Greek for *again* also means *from above*; also in verse 7.

Nicodemus was part of the religious elite, a member of the Jewish ruling council, and a teacher of Moses' Law. He perhaps had the equivalent of a Doctor of Theology degree today. Yet Jesus said he needed to be born again.

It is clear that merely having head knowledge does not save; furthermore, just going through the outside rituals of the faith, even as a highly regarded clergy, does not save either.

You may have attended church all your life, gone through all the motions of church activities, and might even recite all the Scriptures, but in the end, it is the heart that counts.

Have you genuinely admitted that you have sinned? Have you believed and accepted Jesus as your Lord and Savior from your heart?

"I Just Wanted to Please My Grandma"

I remember vividly one student's comment in my World Religions class. She said, "I attended church while I was a kid, just to please my grandma."

It seems often, from the courses I taught, that many who grew up in Christian homes or communities, treated the faith just as a tradition, or part of their culture. And as soon as they left home, they no longer practiced it.

Unfortunately, I am afraid that such persons are Christians in name only. Some call them "cultural Christians".

Nevertheless, it is not too late. If, for any reason, you are not sure if you are saved, you can tell God that you want to be sure of your salvation and ask Him to help you in this regard.

I believe that God will answer your sincere prayer since, as mentioned before, "The Lord … is patient with you, not wanting *anyone* to perish, but *everyone* to come to repentance" (2 Peter 3:9).

Every person is precious in God's eyes, even in the eyes of all angels in heaven! (Luke 15:10).

Are People in the Catholic or Eastern Orthodox Churches Saved?

As spoken of earlier, I believe that there are indeed born-again Christians in the Catholic, Eastern Orthodox churches, or other churches, as long as they admit that they have sinned against God, believe that Jesus was sent by God and died for their sins, and confess that Jesus is their Lord and Savior from their hearts.

Such persons, according to the Scriptures, are indeed saved.

Nonetheless, just to reiterate the pitfall of being a cultural Christian, especially if one grew up in a particular environment such as Italy, where Catholicism is predominant, and Greece, where Eastern Orthodoxy is the expected norm.

In short, if you do not just go to church simply because that is what everybody else is doing, but because you genuinely believe, you are certainly saved!

33 - SEEK AND YOU WILL FIND

God Will Open the Eyes of Those Who Hunger for Truth

Dear friends, if you still have questions, you can ask your Christian friends or church pastors, read the Bible, and check out many excellent books about Christianity.

But above all, *humbly ask God to open your eyes and your mind,* so that you will be able to discern right from wrong, truth from falsehood, and comprehend what you see, hear, or read.

As cited before, Jesus promises us:

"So I say to you: Ask and it will be given to you; *seek and you will find*; knock and the door will be opened to you" (Luke 11:9).

He also assures us:

"[6] blessed are those who hunger and thirst for righteousness, for they *will be filled*. [8] blessed are the pure in heart, for they *will see God*" (Matthew 5:6, 8).

Prophet Isaiah urges us:

"[6] *Seek the Lord while he may be found*; call on him while he is near. [7] Let the wicked forsake their ways and the unrighteous their thoughts. Let them turn to the Lord, and he will have mercy on them, and to our God, for he will freely pardon" (Isaiah 55:6-7).

God promises that He will open the eyes of those who seek Him, and they shall see the truth!

However, He Will Oppose the Proud and the Arrogant

1 Peter 5:5 warns:

"⁵ ... All of you, clothe yourselves with humility toward one another, because, 'God opposes the proud but shows favor to the humble.'" [a]
Footnotes
    a.   Prov. 3:34

1 Corinthians 1:18-25 cautions:

"¹⁸ For the message of the cross is foolishness to those who are perishing, but to us who are being saved it is the power of God. ¹⁹ For it is written: 'I will destroy the wisdom of the wise; the intelligence of the intelligent I will frustrate.'
"²⁰ Where is the wise person? Where is the teacher of the law? Where is the philosopher of this age?
"Has not God made foolish the wisdom of the world? ²¹ For since in the wisdom of God the world through its wisdom did not know him, God was pleased through the foolishness of what was preached to save those who believe.
"²² Jews demand signs and Greeks look for wisdom, ²³ but we preach Christ crucified: a stumbling block to Jews

and foolishness to Gentiles, [24] but to those whom God has called, both Jews and Greeks, Christ the power of God and the wisdom of God.

"[25] For the foolishness of God is wiser than human wisdom, and the weakness of God is stronger than human strength."

Please give yourself a chance and do not give up. Humbly seek the truth, and you will find it. And the truth will set you free! (John 8:32; 14:6).

God Is Sad When People Do Not Want to Be Saved

I am so touched whenever I read this passage about Moses, who speaks for God and cries out:

"This day I call the heavens and the earth as witnesses against you that I have set before you, life and death, blessings and curses. Now *choose* life, so that you and your children may live" (Deuteronomy 30:19).

Jesus also mourns:

"Jerusalem, Jerusalem, you who kill the prophets and stone those sent to you, how often I have longed to gather your children together, as a hen gathers her chicks under her wings, and you were *not willing* "(Luke 13:34).

God desires that all will repent and be saved. However, He will not force us to do what we will not do genuinely from our heart.

As cited for the discussion on the subject of church and state in Part Three, Jesus says:

"²³ Yet a time is coming and has now come when the true worshipers will worship the Father in the Spirit and in truth, for they are the kind of worshipers the Father seeks. ²⁴ God is spirit, and his worshipers must worship *in the Spirit and in truth*" (John 4:23-24).

God's love for us is a voluntary relationship, not a forced one. He wishes that all would be willing to accept his saving grace, but many have rejected him. And unfortunately, many more will do so in the future (Matthew 7:13-14).

Our Opportunities to Believe Is Not Unlimited

It will end when we die, or when Jesus comes again to judge the world.
Nobody knows for sure in advance when we will die. We may have a fatal accident tomorrow, or we may suddenly fall ill and die in a short time.
As for the end of the world, when will it come?
Although no one knows the time (Mathew 24: 36), in addition to the signs as indicated before (Mathew 24: 4 – 8), such as great distress (wars and natural disasters), Jesus says,

"And this gospel of the kingdom will be preached in the whole world as a testimony to all nations, and then the end will come" (Mathew 24: 14).

It is remarkable that today's advanced technologies have enabled us to instantly connect with others worldwide, with satellites, the internet, smartphones, and apps like Skype, FaceTime, and Zoom.

Given that the tools for the gospel to reach all nations are now easier to use and readily accessible, it could mean that the day of reckoning is closer than ever before.

Hope to See You All in the New Heaven and the New Earth

May all of us choose to receive God's love, and the new, joyful, eternal life, by accepting Jesus Christ as our personal Savior, <u>before it is too late</u>.

"See You at the Gate!"

A couple of years ago, my wife and I attended a book signing event by Mr. Don Piper, the author of *90 Minutes in Heaven* (Grand Rapids, MI: Revell, 2015). He wrote on our copy, *"George and Margaret: See you at the gate!"*

Yes, it is also my sincere hope that my family, my parents, and grandparents; those loved ones, relatives, and friends of yours who believed; those Western missionaries who went to Taiwan; those Christians, like Robert Morrison and James Hudson Taylor, who devoted all their lives, sharing the love of Jesus in China; and together with Don Piper, who wrote about his personal spiritual experiences to encourage all the people of the world, all will see you at the gate!

"A GREAT MULTITUDE"

Apostle John says that in the new Heaven, we will see:

"[9]... a great multitude that no one could count, from every nation, tribe, people, and language, standing before the throne [before God, the Father] and before the Lamb [God, the Son] ... "

"... [17] For the Lamb at the center of the throne will be their shepherd; 'he will lead them to springs of living water.'[a] 'And God will wipe away every tear from their eyes'[b]" (Revelation 7:9, 17).

Footnotes
    a. Isaiah 49:10
    b. Isaiah 25:8

Tens of millions of brothers and sisters in Christ throughout history like Abraham, Moses, Isaiah, the Apostles, Martin Luther, Johannes Kepler, Galileo Galilei, Martin Luther King Jr., and many others; Blacks, Whites, Browns, and others; the rich and the poor; men and women; will also see you and celebrate with you in the new Heaven.

It is a place where there is no more injustice, death, mourning, crying, or pain; instead, there is God's eternal justice, peace, love, and joy!

I conclude my book by sharing with you this triumphant song, entitled, *"He has made me glad (I will enter His gates)"* (Praise 15 - He Has Made Me Glad ℗ 1999 Maranatha! Music).

Search YouTube for the song, and enjoy!

www.ingramcontent.com/pod-product-compliance
Lightning Source LLC
Chambersburg PA
CBHW032031150426
43194CB00006B/232